Making It Big in the City

Also by Peggy Schmidt

Making It on Your First Job:
When You're Young, Inexperienced, and Ambitious

Making It Big in the City

A Woman's Guide to Living, Loving and Working There

PEGGY SCHMIDT

Coward-McCann, Inc./New York

646.7
5353
Cop.1

The author gratefully acknowledges permission from the
following sources to quote from material in their control:
    Welbeck Music Ltd., London, England, for "Down-
town," words and music by Tony Hatch, © copyright
1964 by Welbeck Music Ltd. Sole selling agent MCA
Music, a division of MCA Inc., New York, N.Y., for
North, South, and Central America. All rights reserved.
    Colgems-EMI Music, Inc. for lyrics from "So Far
Away," by Carole King. Copyright © 1971, Colgems-EMI
Music, Inc. Used by permission. All rights reserved.
    Gerard Alessandini for lyrics from the song "Ambition,"
from the musical comedy *Forbidden Broadway*.

Library of Congress Cataloging in Publication Data

Schmidt, Peggy J.
    Making it big in the city.

    1. Women—United States—Case studies.   2. City and
town life—United States—Case studies.   3. Women—
Employment—United States—Case studies.   4. Intimacy
(Psychology)—Case studies.   I. Title.
HQ1426.S334   1983   646.7   82-25264
ISBN 0-698-11228-8

PRINTED IN THE UNITED STATES OF AMERICA

Acknowledgments

I am most grateful to my agent, Elaine Markson, who introduced me to my editor, Thomas Ward Miller, whose encouragement and editing expertise were invaluable.

Many thanks go to the women whose stories appear in this book, and Betsy Nore and Sylvie Garant. They gave generously of their time and shared details about their lives in the spirit of providing information and encouragement to others who are facing similar challenges.

I am also indebted to Amy Levin, Kitty Ross, and especially Judsen Culbreth at *Mademoiselle*, who helped develop the Urban Experience Survey. The findings, which were first published in the March 1983 issue of *Mademoiselle*, added depth to the book. Michael Lenaeur, of Chilmark Research Associates was most helpful in the design of the survey and the interpretation of the data.

Wendy Bowis, who assisted me in researching the book, was a cheerful and loyal supporter. Her meticulous work provided rich resource material which helped refine the ideas in this book. Many thanks also go to my longtime friend, Kate White (the only transplanted New Yorker I know whose hometown honored her with a namesake day), whose manuscript suggestions reflect her editing talent. I am especially grateful to Joe Tabacco, my first critic and main moral support throughout.

I very much appreciate the advice and opinions of the following professionals:

Lawrence Balter, Psychotherapist and Professor of Educational Psychology at New York University;

Eli Ginzberg, A. Barton Hepburn Professor of Economics at the Graduate School of Business at Columbia University;

Muriel Goldfarb and Dan Rubinstein, Psychotherapists and Co-Directors of Seminar Associates, New York City;

Dale Hill, Psychologist in private practice in Houston, Texas;

Larry Long, Chief of Demographic Analysis Staff, Center for Demographic Studies at the Bureau of the Census;

Phoebe Prosky, Family Therapist at the Akerman Institute for Family Therapy and in private practice;

Bernie Tessler, Psychotherapist with Transferee's Advisory Programs, Jericho, New York;

Loretta Walder, Psychoanalyst in private practice in New York City;

Robert Weiss, Professor of Sociology at the University of Massachusetts, Boston; lecturer in sociology at the Harvard Medical School and Department of Psychiatry at the Massachusetts Mental Health Center;

Gerda R. Wekerle, Faculty of Environmental Studies, York University, Toronto, Canada.

Finally, my thanks to the many who have not been mentioned individually, but whose cooperation in finding interview subjects and in obtaining research information made a significant contribution to the book.

For
My husband, Joe Tabacco,
and my grandmothers,
Loretta Weber Yunker
and Donnabelle Fields Schmidt

Contents

The Lure of Career Opportunities . . . Testing
the Waters . . . Researching the Move . . .
Escaping to a City . . . Moving with or for a Man
. . . Bridging Two Worlds

BOXES: Where to stay temporarily
Calculating the costs of relocating
Should you keep your car?

Lining up a Job Before You Move . . . Looking
for Work Once You Arrive . . . Settling for Less
. . . How Where You Work Affects Your Social
Life . . . Supporting Yourself While You Pursue
a Financially Unrewarding Career

BOXES: The top ten cities for artists
Guides to finding the right job
"Temp" work to tide you over

Break from Home . . . The Freedom of Being
Your Own Person

BOXES: Staying in touch with family and friends
How to establish financial independence

The Attraction—and Pitfalls—of Being
Dedicated to Your Job . . . Learning to Compete
. . . Surviving—and Making the Best of—Career
Letdowns

BOXES: Top cities for ambitious women
How to compete effectively

The Loneliness of Emotional Isolation . . .
Where Have All the "Good" Men Gone? . . .
Relationship Roadblocks

The Most Common City Crimes . . . Developing
Street Smarts . . . Protecting Yourself Inside
Your Home . . . Living with the Fear of Crime
. . . The Aftermath of Crime

BOXES: Caution: The best crime preventive
Riding mass transit—six safety rules
Five ways to discourage a burglar

Going Home to Heal . . . Retreat to the Past . . .
Getting a Perspective from a New City

Introduction

〴〴

I arrived in New York City at age nineteen without a map, a contact, or the knowledge that my prearranged apartment bordered on one of the city's worst neighborhoods. Over the summer, I took two courses at Columbia University, supported myself with an art gallery job in the East Village and met writers who actually earned a living from their work. They encouraged me to come back after graduation if I wanted to do the same. I followed their advice despite gentle protests from my parents who felt New York City was too tough a place for a young woman who, having grown up among straight-talking Midwesterners, trusted even strangers.

Eleven years of living in a big city has confirmed that there is no other place that offers such advantages: The opportunity to get paid to do what I most enjoy, the excitement of living in an international capital, and a smorgasbord of interesting friends and experiences. A city, regardless of its size, is a macrocosm of many small towns in which you can build an extended family of friends, professional contacts and acquaintances. That realization didn't dawn on me for years, during which time the aggravations of city living tried my resolve and sometimes forced me to deal with them single-handedly. There have been times when I felt like leaving, but I'm glad I didn't.

Many women in cities today, like me, grew up in suburbia or small towns but have fallen in love with an urban life-style. Between 1975 and 1980 (the latest period covered by Census Bureau statistics), the number of people between the ages of

22 and 29 who moved to cities increased substantially. Five million women became city residents, joining the 20 million women already living in cities. This trend bucks the general population movement out of cities, most of which have been shrinking for decades.

The number of young, upwardly mobile women is particularly high in four cities—New York, Washington, D.C., Boston and San Francisco—the centers for government, many of the performing arts, leading educational institutions, finance, the publishing and fashion industries, and the headquarters of many of the Fortune 1000 firms. I traveled to those cities and five others (Cleveland, Los Angeles, Miami, Toronto and Chicago) to interview women who had come there to find themselves and their fortunes.

The attraction of big city living in the '80s goes beyond the traditional ones—an active social scene with plenty of opportunities to meet men whose background and ambition make them desirable partners, the profusion of cultural activities and plenty of people who share similar interests, however eclectic. The city-bound woman today is likely to be a member of the baby-boom generation—she's well-educated (or about to be), serious about her career and interested in making it on her own, financially and psychologically.

The big city has it all—the greatest number of professional opportunities which pay the best salaries; a social milieu in which life-styles that find much less acceptance elsewhere can flourish; the chance to prove to oneself (and the folks back home) that you can achieve success, even if it's in a field that is not thought of as being a "normal" way to earn a living.

Few of the women I interviewed had an easy time making the adjustment to city living; in fact, these women often experienced traumatic personal setbacks. But they survived them, learned from them and often turned them into positive experiences. After having lived in a city from two to twelve years, most of them now think of themselves as "city people," and have achieved far more than they ever dreamt possible when they first arrived. None of them are household names, but many of them are highly successful; some are still struggling to make it big in the city.

The majority of city-bound women are between the ages of 18 and 29, the period when we make more moves than at any other time in our lives. While young single women have traditionally been the most likely candidates to move to a city, there are two new groups of women who are discovering that urban living has a lot of offer them.

Working wives and mothers who are part of a dual-career couple are an increasingly visible segment of a city's population, and many of them relocate because of their career or their husband's. From a financial point of view, they are the luckiest city women. Being part of a two-income partnership, they can afford a nice place to live, frequent nights on the town, vacation escapes when they need them. And the working mothers who are part of a dual-career couple have the unusual benefit of being able to afford child care and private schools while having more time to be with their children than were they to continue working but live in the suburbs.

Another group of city-bound women is suburban divorcées, whose new marital status makes staying in a family environment less desirable. In fact, 60 percent of all marriage-related moves into a city from the suburbs involve people who get divorced.

I interviewed over 50 women who fell into these three categories. Their stories are featured throughout the book. Through their successes and failures, you can learn about the best and worst aspects of city living and ways to handle some of the situations you'll undoubtedly be faced with while living in a city.

Equally relevant are the findings from a 69-item questionnaire sent to *Mademoiselle*'s Career Marketing Board. It was completed by over 500 panel members, 323 of whom live in a city. The candid and often surprising answers given by survey respondents appear throughout the book, and the questionnaire is referred to as the "Urban Experience Survey."

Although this book is written for women, men have asked, "Why didn't you write it for us, too?" In fact, many of the adjustments, challenges and problems endemic in a move to a big city are ones faced by both sexes (and men will find many of the chapters useful). There are two issues, however, that make city living an essentially different experience for men and women, namely safety and acceptance.

The first issue is clearcut: women are more vulnerable to crime than are men. The second difference, that of acceptance, is one most of us would like to think is as passé as the nineteenth-century notion that public places were an immoral domain where women were at risk (in fact, their mere presence in public places often provoked violence and anger). But the fact remains that it is still easier for a man on his own to cope with city living—financially, emotionally and socially—than it is for a woman. Fortunately, that is changing as an unprecedented number of women, armed with their degrees, are heading to cities, where they're playing a more influential role than ever in the work force and housing markets.

The special problems of women in the city—and the impact that they're making in terms of the revitalization of cities—have long been ignored by policymakers and experts who study urban life. Only in the last five years has research about women in American cities been conducted by urban sociologists, labor economists and environmental psychologists, many of them women. Relevant findings from these studies have contributed to ideas in this book.

Knowing what to expect and discovering that you're not alone are two of the biggest comforts in making a smooth transition from a rural, suburban or college setting to a city. Realizing that other women have faced and solved similar problems can be reassuring when you're questioning the soundness of a decision to live or work in a big city.

STAGE ONE

Moving In

⌳⌳⌳⌳⌳⌳⌳⌳⌳⌳⌳⌳⌳⌳⌳⌳⌳⌳⌳⌳⌳⌳⌳⌳

> When you're alone and life is making
>   you lonely,
> you can always go *downtown*.
> When you've got worries, all the noise
>   and the hurry
> seems to help, I know, *downtown*.

ONE OF THE REASONS why cities are so attractive to those of us who grew up in suburbia and small towns is precisely what Petula Clark sang of when she made the hit song, "Downtown"—they're a place where exciting things happen, where there's no room for boredom, no time to worry about insignificant problems.

Beyond the fast pace, bright lights and the chance for adventure, there are the more pragmatic opportunities that cities hold for women: the possibility of finding a job doing what you most enjoy (and which may not even be translatable into a job in a smaller place); the potential to make a name for yourself, to earn a good income, to work for and among the best and the brightest.

City living itself is an enticement to most women who have grown up in a single-family home, usually surrounded by a yard and sometimes even more open space. The closeness and walkability of buildings, stores and restaurants in some cities is a plus for those of us who have grown up going to most destinations in a car. And the idea of living among, if not in, build-

17

ings whose architecture belongs to another era is very appealing.

Images alone, of course, are not substantial enough reasons on which to base a decision to go to a particular city. If you investigate what a move to a city involves before you make the commitment to come for good, it's more likely that your expectations will be met than will those of someone who arrives with only a suitcase full of dreams.

The first stage of city living, that of moving in, is an exhilarating one. It's the beginning of an adventure, the promise of a new life, the excitement of seeing how well you can handle yourself in different surroundings. The choices are overwhelming. Where you work, who you associate with, what you do in your free time is all up to you. There's no pressure to conform to what other women your age or in your position ought to be doing—the city is non-judgmental.

Living in the big city is a way of breaking away, of becoming your own person, even if you're already technically an adult. You'll find yourself in situations you've never been in before, having to make decisions and define your values.

There's no question that those who come to cities are not as satisfied with the status quo as women who stay closer to home. They want more in their lives than security and a comfortable family situation. Most of the women moving to cities today are products of suburbia, and many understood at a young age what isolation was all about by observing their mothers' lives. The city offers women many more options to plug into daily life, whether they're single, married or divorced. It also provides opportunities to experiment and adopt less traditional life-styles.

Beyond the freedom, there is the potential for excitement, stimulation and self-development: discovering that your special talents can earn you the respect and even adulation of others; realizing that the social position you were born into doesn't limit the circles you can travel in; finding out that others think your humor, your intelligence and your way of seeing the world are wonderful and make you worth knowing. Cities are places where fairy-tale fantasies can come true in small and big ways. But they don't come true overnight, or without efforts to put yourself in circumstances that can permit them to become a reality.

The images each of us has about a city through visits, media exposure or reading play an important role in our wanting to move there as young adults. While fantasies provide the fuel necessary to propel you through the moving-in stage, they can lose their energy if they're not tempered with reality. There are potential problems to consider, including:

• How will I find a job?
• What kind of an apartment will I be able to afford?
• Will I be able to keep my pet?
• How will I learn to get around on public transportation?

And there are the less tangible factors that will affect your happiness:

• Will I be able to make new friends?
• Will I enjoy being on my own?
• How long will I feel like an outsider?

The three chapters that are a part of this section talk about the dreams and down-to-earth information that you'll need if you're seriously considering a move to the city.

1

Making the Decision to Move

FROM HER VANTAGE POINT onboard a yacht which moved leisurely around the majestic boats in New York City's harbor, twenty-year-old Wanda Urbanska felt she had sailed into the pages of a history book. The excursion was one of her first press trips since she had become a summer intern at *Newsweek*. It was also the year of the Bicentennial, and the tall ships were making their maiden voyage to the city.

Wanda was on her own for the first time in a city she had fallen in love with through magazines which depicted chic young women rushing off to their interesting jobs in buildings so tall that they seemed like stairways to heaven.

Several months ago, as she hurried between classes on the Harvard University campus, she would have found it hard to imagine that she would be commuting from a dorm room in the Village to a job at one of the leading newsmagazines. But her essay and college credentials had landed her a position that opened doors she had never imagined walking through.

"New York seemed so vast and complicated," remembers Wanda, "But it was a place I wanted to see firsthand, having graduated in a high school class of eighty-three students. I desperately wanted to escape life in a small town. Once I arrived, I kept asking myself, 'Can I fit in here?'"

She did, even more so than she had imagined. One night, two editors at *Newsweek* invited her to attend the premiere of a new film and a reception afterward at the Four Seasons restaurant. "I was decked out in my most daring outfit—a black jumpsuit with a deep V-neck and tiny spaghetti straps. I was standing around with a drink in one hand and trying to appear unfazed by the number of celebrities in the room when a good-looking guy in a tux signaled me to his table. 'Are you an actress?' he asked. I said, 'No, I'm not.' He asked me if I would join him and another man at the table, whom I knew looked familiar. But I couldn't place either one of them. I thought it would be better if I stuck close to my bosses, so I declined. Do you know how bad I felt about not taking them up on the invitation when I learned that the man who had approached me was John Travolta and his buddy was Arnold Schwarzenegger?"

Wanda's exposure to famous, smart, ambitious people during her internship convinced her to return for good when she graduated. But when June 1978 rolled along, she found herself self-exiled to the less-threatening but slow-moving environment of her mother's home—Orono, Maine. "I wasn't sure what I really wanted to do. Writing fiction was what I loved doing and had been recognized for in college. But I knew that wasn't a marketable skill for a recent graduate. I was scared of going back to the city because I realized life would be different when I returned. Everything had been taken care of for me during my internship, but the next time I knew I would be on my own." At summer's end, Wanda packed her bags and headed to the city, because she needed to prove to herself that she could make it.

Wanda's indecisiveness about making a move to a big city is not unusual. Like most women who contemplate re-establishing themselves in a place much more populous and different in style from where they grew up, Wanda was at a major crossroads in her life. She was leaving behind her comfortable college existence and taking on the challenges of the real world—a competitive job market, earning a decent income and living on her own.

The Lure of Career Opportunities

"For women in particular, the large city offers job options unparalleled anywhere else," says Dr. Eli Ginzberg, one of the country's leading labor economists. Dancers, actresses, singers, musicians—all of those in the performing arts for whom audiences are a component of their work—have traditionally found that urban centers are where the jobs are. And those in the visual arts and communications—writers, artists and photographers, to name a few—find their options vastly improved in a city as well.

A new and growing group of women—those who are entering male-dominated professions—are likewise finding cities places where their ambitions stand a chance—cities have historically been more accepting of working women. (Women now compose 34 percent of law school graduates, 25 percent of medical and business school graduates, and 10 percent of engineering school graduates.)

In cities whose economies have historically been based in manufacturing (and which have by definition excluded women if not in job opportunities then in lack of appeal), a renaissance is occurring: in many, including Baltimore, Cleveland and Chicago, it is jobs in the service sector (where most women work) that are growing most rapidly, turning what used to be known as blue-collar territory into the land of the white collar.

Aside from the lure of jobs, the attraction of big city living is as much the opportunity to create a new self, to discard those aspects of your image or personality that you feel you've outgrown—or that you never thought were fair assessments of your true self anyway. In the big city, your past is your personal vision of the events that shaped your life, not someone else's interpretation of them.

Testing the Waters

Most city-bound women have had some exposure to big cities aside from what they read or hear about them in the media. Eighty percent of the women in the Urban Experience Survey said visits with families or vacations were occasions when they had a chance to peek through a window much bigger than the ones in their hometowns.

Very little research has been done on why young adults who have grown up in suburban or rural communities come to cities. But environmental psychologist Sylvia Fava has been examining that phenomenon and has come up with one preliminary finding: That those who settled in cities, generally speaking, had undergone "urban conditioning," that is, they had a chance to form their own opinion about city living, usually during their college years when they may have done an internship or gone to school in or near an urban setting. The results of the Urban Experience Survey confirm that theory—more than a third of the respondents got their first exposure to city living in college.

Survey Finding

What was your exposure to city living before moving to one?

Visits to cities with parents or friends on special occasions	81%
Career internships or going to college in a city	36%
What I read or heard	32%*

*Percentages total more than 100% because multiple answers were accepted.

If you're considering a move to a city but have never spent time there beyond short visits, it's a good idea to put yourself in a situation in which you'll be able to judge whether you and city life are right for each other. That's especially important if you're moving to a city whose culture and geography is much different from the one to which you're accustomed.

At age 19, Mary Alice Kellogg had never been further east than the Rio Grande. It was the summer of '69 and she was slinging hash on a guest ranch in her hometown of Tucson, Arizona, center of the saguaro cactus universe. She was a journalism major at the state university there, and she knew enough about the media to understand that the people at the top of the profession were on the East Coast. But that was a good 2,000 miles away, and all her relatives were on the West Coast. When the owner of the guest ranch, who was an advertising executive from Baltimore, came to visit that summer, she saw her chance to connect with someone who might help her.

"I walked up to him one morning after breakfast and said, 'I'd like to talk to you about jobs in advertising,' the old college student ruse. After a twenty-minute discussion, he offered me a job—in Baltimore. My response was, 'Gosh, I'll have to ask my mother.' He said he would pay me sixty-five dollars a week and my air fare to Baltimore—and that he wouldn't be my daddy."

Her outward show of bravado in the exchange of good-byes with her mother and boyfriend quickly crumbled once she boarded the plane. She was going to the East, that wicked place (or so folks in the West thought) where people knifed one another over a candy bar. Tears of fear gave way to tears of wonder when she stepped off the plane and saw more green than she'd ever imagined possible. But her boss-to-be, who had come to pick her up, wasn't sure why she was crying and tried to cheer her up: "Hey, you're going to have a great time in Baltimore. You're gonna learn everything there is to know about the ad business and you're gonna run the world."

The summer turned out so well that she returned the following summer as well, staying in the same women's residence, the Business Girls Lodge of the Methodist Church, she had the year before.

Where to Stay Temporarily

There are many alternatives worth considering between an expensive hotel and a park bench. The following housing options are relatively inexpensive and are listed from the least to the most costly. Since rates vary widely, they are not included here.

University Dorms and Fraternity Houses. Rooms on or near campus are often available only during summer months. Students and recent graduates are given priority over others (at some university housing, it's a requirement). There is sometimes a minimum stay requirement of several weeks, and you may be required to sign up for a meal plan, which costs extra. But the cost is low and the company is convivial. Check with the Housing Office of the university for more information.

Women's Residences. Many of these residential hotels for women have been in existence for decades and are presided over by a housemother, who is often called the "resident director." They're often conveniently located in the downtown areas and are among the safest types of temporary housing, since there are usually strict policies about male guests (some have strict curfews as well). Rooms are rented on a weekly basis, and meals are sometimes included in the price. Since many residences run a switchboard, you may not be able to make or get phone calls after certain hours, and you may have to share a hallway phone. Contact the Chamber of Commerce for names of residences in the city to which you're moving.

Y's. If you want to have access to athletic facilities, a YMCA or YWCA may be a good choice. Some Y residences house both men and women, although they're on separate floors. Daily rates apply at most Y's. Rooms sometimes come with private bath. Most are at desirable downtown locations. Y's are listed in the phone book.

Bed and Breakfast. An English concept that is becoming increasingly popular in this country, Bed and Breakfast gives you the option of staying in someone's home. Vacationers and business travelers often take advantage of this overnight option, but many hosts are willing to let their rooms for weeks or months. You must fill out an application form beforehand, which asks for references. Bed and Breakfast hosts are numerous in California, and can also be found in Seattle, Las Vegas, Chicago, Boston, New York City and Washington, D.C. For more information, write: Bed and Breakfast International, 151 Ardmore Road, Kensington, CA 94707, or call information to find out if there's a local Bed and Breakfast placement agency in your city.

Subletting an Apartment. Renting someone else's furnished apartment while they're away is ideal, particularly if all you've brought to town are a couple of suitcases. Three-month sublets are often available over the summer, and longer and shorter ones are somewhat less easily found at other times of the year. Sublets are advertised under the "Apts. Furnished" heading of the real estate section. (College newspapers are a good place to look for summer sublets.) But since many leaseholders prefer to sublet their apartments to people they know personally or through a connection, it's a good idea to ask everyone you know if they know of an available sublet. In some cities, tenants are not permitted to charge subtenants more than a certain percentage (often 10 percent) above and beyond their normal rent.

Singles Complexes. This is a good option if you want to take your time researching neighborhoods before you move in permanently. Apartments are often rented fully furnished, and month-by-month leases are available. Sports facilities and equipment, a game or recreation room and organized activities are standard fare. Most of the residents are in their twenties and thirties and are usually single.

Summer jobs and internships are probably the two best ways to investigate city living. If you're able to arrange a structured situation as Wanda and Mary Alice did you have the built-in advantages of a roof over your head, a group of new friends and enough money to take care of your living expenses for the time you plan to be there. But setting up a job or living situation usually entails researching your options beforehand and making plans far in advance. If you're able to do that you'll be free to think about and deal with the pace of city living and decide whether it's for you.

A Trial Run on Your Own

Many of us who have dreamed of living in cities, however, are more inclined to seize an opportunity that presents itself, which can mean dealing with unforeseen problems once we arrive. I hadn't wanted to spend another summer working as a secretary in a boring office in my hometown, so when a college friend offered me a ride to New York, I took it.

I had lined up a place to live—a college dorm room on the Columbia University campus. I had signed up for two summer courses, but I needed a job if I hoped to afford an entire summer in New York City. I followed up on job notices posted at the school, only to find that the first one I went out on was for "models" who were expected to be available for more than just photography. I was shocked at the idea, although the young man who interviewed me assured me that many co-eds made good weekly salaries working for him. I declined. Although the job I finally landed was a secretarial position, it was in a setting I wouldn't have found in Ohio—working in an African art gallery, among wooden sculptures decorated with cowrie shells, some of which still contained the spirits of the people who once used them, or so claimed the young artisan who repaired the damaged artifacts.

Aside from the insecurity of arriving in a city with only enough money to carry me through six weeks, the even bigger problem I discovered once I arrived was that I knew no one, and I was much too intimidated by the bus and subway systems to tackle exploring the city on my own. I didn't venture beyond the immediate vicinity of the campus for two weeks, at which time I met several people from school who were willing to show me how to get around town. When I returned to the city eight months later, I was better prepared to negotiate its neighborhoods via public transit.

Researching the Move

Not everyone has the luxury of being able to give the city they're considering a trial run. But because it's easy to romanticize what life will be like once you arrive (cozy apartment in a Victorian house, a great job as a retail buyer and a busy social life), it's important to think through all the possible scenarios of what might happen *before* you ever pack your bags. Be sure to consider:

1. Who do you know in the city? Whether your contacts are friends, relatives, or alumni, what, if anything, can you depend on them for? It's one thing if the relative is a sister or brother, but beyond that close relationship, it's shortsighted to assume anything when it comes to getting help from those you know. Don't rely on promises of introductions from them; plan on having to track down most of your own leads.

Even if someone you know or are related to offers you a roof over your head, how long can you expect to stay and still be considered welcome company? When people say, "Feel free to stay until you get settled in," what they really mean is, "Start looking for your own place right away." And since most city-dwellers are short on space (even if they're big on generosity), it's understandable that short stays are considered polite, long stays insensitive.

2. How will you feel about spending time alone? Unless a friend or relative is making the move with you, you'll no doubt find yourself with more free time and fewer people to share it with than ever before. If you grew up in an active household and never wanted for friends, you might be surprised to find that loneliness is just around the bend.

3. What are your chances of finding a job in your field?

Even though cities are good places to find work, there may be few opportunities in your particular field. Houston is not the place to go to if you're hoping to work as a fashion designer; Atlanta isn't the place to be if you want to get into television programming. Competition is another factor to consider; if you're not accustomed to going after what you want with a great deal of enthusiasm, energy and hard work, you'll be in for a surprise in most cities, which abound with people who are.

4. What kind of financial reserve do you have should the worst case scenario occur, namely, looking unsuccessfully for a job and discovering that even inexpensive living costs more than you had anticipated?

Calculating the Costs of Relocating

Many first-time movers find themselves in a financial bind soon after arriving because they didn't expect or plan for many of their settling-in expenses. If you want to avoid calling home for help or taking the first job that comes along simply because you need the money, figure out how much the move and related costs will run. Because costs vary widely from one city to another, estimates or ranges are provided only for standard items.

You should also add on to this total figure how much you'll need to live on for a month or two (the time you should allow for finding a job if you don't have one waiting for you).

ITEM	ESTIMATED COST
Transportation	
Your own	_____
Your belongings (check into: UPS, U.S. Mail, rail or private movers)	_____
Lodging	
Temporary place to stay	_____
Real estate or broker's fee (one month's rent to 20% of a year's rent)	_____
Security deposit on apartment (one month's rent)	_____

Telephone installation (if you don't
have a credit track record, you may
have to pay a refundable deposit fee of
up to $100). Installation charge fee
(can be as much as $28)   _____
Renter's insurance (for $10,000–
$25,000 of property and liability
coverage—$68–$139 a year. Payments
can be made over several months)   _____
Crime deterrents (new door locks, win-
dow gate or bars, burglar alarm)   _____
Apartment furnishings
Furniture   _____
Linens and towels   _____
Dishes, pots and pans, cooking utensils _____
Household supplies   _____
Miscellaneous
Car registration ($25–$50)   _____
                       TOTAL MOVING EXPENSES _____
MONTHLY LIVING EXPENSES
Rent   _____
Telephone   _____
Gas/electricity   _____
Food   _____
Entertainment   _____
Transportation   _____
          TOTAL OF 2 MONTHS' LIVING EXPENSES _____
PLAN ON LEAVING HOME WITH: GRAND TOTAL _____

Escaping to a City

Women who head to a city with specific goals in mind stand
a better chance of acclimating well to their new environment
than do those who are running away from an undesirable situation—an unhappy relationship or overprotective parents, for
example. The younger and less experienced you are, the more

likely it is that the elusive grown-up and independent self
you're seeking will elude you as much in a city as it has in your
hometown. Moving to a fast-paced place doesn't speed up mat-
uration so much as it tests the strength of already acquired
traits.

Even if you're well beyond your late teens or early twenties,
viewing a fresh start in a new city as a panacea for your problems is myopic. Inner crises usually demand resolution before
you can settle anywhere and feel happy with your life.

But if you're what Gail Sheehy has defined as a "path-
finder"—someone who has the ability to successfully navigate
through trying circumstances, which may be beyond her control—you may be able to use a drastic change in environment
to resolve inner conflicts.

At 26, Sherry Richardson* felt twice her age. She had already been married eight years and had a preschool son. She
had never quite been able to break away from her mother, who
seemed to demand more and more attention and favors of her
as time went on. And that in turn caused friction with her
husband.

Most young women go through the first passage to adult life
between the ages of 18 and 22 as they separate out their own
identity from their parents' and leave the security of home. But
in Sherry's case, that stage of development didn't start until
age 26. By then, she felt like a prisoner wearing the costume of
a suburban housewife in her Columbus, Ohio, home. She
raised roses, discussed books at a local literary club and tried to
eat her way to peace of mind. She got bigger—eventually
wearing a size 20½ dress—but her frustrations didn't shrink.

Miami had enchanted her from the time she'd first visited it
at age 15. Each time she returned to visit as a married woman,
she found that in the company of palm trees stirring gently
under blue skies, the pressure that she felt to please a demanding mother and a neglected husband seemed to drift out to sea.

After taking a cruise out of Miami with her husband, Sherry
and her preschool son stayed behind with a cousin who lived
there. Three months later, Sherry told her husband she

*A pseudonym.

wanted to stay for a year to sort out her problems. "He accepted my decision because he was as sick of the bickering between us as I was," remembers Sherry, whose attractive figure (now a size 12) makes her look younger than her 38 years.

Why did Sherry succeed in making a difficult transition when others may have failed? Her expectations about what life would be like in Miami were realistic. She had no illusions about the fact that she'd have to support herself (something she'd never done in her life before); that she'd be lonely at first (she'd never lived anywhere else but Columbus); that she would eventually have to face up to the fact that her marriage wasn't working out. Looking back on it, she says, "We were just two nice people who got married too young." And Sherry had two personal goals: caring for her son on her own and getting herself back in shape.

Her "can do" attitude made all the difference in her building an impressive career from scratch at age 26 (she now owns her own public relations firm in Miami), discovering that she thrived in a cosmopolitan environment which was the juncture of North and South American cultures (she began learning Spanish soon after her arrival), and liberating a long-repressed sense of adventure (she and her son hitchhiked their way through several Central American countries).

Survey Finding

What was your main reason for moving to the city in which you're now living?

	Single Women	Married Women
To find a good job	30%	6%
To get a good education	11%	9%
For adventure's sake	11%	6%
To be with my boy-friend/husband	5%	49%
To get away from an un-happy home situation	2%	2%
Other	42%	28%

Moving with or for a Man

Women today are much less inclined to follow the man in their life as he pursues his career dream, particularly if they are single. Only 4 percent of the women surveyed said they moved to be with their boyfriend. That's because women are just as interested in establishing themselves in the job market as men are, and unless their partner is willing to take their needs into consideration, they're probably better off alone for the time being. Still, there are some women who elect to move to a city of their man's choice. They may feel his career is more important, haven't yet defined their own career dreams or are dissatisfied with their current job situation.

Half of the married women in the Urban Experience Survey moved to a city to accommodate their husbands' plans. But a growing number of couples are making the decision of where to move a mutual one. One in four women interviewed in depth for this book moved to a city with a man. Half of those who moved with their husbands subsequently got divorced. Of those who moved with their boyfriends, one eventually married the man with whom she moved, another is still with her boyfriend; the third couple split up.

The message behind these numbers, says psychotherapist Phoebe Prosky, is that the fate of a relationship depends greatly on the strength of the commitment of the partners to each other at the time of the move and the flexibility of each individual to adapt to a new situation.

One of the couples whose marriage survived and ultimately prospered as a result of the move was Vicki and James Madara's. It was a foregone conclusion that Jim would be doing his surgical residency at a Boston hospital the year after Vicki's graduation from an art college in Philadelphia. It was 1975, and getting married was not considered the thing to do right after college, let alone subjugate one's own career plans to a man's. "No one offered me any encouragement to get married—including my roommates, my mother or my sisters," Vicki remembers.

The transition from being single and in school to getting married and looking for her first job in a city she'd visited on only several occasions was extremely difficult for Vicki, who was 22 at the time. Being at an age where it is easy to think that one can take on almost any challenge and succeed, Vicki made the best of the situation. She found a design job at a contract furniture dealer, which proved to be a stepping-stone to becoming director of the design department there. Because her husband put in long hours in the hospital, she, too, worked overtime. "I didn't take the initiative at first to explore the city, partly because I had no one to do it with," she remembers. "Had I been single, however, there would have been more opportunities, since men did ask me out."

Their determination to make the marriage work while building their respective careers kept the momentum of the relationship going long after the veneer of romance had been shaved thin by the realities of coping with everyday problems.

Some couples, like the Madaras, have the emotional security to deal with major changes in their life in their early twenties. Part of that adaptive mechanism depends on the number of moves made as a child or adolescent. Another determinant of whether a relationship that is transported to a big city will survive is whether the person who is asked to leave feels she is leaving behind something important.

Candidates for a Post-Arrival Breakup

Many young women still find themselves entering into traditional relationships with men—ones in which the husband or boyfriend makes the major decisions, which the women are "free" to take or leave. When they're in love, most women see no other choice than to accept the decision, even if it ignores their needs. (The unspoken choice is to risk losing the man, one that most women don't feel confident enough to take.)

"If a woman feels she is being forced to leave behind things that are important to her, the resentment she feels is likely to grow rather than subside," says psychotherapist Prosky. Any move that separates a person from familiar surroundings, family and friends is potentially traumatic. But when a relocation also includes adjusting to life in a big city, the effects on a relationship can be catastrophic.

Nima Grissom was born in a suburb of Dallas, where she lived until she went to college in San Antonio, some 240 miles to the north. Accepted at the Medical School at the University of Texas, she spent four more years there. Nima fell in love with a fellow medical student, whom she married at age 24. It was a happy, if challenging, time in her life, building her home nest, expanding her group of friends, feeling a sense of accomplishment as she conquered microbiology and anatomy and physiology, one of five female members of her class.

Then, in September of 1978, her husband dropped the bombshell. He'd landed a residency in San Francisco for the following spring. Nima would also be doing her residency, but spots in surgery were much more available than were those in his specialty.

Nine months later, she said good-bye to her friends and gazed wistfully at the roomy ranch home surrounded by plenty of space that she knew she couldn't replace in San Francisco. Being a homebody who felt most comfortable when she knew where everything was, she was terrified of the unknowns that lay ahead. True, she'd lined up a residency for herself at a good hospital and she would, after all, be with her husband. Still, she felt like Dorothy in Oz, swept away by forces beyond her control, her only goal to find her way back home as soon as possible.

The apartment Nima and her husband found in an old Victorian house in the Western Addition section of the city was charming enough, but they later realized that the neighborhood was not in what was considered a safe area. With both of them on rotating shifts, which demanded an overnight tour of duty every third day, Nima and her husband saw less and less of each other. Nima realized that she enjoyed the time she spent alone more than the time they spent together. Nine months after they arrived, the couple split.

Nima and the other women I interviewed who opted to relocate with a boyfriend or husband ended up falling in love with and adopting the city to which they had moved. The transition was rarely a smooth one, since even the ones whose marriages sustained the move inevitably underwent change. In fact, in two cases, when the husbands wanted to move back to their previous residence for business reasons, their wives, who had begun building their professional life rather successfully, talked them into staying. Had these men been less flexible or sensitive to their wives' needs, their marriages might not have withstood another uprooting.

Should You Keep Your Car?

There are only a handful of American cities—New York, Boston, San Francisco, Chicago and Washington, D.C.—in which a car is usually not a necessity and is often a luxury. If you plan on living and working within reach of good public transportation, it's wise to think twice about holding onto your wheels for three reasons: expense, hassle and safety.

Parking. The cost of garaging your car can put you on the road to bankruptcy if you live in a highly congested area where space of any kind is at a premium—for example, in Washington, D.C.'s Georgetown. A less expensive alternative is an open parking lot, but they are usually situated on the perimeter of a neighborhood or a downtown area. You may have to walk a distance or take a cab to get there, and even during the daytime, they're not always safe for a woman alone on foot. Unless they're well lit and attended by round-the-clock security guards, parking lots are easy pickings for thieves. A third possibility is to park your car on the street. It may be free, but chances are you'll have to move it regularly (for street cleaning). Should you forget, you'll end up with a ticket or a tow.

Parking Tickets and Towing. Not only are they more expensive ($15–$35 depending on the offense), but they're often given for the slightest infraction because parking tickets are a big source of revenue for city governments. "Limited" and "no parking" zones abound in downtown areas and residential neighborhoods of cities.

You almost have to figure in a few tickets or a most costly tow in the annual cost of keeping your car if you often park it on the street.

Insurance. Premiums are higher in cities, primarily because of the increased risk of theft. You can keep your insurance costs down by increasing your deductible. Or, if you have a used car that has seen better days, you may want to forgo collision insurance, which may reduce your premium by as much as a half.

Registration Fees. If you've relocated to another state, you'll have to re-register your car there within a set time period, which is often 30 days after you arrive. (If you neglect to do so and your car is parked on the street, you risk being ticketed.)

Gas and Maintenance Costs. Plan on paying more per gallon if you tank up in the city, where gas stations are less plentiful and can get away with charging more. If you do much city street driving, your car will need attention more often because of less than adequate road conditions. Repairs are often more costly in the city, once again because there are fewer big store service centers or even small repair shops.

Theft and Vandalism. If you have a late-model car or even a desirable older model, it's advisable to keep it in a garage or guarded lot. Cars parked on the street are prime targets for car thieves, many of whom operate in big cities. In 1979, the cities with the highest motor vehicle theft rate were Boston, Houston, New York, Los Angeles and Cleveland, according to *Places Rated Almanac.* If your car isn't anything special, but it has a tape cassette player or a new tire in the trunk, it may be broken into. The cost of replacing a shattered window or punched-in trunk lock often exceed the cost of what was taken from the car.

Despite the risk, expense and hassle of owning a car in the city, there is a big plus in being mobile—the freedom of being able to get out of town on the weekends. Whether you defer that luxury until you're better situated financially depends on your needs.

Bridging Two Worlds

Even the most adventurous city-bound women need to maintain a connection to their roots. For it is the world they're leaving behind that has given definition to their identity, and until there are new "important others" in their life who can reinforce their self-image, it is people from the past whose opinions matter.

If one or more people whom you know from back home are living in the city to which you're moving, getting through the first few months is bound to be much easier. Because you're both members of the same tribe, there is an appreciation and understanding of your perception and ways of coping with unfamiliar territory. That bond of shared experience, whether the person is a friend or relative, your age or much older, can be a great comfort early in your stay. He or she is a shoulder to cry on, a friendly voice on the telephone, a trusted resource for information and advice.

Having Family in the City

Washington, D.C., is a long way from Kennard, Indiana, a farming village, where Penny Farthing grew up. Although her mother was a schoolteacher, Penny's career choice was more influenced by uncles on both sides of the family who were lawyers.

After her first year of law school at Indiana University, Penny accepted a job offer from her favorite uncle who ran a successful law practice in suburban Virginia, just 30 minutes from the nation's capital. It was her first experience living outside of her home state. Two summers of working for her uncle's firm and exploring Georgetown and other city neighborhoods convinced Penny that neither Kennard nor any other place in Indiana was going to offer her the opportunities and excitement that Washington did. She arrived there in the spring of 1970, having accepted a job offer from a federal agency that interviewed on campus.

She accepted her uncle's invitation to stay in his suburban home while she looked for an apartment. Just as he had so carefully orchestrated her introduction to job options in one of the country's leading law centers, he now laid the groundwork for her to make the cultural leap out of the land of beef and potatoes to the world of blue crabs and Brie.

Her uncle tended to her social life, introducing her to the son of one of his associates—a law student who knew Washington well. "He took me to all kinds of places and really helped me get to know the city. It wasn't a wildly romantic relationship. But he was a good companion, and from a practical point of view, it really helped smooth my transition into life on my own in a big city," says Penny.

Penny was lucky in the sense that she not only had a member of her own clan looking out for her, but a key social contact her own age with whom she had something in common. For the woman who comes to a city "cold," finding the first few people upon whom she can rely for anything beyond directions is a difficult task.

Coming to the City with a Friend

One way to avoid having to rely entirely on strangers or people you barely know to be the building blocks in your new world is to make the move with a friend. The women interviewed for this book who had traveled to a big city with a college roommate or friend were unanimously more upbeat about the adventure of it all because they could share their triumphs and disappointments. They didn't have to face the prospect of going out alone, and meeting new people was a situation whose results they could compare and joke about.

Still, unless you and your friend have similar motivations and interest in coming to the same city, the situation may backfire. Before getting caught in the excitement of planning a move, it's a good idea to ask yourself:

• What are my reasons for moving to this particular city?

- Would I consider moving there on my own? Should my friend change her mind once she gets there, would I have the determination to stay and try to make things work out on my own?
- Are the two of us capable of sharing tight quarters?
- Do we have similar financial resources and attitudes about spending money? (If you don't, you may find yourself going off in opposite directions soon after you arrive.)
- How have I reacted to crises in my friend's life which she's shared with me (and vice versa)? They're inevitable, if only on a minor scale, in the first year of living in a city.

Like any relationship, a friendship is a delicate balance of meeting each person's respective needs and not demanding more than the other person can give (and still having your needs met) while being capable of giving what the other person requires. Drastic changes in environment and life-style can put the most longstanding friendships on shaky ground, so it's best to know that taking that route as a way of insulating yourself from the loneliness of not knowing anyone has its risks, too.

2

Landing a Job

∞∞

MOST WOMEN MOVE to a city with the expectation rather than the certainty of finding employment. How fast you find a job can make a big difference in how quickly you adjust to life in a new place because work is the focus around which most of us build our day. If you're a recent graduate or have never taken a long break from work, it's especially important to have the structure of a job in your life, or you'll feel out of sync with the work-oriented pace of the city.

Even though job opportunities are extensive in major cities, it's a good idea to research what's available in your field before you actually come. Several of the women interviewed for this book discovered to their surprise that the city they had moved to was not a good place to begin serious careers—either because the competition was too stiff or there were simply too few opportunities.

Choosing a city because you like its ambience and style of living are valid reasons to move there, but that may mean you have to make trade-offs in your work. Boston, for example, is a popular post-college place to settle. But many recent graduates find they have to scale down their employment expectations to match the realities of the highly competitive job market there.

Financial considerations are another aspect of your job search that require planning. Count on spending at least two months looking for a job in your field. That means you should either save enough money to cover your living expenses before you leave home or be willing to work part-time once you arrive.

Survey Finding

Did you rely on financial help from family or friends in order to make ends meet?

Yes	10%
No, I never did	57%
Not now, but I did when I first moved to the city	18%
Not now, but I did when I was unemployed or underemployed	14%

Lining up a Job Before You Move

After teaching for a year in a regional high school in a small town 30 miles north of Boston, Gale Smith was ready for something more adventurous. She didn't quite know what she wanted nor where it was, but she was in a "I'm ready to move on" frame of mind when she went to a regional trade show/convention for teachers in 1972.

She met the president of a graphics art company there, who wanted to know if she'd be interested in a marketing position with their company.

A month later, she was living in an apartment on Wisconsin Avenue in Washington, D.C., a city which she barely knew but was determined to conquer. But even at 23 and without any experience in business, Gale realized that unless she knew what it would cost her to operate the company's business out of her apartment (the company was based in Massachusetts), that she might sell herself short. So she asked the company to pay her way to Washington so that she could investigate her expenses firsthand. "I figured in everything I could think of—my rent, car payments, telephone answering service—to use as the basis of my salary negotiation," explains Gale. "When you're leaving a comfortable situation for an unknown and potentially stressful one, it doesn't pay to put yourself through the aggravation if you're going to end up making less after taxes than what you're currently making." After several negotiating sessions, she walked away with the job and a salary that was $5,000 a year more than what she'd been making as a teacher.

Pinning down a job long-distance is usually limited to those who have extensive experience, a professional degree or great contacts. And, like Gale, they have to be risk-takers—she didn't know how financially stable or successful the company she joined was at the time (although she later developed her financial savvy and became a stockbroker).

Soon-to-be graduates stand their best chance of connecting with employers in various cities through the placement offices at their schools. Still, the employers most likely to interview students are those in fields in which the demand exceeds the supply of good candidates—computer science, engineering, accounting and nursing, to name a few. Even if your chances of working for a visiting employer are not great or the companies who come to your campus are not your top choices, interviewing with them is one way of getting a handle on just how available jobs are in a city to which you'd like to move.

Long-Distance Job-Finding Strategies

How do you even start looking for a job in Denver, for example, if you're living in a small town in the Midwest? Tracking the help-wanted ads in the Sunday newspapers from that city is the best way to get an idea of what's available and what the going rates for salaries are. The *National Business Employment Weekly*, published by *The Wall Street Journal*, is a good source for jobs in business and a wide variety of other fields including health care, engineering and computer science.

But even if you find opportunities for which you're qualified, you still face the biggest problem of the long-distance job hunter: you can't simply come by for an interview. And unless your experience makes you a highly desirable candidate, count on having to pick up your own transportation expenses (which may be tax deductible).

Many employers are reluctant to contact out-of-town job hunters because they're unsure of how serious you are about the move or if you're capable of making the adjustment (if you have no family or school ties to the area). The only way to be seen as a serious candidate is to make yourself available for interviews by making a trip to the city, which you may be able to combine with taking a vacation there. If an employer knows you'll only be in town for a limited time, he may be more flexible about accommodating your request for an interview. (If you're in your last year of school, spring break is a good time to establish contacts in the city to which you hope to move after graduation.)

It's overly optimistic to expect that you'll actually be offered a job during an initial job exploration trip to a city, although fate may conspire in your favor. It's more realistic to assume that this is a time to assess possibilities and establish contacts with whom you can keep in touch. Most employers want to interview people who, if they're not available immediately for employment, can start in two to three weeks. If you're currently working, giving your employer notice and making a long-distance move usually take longer than that.

If you have contacts—friends, relatives, alumni from your school—who understand what kind of job you're looking for and are in a position to keep you informed about openings that may come up, you'll have an edge over the job hunter who is coming in cold. The best job openings are ones that are passed along through word-of-mouth. The chances of news of a television production job in Los Angeles filtering out to Kansas City are almost nil, for example, unless you have a contact in Los Angeles who is tuned into the media grapevine.

Besides friends, another way to plug into a city far from where you now live is to contact alumni who live and work there (talk to your school's alumni or placement office for names), professional organizations to which you have a legitimate connection or women's groups which offer job counseling or advice. Trade journals and magazines might be more useful if you're looking for work in a more specialized area.

The Top Ten Cities for Artists

If you hope to work in any area of the arts, your chances of finding employment are better in cities where people already working in your field live. Granted, the competition is keener, but the chances of finding work are greater in cities because they can attract the biggest audiences and are where the businesses who market the work of artists are located. There are more people in every artistic field working in New York City or Los Angeles than any other cities, although Chicago, Washington, Philadelphia, Detroit, San Francisco and Boston also have significant artist populations.

Those in the performing arts—actors, musicians, stage producers and directors—are more heavily concentrated in urban areas than are those whose work doesn't demand an audience. The following charts show the top ten cities where artists in ten fields live. (The term "artist" includes a wide array of artistic professions grouped together for counting purposes by the Bureau of the Census.)

Artists	*Actors*	*Architects*
New York City	New York City	New York City
Los Angeles	Los Angeles	Los Angeles
Chicago	Chicago	Chicago
Washington, D.C.	San Francisco	San Francisco
Philadelphia	Washington, D.C.	Washington, D.C.
Detroit	Boston	Boston
San Francisco	Philadelphia	Philadelphia
Boston	Baltimore	Detroit
Minneapolis	Dallas	Seattle
Dallas	Seattle	Dallas

Authors	*Dancers*	*Designers*
New York City	New York City	New York City
Los Angeles	Los Angeles	Los Angeles
Washington, D.C.	San Francisco	Chicago
Boston	Detroit	Detroit
San Francisco	Chicago	Philadelphia

Chicago	Honolulu	San Francisco
Minneapolis	Las Vegas	Boston
Baltimore	San Diego	Paterson
Philadelphia	Washington, D.C.	Newark
Detroit	Baltimore	Washington, D.C.

Musicians and Composers	*Painters and Sculptors*	*Photographers*
New York City	New York City	New York City
Los Angeles	Los Angeles	Los Angeles
Chicago	Chicago	Chicago
Philadelphia	Philadelphia	Washington, D.C.
Detroit	Detroit	Philadelphia
San Francisco	Washington, D.C.	Detroit
Boston	San Francisco	Boston
Washington, D.C.	Boston	Minneapolis
Minneapolis	Minneapolis	St. Louis
Miami	San Diego	Baltimore

Radio and TV Announcers
New York City
Los Angeles
Washington, D.C.
Chicago
San Francisco
Philadelphia
Boston
Pittsburgh
Detroit
Miami

Source: National Endowment for the Arts.

Looking for Work Once You Arrive

One of the disadvantages of arranging a job long-distance is that the temptation to take the first quasi-interesting job that comes along is strong. It is, after all, your passport to life in a new city, and if you're like most people, you wait until the last minute (i.e., when you can no longer stand being where you are or your student status is about to change imminently) to try to set something up.

Once you've arrived in a city, however, you have a better perspective on the range of jobs available and can better make small judgments (for example, whether the employer is in a desirable location) that will contribute to your satisfaction with a job. If you're determined to get a toehold in a particular field, it's smart to try to work for an employer who is considered a leader in that city (and beyond) and to go for an entry-level position that will help you prepare for the dream job you eventually hope to get.

When, at age 19, Marsha Appel walked into the offices of the *St. Paul Dispatch,* she wasn't at all sure why anyone there might want to hire a college dropout. She had just moved to one of Minnesota's Twin Cities from the college town of Ames, Iowa, with her new husband, whose promised job had fallen through. Marsha couldn't afford the out-of-state tuition fees at the state university, so she had to look for a job to establish her residency. Why not look for something in the field she hoped to eventually go into—journalism—even if it meant she had to work as a janitor?

"I was absolutely amazed when they gave me a job as a receptionist in the sales department. It was a beginning that I never thought would happen so easily. I soon realized, however, that I was seen as a cute young thing rather than a serious aspiring journalist, which, combined with my new role as a suburban wife, made me feel incredibly misunderstood and lonely," says Marsha.

Marsha had successfully identified a top employer and found a job with the company, but what ultimately led to her dissatisfaction with her job seven months later was that she hadn't started in the right department. There was no way that learning the ropes in advertising would hone her skills as a reporter.

"I quickly learned that unless you asked for what you wanted, you'd never get anywhere," Marsha remembers. "So I marched up to the editorial department and said, 'I really want to be in this department and I'll be happy to work as a copyboy.' Again, much to my surprise, the editor said, 'Okay.' Six weeks later, I was working as a newsclerk—the title for a junior re-porter—in the business section."

Tall, fair-haired and pretty, Marsha is one of those people whose enthusiasm is readily communicated to the people she meets, which is why she had few problems getting hired into a competitive field. (She stayed at the *St. Paul Dispatch* for four years, working full-time and earning her degree at night.) Good luck and charm can be a big help in getting hired, but it's to your advantage to understand how people are hired into jobs in the field you hope to break into so that you can make the necessary preparations before or as soon as you arrive in the city.

It's particularly important to understand hiring procedures in competitive or glamour fields—television broadcasting, modeling, magazine and book publishing, to name a few. Even in a large city, these businesses are small and tough to break into. That's why, for example, many recent graduates who want to make it in publishing or those who have worked in the field outside cities, take a six-week course (the best-known ones are offered by Radcliffe, the University of Denver and New York University) during which time they learn how books and magazines are put together and, even more importantly, meet professionals in the business. Most hiring (in any field) is a question of whether the interviewer likes you (assuming, of course, that you're qualified for the position). Developing con-tacts with people who have the power to hire you or recom-mend you to someone who can is the quickest route to finding employment.

Guides to Finding the Right Job

Looking for a first or new job is tough enough when you're on familiar turf. But pinpointing the employers that should be on your "to contact" list in a new city can seem like an overwhelming task unless you know where to be-gin. The following books can help you organize a systema-tic job campaign, determine what kind of salary you can negotiate and get you off to a good start in your career.

The Job Bank Book Series by Bob Adams, Inc. There are four editions available: Metropolitan New York, Chicago, Boston and California. Essential information about major firms is provided, including: address and phone number, description of the company's products or services, name of major personnel officer. In addition, entry- and middle-level positions and their requirements are listed for most companies. ($9.95 each)

The National Job-Finding Guide by Heinz Ulrich and J. Robert Conner (Doubleday/Dolphin). Similar kinds of information about 500 corporations nationwide is cross-indexed in this guide by type of company and location. Career counseling and placement services for women are listed by city and state in a special section. ($12.95)

The American Almanac of Jobs and Salaries by John W. Wright (Avon Books). An in-depth research report on what workers in virtually every field make. Salary breakdowns are often given for specialties within fields, geographical areas and level of experience. ($9.95)

Making It on Your First Job by Peggy J. Schmidt (Avon Books). A step-by-step guide from deciding what you want to do, to developing a comprehensive job-finding strategy to establishing a good relationship with your boss. ($2.95)

Settling for Less

Even the best-plotted job campaign may fail to produce results quickly enough. So it's smart to have a backup plan so that you don't find yourself packing your bags before you've had a chance to prove that you can make it.

Sue Sheets came to Washington, D.C., with the dream of working for the State Department or Foreign Service. She was bilingual, having taught French to junior high school students for two years, and had taken courses in public administration after graduating from college. Realizing that office skills might also be useful, Sue took an eight-week secretarial course the summer before she and her twin sister, Ann, made the move to Washington, D.C. Sue had no idea, however, of how competitive their examinations were. After taking them, she suddenly knew she wouldn't be heading to some romantic outpost in a French-speaking country. After several weeks of unsuccessful job hunting, Sue decided to waitress because it paid good money and allowed her the flexibility of continuing to look for work.

The psychological impact of having to accept work that may have at one time fit in well with your status in life but no longer does can take its toll. It's particularly difficult to go back to a job you may have had as a student once you've actually worked as a professional. The only way to keep your spirits up and your self-confidence intact is to push ahead with your job campaign, which is what Sue did. Armed with a list of all the French companies with U.S. subsidiaries from the U.N., she systematically contacted all that were in the metropolitan D.C. area.

A copy of her résumé happened to arrive at Aérospatiale, Inc., the U.S. corporate sales office for the largest aircraft manufacturer in France, the day that three people—almost half of the company's staff—had been fired. Sue was hired in a part-time capacity and continued to work as a waitress until the French company expanded her job to a full-time position several months later.

Reality Testing

The best way to avoid having your expectations about a first job dashed is to subject them to a reality test ahead of time. Even if you have work experience, you can't assume that you'll automatically be able to get a position similar to the one you now have in a new city. Talking to people who work for companies or agencies similar to one you would like to work for can help you gauge your chances of finding a position. Find out, too, if there are licensing or state examination requirements you have to pass before you'll be considered for employment.

The other option, of course, is to take a full-time, permanent position even though it's not the job you want because it may pay more or carry more professional prestige. The two major disadvantages of going that route are that you're limiting the time you have available to continue looking for your first-choice job (most of which has to be done between nine and five), and you're putting yourself in the potential dilemma of having to tell an employer you're leaving (should a job you want come through) before he's been able to recoup his initial investment of hiring you.

When Self-Employment Makes Sense

Another possibility is to try to work free-lance or start your own business—both of which are difficult even when you are already well established in a city. Terrie Temkin had three years of work experience under her belt when she moved to San Diego from Milwaukee, Wisconsin. She had worked as a speech communication instructor for two years, a job which she hoped to continue in a college or hospital setting on the West Coast. Everyone in town had a master's degree, or so it seemed, as Terrie made the rounds of personnel offices and employment agencies. Even though she had an education specialist's certificate in addition to her master's degree, the number of qualified people looking for similar jobs (many of whom had better contacts than she did) worked against her.

Summer had come and gone, and so had Terrie's savings. She began accepting money from her parents in order to live while she continued her job search. "I wanted to be independent but not badly enough to take a waitressing job," remembers Terrie, who felt a little guilty about her parents paying her rent even though she was 25. The only option that would allow her to continue using her training and experience was to go out on her own. Teaching interpersonal communication courses through the continuing education divisions of local high schools and colleges proved to be the best way to earn her bread and butter money. Meanwhile, she began building her reputation and extra money by working from time to time as a consultant to hospitals, medical schools and social service agencies. It wasn't until she had been in California three years that Terrie began working in a full-time job as a staff development specialist, doing training in a hospital that had been one of her clients.

A move to a geographically desirable area often means taking a less exciting job—or as was Terrie's experience, having an extremely difficult time finding a job commensurate with the one you had in your former residence. Job opportunities in Sunbelt cities have often been exaggerated in the media, and those who set off in search of them are often surprised to find the competition for the good jobs absolutely staggering. That's particularly true of white-collar jobs, which women are more likely to pursue.

How Where You Work Affects Your Social Life

It was on a hot, lazy afternoon in Mobile, Alabama, that dental assistant Jeffry Culbreth found out that she had gotten a job working as a secretary in TV celebrity Gene Shalit's office. She had interviewed for the job over the phone, and been offered it because her older sister, Judsen, who lived in New York and did free-lance research for Mr. Shalit, had convinced him that Jeffry would be perfect for the job.

Jeffry gave her employer four hours' notice and hopped on the next plane to New York. She was on her way to a job working for a man whose face was seen by millions every day. That alone was enough to charge her imagination, to make her believe that her life, too, would be touched by the magic of television. She was sure she would be meeting exciting people, going to interesting places and dating fascinating men.

What she hadn't stopped to consider, or even ask about, was what the office situation was like. When she arrived, she was surprised to discover that although she was working in an attractive townhouse in midtown Manhattan, there were only six in the office, counting the large cat who acted as if he were the television star. Besides Mr. Shalit, there was only one other man.

"We were several blocks away from the NBC studios where all the action was and our boss was often out of the office. It was as if we were a satellite operation and our orbit rarely brought us close enough to really feel that we were a part of the excitement, too," says Jeffry.

When Gene Shalit eventually moved his personal offices into quarters in Rockefeller Center some five years after Jeffry had started working for him, she noticed the difference immediately. "The stimulation of being around a lot of different people, even if you don't directly work with them, was much greater. I got to meet and know the people whom I had spoken to on the phone frequently," explains Jeffry, who has worked for Mr. Shalit for six years.

Before accepting a job, it's a good idea to consider how important the people you meet at and through work will be in terms of establishing your social network. If the job doesn't provide one or more of the following possibilities, you may find that even though you enjoy the work itself, you won't feel connected:

1. *A substantial number of employees working in jobs at your level.* If there are others your age who share similar backgrounds or experience, you'll have a built-in network of peer advisors and sympathetic souls with whom you can commiserate and celebrate.

2. *Regular contact with clients and customers.* The wider your circle of acquaintances, the greater the possibilities for broadening your social base, so long as you have something in common with the people with whom you come into contact.

3. *Frequent interaction with people in other departments.* Even in a large company, you can find yourself seeing the same old faces every day, particularly if your department is "staff" rather than "line," which means that your job supports the jobs of those whose work is directly connected with the company's service or products.

4. *Other women or professionals at your job level.* While it doesn't make sense to turn down a job offer on that basis alone,

knowing that your social life will develop outside work may motivate you to hook up with a professional group sooner rather than later.

Supporting Yourself While You Pursue a Financially Unrewarding Career

So you have your heart set on becoming an actress or a dancer or a musician or any number of other professions where regular work is a luxury, or the work you do get is often better for the ego than your pocketbook. How are you going to survive the expensive life-style of the big city if you're not married to an investment banker or you're not independently wealthy? There's always mom and dad. But the problem with money from home is that it usually doesn't come without strings attached. Besides, moving out on your own by definition means supporting yourself, which is why most women whose ambitions don't allow them to make a decent living usually moonlight to pay the bills.

Nothing in the world was more exciting to Janis Carr than being onstage. She had majored in theater at tiny Allegheny College in Meadville, Pennsylvania, and acted in many productions there.

Soon after graduation, several friends from college called and convinced her to come to Chicago to become the fourth member of a comedy group called "The Unnatural Acts." They performed in theater space donated to them by a supporter and passed a hat to collect donations. It was a heady time for Janis and the other members of the troupe, whose performances were crowded and well received. "I was on top of the world. We were doing original comedy material and making people laugh. It was at a time when *Saturday Night Live* was doing well and we very much identified ourselves as having the potential to make it as big as the players in that show had," says Janis.

Still, the money they collected didn't cover their living expenses, let alone the cost of their props and costumes. Janis volunteered to do what she had vowed was a compromise—to work in an ordinary job so that two of her partners could spend their days writing material for the group. "At the time, I didn't mind it. I was doing it for the group, which was what my identity was wrapped up in. So working as a sales clerk in a luggage store by day didn't bother me because at night I became a zany comic who bowed to the applause of her audience."

After performing together for four years, the troupe split up. The members decided to go their own ways to pursue their separate dreams. Janis had a difficult time finding hers. For a year she got a job through a grant from the Chicago Council of Fine Arts teaching students from disadvantaged homes how to put on theater productions. The following year, she was paid to be a performer for the Council, and joined a second troupe which performed on Saturday nights. When that troupe dissolved and funds from the Council expired, it was back to the luggage store to pay the rent. Three years later, Janis won a supporting role in a successful theater production, "We Won't Pay, We Won't Pay," and left her sales clerk job.

What can make the transition back to an ordinary job more bearable is working with people whose ambitions and hopes are similar to yours. Knowing that you're not alone in having to put in long hours doing work that does nothing to advance your career can carry you through lean times. And you may learn of work you may not otherwise have heard about. Whatever kind of ordinary job you choose to take, keep in mind that earning top dollar, having flexible hours and doing work you don't consider demeaning are important considerations.

"Temp" Work to Tide You Over While You Look for a Job

If your job prospects look bleak at the moment or you want the luxury of being able to hold out for the job you really want, one option to consider is temporary employment through an agency. Working on an assignment basis can give you the money you need to live and the time you need to keep searching for a good job in your field.

Who Can Get Hired as a Temp. The demand is greatest for those with office skills. In addition to secretarial, clerical and receptionist positions, there are also temporary work openings for accountants, keypunchers, office managers and others with specialized experience. Professionals in the health care area, particularly registered nurses, are being recruited by an increasing number of agencies. Even engineers, computer programmers and others with technical skills are being placed in temporary assignments.

How They Work. When you go to register at an agency (check the Yellow Pages under "Employment Agencies—Temporary Contractors"), you'll be tested and/or interviewed. If your skills, work experience and enthusiasm meet the agency's standards, you'll be put in their active file and called when a job becomes available. Most of the time, the agency will notify you of a potential job several days to a week in advance; sometimes, however, the agency may call and ask if you can report to work that same day. You're not obliged to take every job you're called for, but accepting some assignments at first shows your willingness to work and dependability.

How Much You Can Earn. Aside from the number of hours you work each week, your skills are the biggest determinant of how big your paycheck will be. Word-processing is the highest paid office skill (some agencies offer this training free in exchange for your agreement to work for them for a specified length of time). Good dictation and typing skills also command a good hourly rate. Generally speaking, the more office equipment you know how to operate, the more you'll be paid. Some agencies offer free refresher courses, but none teach basic office skills. Your hourly rate (which is paid to you by the agency, who in turn is paid by the client) does not include any benefits such as health coverage, sick days or paid holidays.

While temping has its drawbacks—the work is often menial and routine and the time on each job is usually too short to get to know your co-workers—the advantage of having income while you look for a job is undeniable. And you may even be offered a permanent position at a company where you're working as a temp.

3

Finding a Place to Call Home

〰〰〰〰〰〰〰〰〰〰〰〰〰〰〰〰〰〰〰〰〰〰〰〰〰〰〰〰〰〰〰〰〰〰〰

WHEN TWIN SISTERS Ann and Sue Sheets moved to Alexandria, Virginia, they decided to live in the Oakwood Apartments, part of a nationwide chain of singles complexes in 20 cities. The complex is fifteen minutes from downtown Washington, D.C., and offers residents a swimming pool, tennis courts, saunas, game rooms and organized activities. It's like a dorm for the post-college baby boom set.

To Sue and Ann, it seemed like an ideal setup until they decided where they wanted to live more permanently. Considering that many of the residents of the complex were at a crossroads in their life—having become recently separated or divorced, or, like them, having just arrived in town—the sisters thought it would be easy to meet people.

"We discovered it wasn't at all easy to make friends with women or men because everyone was going off in their own direction, and the only time you saw people was if they happened to step into the whirlpool at the same time you were there," explains Sue. "And five or ten minutes isn't enough time to really get to know someone well enough to feel comfortable saying, 'Why don't we get together sometime?'" Sue and Ann moved out of the Oakwood Apartments three months later.

While temporary living situations may provide comfortable surroundings, you won't feel at home until you're in a place which you can identify with, either because you like the neighborhood, the kind of people who live in your building, or the physical layout itself. And once you know where you're going to work and how much take-home pay you'll have at your disposal, you'll be in a good position to look for your own place.

The Art of Apartment Hunting

In some cities, tracking down an apartment is as challenging as finding a job because vacancy rates have fallen to their lowest level in years. The unavailability of desirable, affordable housing close to downtown is causing many newcomers to look for apartments in a wider variety of neighborhoods.

Keep in mind that rental rates are based on location, the newness of the facilities and equipment, extras such as athletic facilities and whether or not there is a doorman. (Some states and cities have rent-control regulations, which govern the prices landlords can charge.) Even if you don't have a trust fund or haven't recently won a lottery, you can find a decent place to live if you use several apartment-hunting strategies.

1. *Newspaper Classified Ads.* There's lots of competition for the rentals listed in the real estate section, so it's important to call as soon as you see an ad that interests you. Call the paper's classified ad department to find out which day of the week the bulk of the new listings appear (you may be able to get a hold of that day's paper in advance by checking delivery times at various newsstands). If the place suits your needs (it may take a number of go-sees before you can determine this), be prepared to take it on the spot, or you might find it snatched up by the next person who comes to take a look.

Don't limit your search to daily newspapers. Check weeklies and neighborhood papers for their listings, too. Familiarizing yourself with the prices in the particular neighborhood you're looking in through the classifieds is the best way of spotting a bargain.

2. *Real Estate Brokers*. They're an added expense (fees range from a half-month's rent to 20 percent of your annual rent), but they can save you a lot of legwork. Most brokers specialize in listings in one or several neighborhoods, some of which aren't advertised elsewhere. You can find a broker by checking the classifieds, where brokers advertise a sampling of their listings. Legitimate brokers operate by showing you apartments you've seen advertised or others that are in your price range, and collect their fee if and when you sign a lease. Beware referral agencies who may try to sell you a list of available apartments or who require a fee upfront. Don't hesitate to go to several brokers; some are better than others at matching your needs to the right place, and most will have listings the other doesn't.

3. *Direct Contact*. Scouting out unadvertised places has many advantages—the competition is negligible (and sometimes nonexistent), the location and sometimes even the building is your own choosing, and you pay no finder's fee. The best tactic is to try to talk to the owner or managing agent of a building, since either one has the power to offer you a lease. (The managing agent's name is usually posted near the front door.) Other tenants often know who the owner is or how to reach him. If none seem to be around the day you're there, you can use "Cole's Metropolitan Householders Directory" (available in most libraries), which is a reverse telephone book, indexed by address.

Your next best bet is to talk to the superintendent, who often lives in a big building or nearby. He'll be able to tell you whether apartments are available or when one might be. If you make a good impression and ask whether you can call back, a super (as they're commonly referred to) may be a big help in your getting an apartment. Doormen are sometimes good sources of information, but they usually wield no power in getting you an "in." In some cities where the vacancy rate is very low, apartment hunters are sometimes asked for or voluntarily give illegal "key money" to agents, supers and doormen for their help in securing you a lease.

Finally, don't hesitate to ask people in the neighborhood you'd like to move into for advice. Store merchants, postal carriers and dog-walkers often monitor the comings and goings of residents and may have good leads.

4. *Word of Mouth.* In a tight rental market, the best way to get first dibs on a place is to hear about it, preferably from someone you know who may be able to make an introduction for you. Tell everyone you know what you're looking for. Post notices on bulletin boards at work, in the local laundromat or grocery store. If your college has an alumni association in town, call or write to see if they offer listings or can run your request in a newsletter.

One last caveat: Don't panic and take the first place you see (unless it's a shoe-in). Careful comparison shopping and persistence will land you a place you can live with— and in.

NOTE: Check bookstores for any local publication that may get you started off on the right foot. In New York City, *The Newcomer's Handbook for New York City* by Jennifer Cecil is available for $6.95 plus postage and handling from: TLC & CO., Publishers, 313 West 4th Street, NYC 10014.

The Roommate Question

West 88th Street in Manhattan is located in one of the city's up-and-coming neighborhoods. The four young women who live in one of the brownstones there are probably among the happiest apartment dwellers in the city for they have an ideal living situation: enough space for each to have a bedroom of her own and shared common areas in which they can socialize, entertain and keep each other up on what's going on in their lives.

The night I came to interview them, the four roommates—Giddy Bancroft, Kathy Rasenberger, Angela Fowler and Caroline Davenport—were gathered together in their living room for the first time in several weeks. They sipped glasses of wine and munched on crackers and cheese while they talked about what life in the house had been like for the past 14 months they had lived there.

"I knew that I wanted to live with other people, financial considerations aside, especially in a city like this," says Caroline, who had previously roomed with a friend from college in tight quarters—an experience which seriously damaged their friendship.

"I agree. It's just depressing to come home from work to an empty apartment and find that nothing has changed since you left it earlier that morning," chimes in Angela, who works at an art gallery.

Survey Finding

Have you experienced feelings of loneliness in the last year?

Women living alone	57%
Women living with roommates	51%
Married women	28%
Women living with their boyfriend	27%

"You go through a healing period after you leave your family and graduate from college. You know you're not going to get married for a good long time. It's great to link up with people who become your surrogate family," explains Kathy, who grew up in a family of four sisters and is used to having a lot of activity going on in a house, although she relishes her privacy.

"There are days that go by when we don't see each other because we're on different schedules," says Giddy. "But it's a great feeling to know that someone is likely to be around when you get home from work with whom you can share what happened that day. There are all kinds of crises that happen in a first job, and there's nothing better than being able to share them with someone who sympathizes but who also has a different perspective."

Two of the roommates, Giddy and Kathy, have a long-established friendship dating back to college. Caroline and Kathy went to the same high school, although they were not in the same class. Angela was the only person who had no previous connection with anyone in the house.

How to Rd Rl Est Clsfd Lingo

Aside from crossword puzzle experts, few new readers of real estate classifieds understand all of the terminology used to describe places for rent. Here, then, is a glossary of the most commonly used terms:

Studio apt.—A one-room apartment.
1½ rm. apt.—One room plus a sleeping area
2½ rm. apt.—One-bedroom with a dining area
3½ rm. apt.—A one-bedroom apartment with a living room and a dining area
BR—bedroom
LR—living room
Gdn—garden
Eff kit—a fully-equipped but very small kitchen
Pullman kit—a less than fully-equipped kitchen which is behind folding doors
Dng L—an L-shaped dining room which is an extension of the living room
WBF or wb/fpl—a wood-burning fireplace
expd brk wls—exposed brick walls
bsmt lndry—coin-operated washer and dryer in basement
vus—views (which means the apartment doesn't face a building)
so exp—Southern exposure (which is the sunniest)

hi flr—the apartment is on a high floor, which makes it less noisy and increases the chance of good light
drmn—the building has a doorman on duty
dplx—a two-floor apartment
flr thru—an apartment which runs from the front to the back of the building
avl immed—you can move in as soon as you want

While the foursome do consider each other friends to varying degrees, all have their own sets of friends outside the house, some of whom know and socialize with each other. But it's clear they enjoy the stability their living situation provides, particularly since they're at a time in their lives when men and jobs come and go. "Because we have each other, there's always less pressure when any of us are in a new relationship with a man," says Kathy. "A lot of women who live by themselves, on the other hand, often look to a man to fulfill the unmet needs of having family around."

The house on West 88th Street is not without its problems, which, as is the case in most group living situations, center around daily household matters.

"We all like to keep the kitchens and bathrooms clean. But everyone has walked into the kitchen at one time or another and yelled, 'Goddamnit, it's a pigsty in here again! I feel like a maid in this house.' But you wash the dishes even if you didn't get them dirty and you don't make a production over it. Because if you do, someone else is likely to say, 'Well, you don't go out of your way to clean the bathtub.' All of us are guilty of not cleaning up after ourselves at one time or another."

A small group living situation can be an ideal setup financially and emotionally when you're new to a city *if* you take the time and effort to find the right place and people. It certainly is going to be a more viable possibility if you know people from the past who might be interested in sharing living space or who can recommend people they know.

Living with one roommate is a far more common arrangement. Even though women in that living situation are much happier and somewhat less lonely than women who live alone, only one in five single women who are 28 or younger share a city apartment with a roommate, according to the results of the Urban Experience Survey. Still, there are advantages to sharing space—being able to afford a nicer apartment, feeling safer and having someone to share some parts of your life with.

Survey Finding

How happy have you been in the last six months?

	Very or Moderately Happy
Women living with a room-mate	86%
Married women	79%
Women living with their boy-friend	76%
Women living alone	73%

The single most important consideration in terms of getting along is the size of the living quarters you're sharing. If each roommate has the option of escaping into her own room or suite when she feels like closing off the world (or getting away from a roommate whose habits and interests she does not share), the probability of the living situation working is greatly increased. Of course, that's not always possible, particularly in cities where whole apartments are the size of the bedroom you had to yourself when you were a kid. In that case, it's essential to room with someone whose daily rituals don't rub you the wrong way.

Be aware that there are liabilities unique to moving in with anyone, including:

Relatives. True, your brother or sister is going to be prepared to deal with your idiosyncrasies. And you're going to be able to speak your mind without running the risk of never having them speak to you again. But precisely because the relationship is so comfortable, you may be less inclined to seek out social contacts and begin developing important relationships with others that would be natural if you were living alone or with other roommates.

Your Boyfriend. There are risks inherent in living together when one or both of you is new to a city: it will take longer for you (and him, if he's also a newcomer) to develop friends of your own because you're a unit (which does have its benefits as well); your relationship may be more stressful because you're naturally looking to him (or to each other) for emotional support that came from a variety of people before the move; if you've never lived together before, you have to deal with the double whammy of adjusting to that new situation and different surroundings simultaneously.

Someone with Whom You Work. If your roommate-to-be is someone you see and deal with every day at work, you may find that sharing the same apartment may simply be a case of too much togetherness. It's sometimes a relief to leave work worries at the office, which isn't easy if your roommate is a co-worker.

A Friend. It's one thing to set up house with a former roommate; it's quite another to do the same with a friend. After all, your friendship is at stake, should the scenario of being best pals and compatible roomies not work out as you had hoped. If you decide to go ahead, one way to protect your relationship is to promise each other that if the small annoyances of day-to-day living begin to erupt into major sources of disagreement, that one or both of you will move out.

A Stranger. Most women aren't eager about rooming with someone they don't know unless none of the above options is available to them. If you fall into that category, take heart. It *is* possible to find compatibility with a stranger. Following up on (or placing) classified ads for a roommate is one way to find a roommate. But if you want to be more selective, consider using a roommate service. For a fee, a service will provide you with the names of leaseholders whose roommate needs and preferences are similar to yours. (If you're listing rather than looking for an apartment to share, the fee is usually less.) Keep in mind that it's necessary to discuss everything you can think of that may surface as an issue in your living together in order to make a good match. Before you decide on working with any roommate service, check with the Better Business Bureau or a local consumer protection agency to find out if there have been complaints lodged against it.

What to Ask Prospective Roommates

If you're thinking of moving in with anyone other than a relative or former roommate, it's smart to try to determine the chances of the arrangement working out beforehand. Prospective roommates whose backgrounds are similar to yours (where you grew up, went to school) are the most likely to share your home and hearth values. And having similar expectations and feeling comfortable talking to one another about your likes and dislikes make all the difference in your roommate relationship working out.

Personal Habits
Does she smoke? Do you feel differently about cigarettes or marijuana?

Is she a night person, or does she get up with the sun?

What are her musical tastes and will you be forced to share them (either because there is only one stereo or the walls are thin)?

Does she spend a lot of time on the phone?

Social Life
Does she have a boyfriend? (This could be an advantage if she spends time at his place and you enjoy having the apartment to yourself. On the other hand, it may mean there is one more person lining up at the shower or your getting displaced from your own bedroom.)

Will she be entertaining friends in the apartment frequently?

Does she want companionship as well as just someone to help pay the rent?

Money
Who's name is on the utilities and phone bills?
Who is responsible for seeing that the rent is paid?

How will the cost of food and supplies be divided?

Is she willing to pay for cleaning damages to your property that are caused by her visitors?

Is she willing to split the cost of renters' insurance?

Housecleaning

Is she willing to alternate regular cleaning of shared areas? (Bathrooms are particularly tricky. As petty as it may seem in a preliminary conversation, the issue of bathtub rings is better brought up then than when you feel like throwing a can of scouring powder at your roommate.)

Has she ever had to clean anything other than her own room before? (Beware of roommates who don't know the difference between ammonia and floor wax).

What's her tidiness tolerance level? Find out if she's the type who can ignore the mess around her all week until she has the time to take care of it or whether she picks up after herself immediately.

Work Schedule

Do you work the same hours? If not, you may find that your comings and goings disturb one another.

Does she travel frequently? Being out of the apartment may be a plus or a minus, depending on whether you're counting on her company or looking forward to extra periods of privacy.

Miscellaneous

Does she have a pet and can you live with it (or vice versa)?

When Should You Live Alone?

While it's true that you're more likely to experience pangs of loneliness if you're living alone, it's the living arrangement preferred by over one-third of city women in their twenties and thirties. More women than ever make enough money to afford their own place, and the freedom to do as you please is irresistible.

Even if you feel that having shared a bedroom with a sister, lived in a sorority house or having had previously unsuccessful roommate experiences cured you of ever wanting to live with someone (except a man whom you loved), consider the following points before you make a final decision:

1. *Have you ever lived alone in a similar situation before?* That's the single biggest determinant of whether you're equipped to handle the new stresses that being completely on your own and in a new city can generate. If you know what it's like to have to depend on yourself to pay the rent, buy the groceries, keep the place habitable, come home to yourself and deal with frightening situations (i.e., obscene phone calls in the middle of the night), you'll be better equipped to handle the stresses of living alone in a new city.

2. *Do you have friends nearby whom you can call or drop in on?* Knowing that comfort or help is just around the corner can mitigate loneliness or fear. One ideal solution is to move into the same building or block where a friend or someone from work whom you like lives.

3. *Are you willing to trade off space or safety considerations to afford living alone?* Privacy is expensive, and unless you've got a trust fund, you may not want to forego other pleasures for the luxury of being able to have your own place. It's likely, for example, that you will have to settle for a studio.

The experience of living alone seems to have become a rite of passage for single women. But you shouldn't feel pressured to get your own place just because your friends are doing it or you don't know anyone in the city to which you're moving. Not everyone is cut out for living alone—certain people need more support than others, which often comes from those with whom one lives.

Melissa Howard had never lived alone before moving to Washington, D.C., after graduating from college in 1976. She was outgoing and made friends easily. So when she got a job in the nation's capital, she had few qualms about leaving her family (who live in a small town in Ohio) or her boyfriend (who moved to Houston).

After staying with a friend who worked for the same organization for a month, Melissa got an efficiency apartment in a high-rise building in downtown Washington. She remembers the next nine months as being among the most lonely in her life. "I was so used to having people around that I was shocked at the emptiness I felt without them. Besides that, my apartment was claustrophobic," says Melissa.

Nine months after she moved in, the building was sold, and the new owners offered $800 to anyone who would move out. Melissa volunteered gladly. In the six years since then she has lived in a variety of roommate situations. "I've found that the ideal situation is having one roommate with whom you get along—my best roommate ever was a man who truly split the money and the responsibilities. I don't think living alone will ever appeal to me. I'd much rather take the risk of trying to live with someone, even if it was a person I didn't know very well," explains Melissa.

Being at the right stage in your life to try living alone makes a big difference in how content you'll feel about it as well. For many women in their early to mid-twenties, living with a roommate or boyfriend is the most affordable and comfortable arrangement. By the time you're in your late twenties and early thirties, you'll no doubt find that you treasure privacy more than you ever did and can afford a nice place of your own. Nearly 75 percent of women in the 29–35-year-old age group live alone and like it.

After five years of living with roommates, I decided to get my own place. There were nights filled with romantic whisperings on my terrace, wall-to-wall-people parties in my cozy living room and, occasionally, silent evenings when I wished a friend would call to ask if I cared to have a drink or when I woke up in a sweat from a nightmare and wished for the comfort of someone else nearby. But the three years spent living alone in that one-bedroom brownstone apartment were a time when I felt I had come into my own, and a time in my life I wouldn't have traded for even the best of roommates.

How to Judge a Neighborhood

Sizing up a neighborhood in a city with which you're un-familiar is not unlike trying to pick out the most interesting men at a large party—looks can be deceptive.

Before you set out with your map in hand, talk to people who are veteran city dwellers for their opinions of the best neighborhoods. Start with people at work since you already have something in common—the same destination five days a week. Another good source of information is friends or acquaintances who are already settled in. If your school has an alumni organization in the city to which you're moving, its members may offer helpful advice. If none of those options is available to you, you might try contacting the chamber of commerce. Even if they don't ordinarily give out such information, you may be able to get the views of someone who answers the phone if he or she seems friendly.

While your take-home pay and whether you plan to have roommates will determine how much you can afford to pay for an apartment, you shouldn't automatically rule out any neighborhood simply because it has a reputation for high rents. There are always relative bargains to be found if you have the time to look and the patience to wait for the right deal. In most cities, it's likely that you'll pay more than a quarter of your gross salary on annual rent if you want to live in a geographically desirable neighborhood. That means cutting back on other discretionary expenses. What then, should you look for in a neighborhood?

Safety. If you've grown up in a place where you've never had to lock your doors or you took minimal precautions, you will probably have a difficult time discerning a dangerous neighborhood from a safe one. The police at the local precinct can tell you about crime statistics in the area and how they compare to other neighborhoods. While no area is immune to crime, the safest ones are those in which many homeowners (rather than renters) live; long-established ethnic enclaves and ones that aren't adjacent to or only blocks away from a high crime area.

Convenience. Your commute to work should be your major consideration. If you're living in a city where it is possible to walk to the center city, give serious thought to whether you want to rely on your feet to get you to and from work (an increasingly popular option in cities where public transportation is lacking in amenities). How close the neighborhood is to activities you'll be involved in in your free time is important, too.

Ambience. Even if you've always dreamed of living in Old Town (Chicago), Greenwich Village, Beacon Hill (Boston) or Georgetown (Washington, D.C.), you may be shocked to find out what the going rates for apartments in the best-known historical neighborhoods are. If charm is high on your list of priorities, it's smart to check out less well-established neighborhoods whose architecture fits the bill and whose rents more closely match your pocketbook. If growing up in the suburbs has made you hungry for more diversity, you might also want to consider moving into an ethnic area where you can immerse yourself in a different culture. Rents tend to be somewhat lower and the sense of neighborhood is strong.

Five Qualities to Look for in a Neighborhood

Once you've collected the opinions of a half dozen or so city dwellers, it's time to take a look at the neighborhoods yourself. So long as you're not living in a car culture city like Los Angeles, it's best to explore on foot. Be sure to look for the following things:

1. *How well maintained the neighborhood is.* The poorer the neighborhood, the more littered the streets and sidewalks are likely to be. That doesn't necessarily mean the neighborhood is a dangerous one; it does mean that your tolerance for dirt should be high if you hope to keep your sanity. Take note of whether the sidewalks are swept or hosed down. Planted trees, gardens and shrubbery are usually evidence of one of two things: a strong block association or the presence of many owner-occupied buildings in the neighborhood.

2. *How well lit and patrolled the neighborhood is.* The only way to get a true feeling is to try to drive or ride through it at night. In fact, it's smart to go at a time when you might conceivably be going home alone so that you get a realistic feeling for what it's like to walk (or drive through) at that hour. The number of police officers you see on foot or in patrol cars is one indication of how well patrolled the area is. Some neighborhood associations hire private security guards, which, statistics show, do cut down on street and property crimes.

3. *The amount of activity on the street.* Not only will the number of people you observe going about their daily routine give you an indication of how bustling or quiet a neighborhood is; it also says something about the safety of the area. If your work or social activities mean you'll be coming home at late hours by yourself, it's reassuring to know that there are other people up and about at that hour—crimes are more likely to occur on a deserted street.

4. *The kinds of people who live in the area.* Whether you want to live in an enclave of young adults like yourself or live in a community in which you encounter a wide spectrum of people is another consideration. It is reassuring to see people like yourself in a neighborhood you're exploring—and it is one indication of whether or not others consider it safe. Beyond that, it's important to notice who else is living there. The presence of families usually means a neighborhood is well established and stable. If the area is an enclave of young adults, the neighborhood's population is probably transient.

5. *Proximity of stores and services.* Don't pull out your checkbook to make a deposit on an apartment before you've checked into how far away essential services are. For example, if you have no laundry facilities in your apartment or building, having a laundromat within reasonable walking (or driving) distance is a necessity. And you don't want to have to go out of your way to get to the nearest branch of your bank, a dry cleaner, the post office, a drugstore, hardware store, late night delicatessen or convenience store.

Living Outside the City

Generally speaking, desirable apartments that are proximate to downtown are beyond the financial scope of most first-time apartment hunters. Ferreting out those gems of places that are geographically desirable and affordable is no easy task, which is why newcomers to cities sometimes consider looking for housing in adjacent communities. Not only do many of them cater to singles, but they also offer more space and greenery, which can be important if you own a pet the size of a Labrador retriever.

If you're considering life in the suburbs (many of which are so developed that they look like or actually are cities in themselves), be aware of the hidden costs—financial and psychological—that living there may entail.

The single biggest expense that many out-of-towners fail to take into account when they're figuring how much they'll be saving in rent is how much extra they'll be doling out to get to their city jobs. The farther from the city center you are (and the more luxurious your means of transport), the more your daily commuting costs will be. If you go the public transportation route, you'll no doubt begin to feel like a prisoner of bus or train timetables, particularly if your social life keeps you in the city in the evening. Like Cinderella, you may have to pull the disappearing act before midnight, which is when many trains and buses slow down or cease operations for the night.

If you're living in a city where a car is a luxury, you may discover that it becomes a necessity if you decide to live outside of it. Most essential services are a car drive away in the suburbs, and carrying the cost of insuring and maintaining a car may take a significant chunk out of your earnings.

Easing into City Living

The advantage of living outside the city is that it can be a way slowly to adjust to the culture shock of being in a large metropolitan area without having to deal with the day-to-day hassles that are part of city living. Ann and Sue Sheets, the twin sisters mentioned earlier, were used to a suburban lifestyle, having spent three years after college living in Stonington, Connecticut. They had both looked for jobs in the city, but Ann's first job was with an art gallery, which was located in Old Town, ten miles from downtown Washington. The two of them soon fell in love with the historic city's cobbled streets and red brick buildings, many of which were built 150 years earlier. It took them several months to find an apartment there, but the wait was worth it. Their spacious one-bedroom with a fireplace and an eat-in kitchen was located above an antique store in the heart of Old Town.

"Old Town has a small town atmosphere, and we found it easy to meet people, many of whom come from different areas of the country like we did. There are even neighborhood bars where you can walk in almost anytime and run into someone you know," says Ann.

An Option for Single Mothers

Divorced women with children face different considerations than those faced by singles moving to a new city. Although there are usually better jobs and more convenient transportation in and around the city, inner-city schools do not enjoy a good reputation and streets and playgrounds are not considered safe by many parents. And while day-care facilities may be closer or more conveniently located to both home and work, there are often fewer facilities and less space, both inside and out, for children to play.

Those were among the reasons why lawyer Alice Jamison* scouted out houses with backyards in Falls Church, Virginia, when she moved with her two-year-old son to the Washington, D.C., area. The suburban community was an eight-mile commute from her office downtown (which can be a 45-minute ride in rush hour traffic). "I wanted my son to be able to grow

*A pseudonym.

up knowing how to throw a baseball," says Alice in explaining her decision. She asked the realtor who arranged the rental to recommend day-care facilities. "The Sisters of St. Joseph ran a day-care center not too far from my home, which was a god-send, particularly since my son was a hyperactive child."

Does she feel her choice was the best one in retrospect? "Absolutely. It's true that it wasn't possible for me to socialize with people after work because I had to get home to pick up my son. But it didn't prevent me from meeting people—it's just that I did it during my workday with the people with whom I came into contact, not at night, which is when I spent my time with my son," explains Alice, who three years after her arrival bought a home in another suburb, Chevy Chase. "Being a Midwesterner, it was very important to me to have a house. I'd never lived in an apartment, and when I relocated, it just made sense to me to reproduce physical surroundings like the ones I had known, which I knew would be positive for my son as well."

STAGE TWO

Shedding Your Stranger Status

><><><><><><><><><><><><><><><><><><><><><><><><><><><><><><><

YOU'VE MOVED IN. You've found a job and a promising living situation. Once the excitement of making a major life transition wears off, however, the hassles of everyday living are bound to creep in. That's hard enough under normal circumstances, but when you're disoriented, small problems can take on the proportions of major crises.

Being a newcomer in an unfamiliar city can be as frustrating as being a tourist in a foreign country. More times than not, you won't know how to get from Point A to Point B without making inquiries beforehand and along the way. Finding a gynecologist, a good hairstylist and the best places to shop can be an exercise in frustration because you're without reliable sources of information. But know that those feelings will dissipate once you get your bearings and are better able to fend for yourself.

Then there's "stone canyon culture shock," a condition which might best be described as the reaction of non-city folk to their newly acquired surroundings: tall buildings, paved surfaces, garbage, crowding and urban noises. (Only a handful of American cities are so well designed and clean that every major aspect—transportation, housing, parks and the downtown area—are a pleasure rather than an affront to the senses.) If you're destined to become a city person, however, you will begin blocking out the more unpleasant sights, sounds and smells.

Chapter Four, "Adjusting to Life in the City," discusses the problems of getting physically oriented, how to deal with strangers and the effect of sensory intrusions on city dwellers.

The first six months in a new city are often a difficult time for another reason: loneliness. Most newcomers don't know many people in their adopted city, and they're often geographically distant from family and friends. It's important to be able to talk to people who understand you when you're experiencing major changes in your life, but finding replacements for family and friends takes time. Those who are moving to cities in different culture zones, that is, areas where customs and values are markedly different from their own, are especially likely to have a difficult time connecting with people.

If you understand that making friends will be easier if you're willing to make the overture and follow up on potential friendships, your circle of acquaintances and contacts will grow much more quickly than if you wait for people to come to you. In Chapter Five, "Connecting with People," guidelines for making friends and meeting men are included.

Shedding your stranger status is a challenge for anyone who moves to a city from a smaller place, but it's a special challenge if it's the first time you've ever been on your own. "Learning to Be on Your Own," the last chapter in this section, explains the challenges of making the break from home and why becoming independent is one of the most important benefits of city living.

4

Adjusting to Life in the City

WHEN NIMA GRISSOM, a native Texan, moved to San Francisco, she felt physically disoriented by the hills, whether she was navigating them on foot or in her car. Learning to park on a 45-degree angle was downright nerve-racking. And the lines one had to stand in at the grocery store, the movie theater or a restaurant were barely comprehensible to someone who wasn't used to waiting. Along with these exasperations were the crowds who seemed to invade Nima's personal space at every turn. It wasn't easy for a Lone Star Stater for whom open space was an inalienable right. If you've never before lived in the area of the country where your adopted city is located or spent much time in similar cities, you can count on experiencing culture shock, as Nima did.

A number of factors can contribute to your feeling like an outsider—the transportation systems, the physical environment, local customs, the appearance and behavior of people who live there. If you understand from the outset that it will take time for you to adjust to things you cannot change, and develop your own style of dealing with those that you can, you'll find shedding your stranger status an easier proposition.

Six Ways to Get to Know Your City Better

Part of the thrill of being a newcomer is that you have license to act like a tourist—to gawk at a city's famous sights, to explore its neighborhoods, to go on organized tours. It's a good idea to spend your free time learning as much as you can about where you live soon after you arrive for several reasons. You'll become an expert on getting around in no time, you'll be able to meet others (especially if you explore on your own), and you'll develop the habit of being adventuresome, which many out-of-towners and even natives never do. The following suggestions will get your exploring days off to a good start:

1. Buy a good map and guide to your city at a bookstore that features a well-stocked travel section. If you have to watch your pennies, get a budget travel book (i.e., *New York City* [or wherever] *on $20 a Day*) that describes inexpensive restaurants and where to get inexpensive theater tickets, among other things. Familiarize yourself with the names and locations of various neighborhoods. Study the names of freeway exits or subway stops you'll be using frequently. *(Flashmaps Instant Guides* are highly recommended. Currently there are *Flashmaps* for New York City, San Francisco, Los Angeles, Chicago, Washington, D.C., and other major cities. They're available for $3.95 by writing: *Flashmaps* Publications, Inc., P.O. Box 101, Chappaqua, NY 10514.)

2. Take a bus tour of the city. It's the best way to get the lay of the land (follow your route on your map). In addition to viewing landmarks, you'll get a sense of which neighborhoods are desirable, expensive, convenient and safe.

3. Drive or walk around on your own. Choose a destination from your guidebook, figure out the best route by consulting your map, then verify your hunch by asking someone who knows. Forcing yourself to pay attention to where you're going (and when to get off) will help you learn your way around faster than if you rely on friends who know the route.

4. Visit the local historical society or museum of your city. In addition to multi-media shows about the city and its people, these societies often feature lectures about and walking tours of various neighborhoods.

5. Collect cards or matches from restaurants and clubs you go to. When you're taken to a place by friends or

colleagues, it's easy to forget where the place was unless you get the address on your first visit there.

6. Review the entertainment sections of the newspaper (which usually appear on Fridays or Sundays) on a regular basis, so that you become familiar with the names of various night spots and can recognize them when people make recommendations to you. Try out as many different places as your time and finances will allow and jot down your impression of them in a notebook.

Getting Around

When asked what the biggest adjustment to city living was, many of the Urban Experience respondents wrote, "Learning my way around the city." For those who have never taken public transportation or negotiated their way through freeway or city street traffic, finding your way around can be intimidating.

Mastering Mass Transit

The scariest transit prospect for those in non-car culture cities is the rapid transit or subway. Aside from some of them being acoustic versions of Dante's hell, subways are disorienting because there are no landmarks, no sun, nothing but manmade signs to tell you where you are. If you don't learn how to ride the train system from friends who've mastered it, you'll have to do it on your own. Even if you're good at reading maps, deciphering the proper direction isn't easy. It's a good idea to validate your conclusion by asking conductors, transit police and harmless-looking fellow passengers for help.

The biggest concern of those who ride subways is fear for one's personal safety. In fact, fewer women than men ride rapid transit systems for that reason, although similar percentages of men and women are victims or observers of crime.

What adds to women's fear is the possibility of harassment. In a study conducted by the Cleveland Rape Crisis Center and Cleveland Women Working, 89 percent of the 1200 women office workers surveyed reported experiences of harassment, ranging from insulting language to minor unwanted physical contact on mass transit. Harassment seems to be a condition relating to how crowded the bus or train is since women riding from 5:00 to 6:00 P.M. were bothered more frequently than were those coming home between 6:00 and 9:00 P.M. But those who came home later were nine times as likely to be a victim of violent assaults.

Negotiating Freeways

If you think that freeway driving was designed for the Janet Guthries of this world, you're not alone. Few driving experiences are more intimidating than wheeling your way through bumper-to-bumper freeway traffic that's moving at 55 miles per hour and discovering that you're three lanes away from the right-hand lane when your exit appears. But missing your exit is a minor problem, which can be remedied by memorizing a freeway map. A bigger one is having your car break down on the highway.

When Elizabeth Haas's rented car broke down on an interstate between Cleveland and Akron after nightfall, she decided to accept the offer of a man who stopped to see what was wrong. He turned out to be a weirdo rather than a Good Samaritan and drove her around for a long time before releasing her unharmed on the highway. "When he refused to take me to a service station, I knew that his intentions weren't good. I tried to remain calm and decided it was better to listen to his problems, which he wanted to share with me. I was finally able to convince him to stop the car and let me out," remembers Elizabeth.

Another potentially dangerous highway scenario is getting scraped by another vehicle. It may be more than an accident. A crime called "bumper" rape has gotten a great deal of publicity in California, where a man was recently sentenced to 151 years in prison for assaulting more than two dozen women in a 30-month period. The modus operandi of a bumper rapist is to bump his car (which is often stolen) into one driven by a woman. When she stops to inspect the damage, he forces her into his car, often at knife point, and rapes and robs her. The advice given by Deputy District Attorney Jacqueline Connor, who prosecuted the case, is to continue driving if your car is bumped and stop at a gas or police station. If you can, try to note the license plate or description of the car and report the incident to the police. If your car is not driveable and you're forced to stop, don't get out or roll down the window. Put on your emergency lights and wait for the other car to leave or the state highway patrol to stop.

Environmental Trade-Offs

For all their architectural marvels—the bridges that span rivers, the sleek buildings that pierce the sky, the sparkling glass and stone facades of cultural institutions—most cities fall short of being environmentally desirable. Their noises are an affront to any civilized eardrum, their litter an eyesore, and they're short on breathable air.

Seasoned city-dwellers seem to effectively block out those assaults to the senses so often observed by newcomers and visitors to the city. Physiologists and psychologists say their response is an adaptive one. When one's surroundings begin intruding on the body and mind, certain processes—metabolic, hormonal and mental—are triggered to equalize those bad effects. The Pulitzer Prize-winning biologist René Dubos likens these homeostatic responses to scar tissue that forms to help heal wounds and check the spread of infection. While the immediate effect is to enable us (or our body) to better cope, the long-run effects may be injurious. The longer you stay in the city, for example, the more you're likely to feel tense and keyed up. According to the results of the Urban Experience Survey, only a third of newcomers who had been in town less than six months said they felt that way, but after a year or two of city living, tension increased to include 70 percent of those who had moved and stayed at that level or higher over a ten-year period.

Noise

The cacophony of city sounds—blaring sirens, honking horns, pounding jackhammers, rumbling garbage trucks—is often more than just irritation. It can be downright stressful, and prolonged exposure to nerve-racking noise can affect your physical well-being.

A study by the Environmental Protection Agency concluded that the urban sound level has doubled in the last twenty years. And in another federal survey, noise topped the list of complaints of renters and home owners in the city.

All of the sounds mentioned above register over 70 decibels, which is 50 decibels below the level at which the ear begins to register pain. But that's small comfort if you're living next to a construction site or commute daily in rush-hour traffic.

It's no surprise that people who move to cities from places where the loudest nighttime noise is crickets singing begin to experience the symptoms of stress induced by noise: feeling on edge, jumpy or irritable.

Earplugs used to be the only solution to noises encountered by the city dweller in transit; now, of course, cassette players with stereophonic headphones not only block out noise but replace it with anything from Bach to Spyro Gyra to the Talking Heads. Walkmans and their competitors are winning an incredible number of city converts, but there is a drawback to being tuned out to one's environment. In the absence of acoustic clues, you cannot always detect danger.

In an article entitled "Noise: The Stress You Can Hear," writer David Martindale explains the relationship of noise to survival. "In the relatively quiet environment of prehistoric times, noises, particularly loud, sudden noises, meant just one thing: danger. . . . By triggering the body's involuntary mechanisms, stress prepared our primitive ancestors to fight when they thought they could succeed or flee in the face of a dangerous threat." Today, the threat is likely to be a passing car, bicycle or would-be mugger. Whether blocking out annoying sounds is worth the risk of eliminating useful sounds of warning is debatable. Already, it is beginning to surface as an issue that may be subject to state or local regulation: The first locality to outlaw the wearing of headphones in the street was Woodbridge Township, New Jersey, in October 1982.

More important than noise encountered while going to and from your destination is noise that invades your home. Studies have shown that when noise interrupts dreams, people often feel tired, tense, irritable or depressed the next day. There are ways to barricade "too thin" walls with sound-absorbing materials such as cork, or buy yourself a noise machine (which produces a neutral whirring sound.) But these "peace at any price" last resorts can be avoided by checking a place for its sound-proofness when you are house or apartment hunting.

The major noise pollutants which can be detected by sight as well as sound are: nearby expressways, intersections, subway stops, schools and playgrounds, police and fire stations, manufacturing firms, gas stations and shopping centers. The unseen ones—airline flight paths, underground train tracks—are worth inquiring about.

You can't determine how noisy a place is during a short daytime visit, which is why it's smart to return during the morning or evening rush hour or to talk to a neighbor about their biggest noise complaints. You may discover that while outside sounds are not a problem, sounds from inside other apartments are. Neighbors who have screaming contests, barking dogs, powerful stereo systems or frequent parties can make your life miserable, and as most complainants in large cities discover, the police usually have too many other more serious matters to attend to.

How to Avoid Sidewalk Gridlock

You may have always thought you knew how to walk, but negotiating crowded city sidewalks is an entirely different skill. There are ways to avoid getting elbowed, pushed or stepped on and to get to your destination more quickly. They include:

1. Wearing comfortable shoes. The trend of well-dressed businesswomen sporting tennis or running shoes on their way to and from work is a practical idea, which had its beginnings in the 1979 New York City transit strike. Not only do flat, cushioned shoes mean more comfortable walking, but without heels it's possible to make the quick pivots, turns and sashays needed in heavy pedestrian traffic.

2. Don't depend on traffic signals or walk signs to let you know it's safe to cross streets. City drivers in general are a lawless group who think nothing of making a turn into pedestrian walkways and forcing those on foot to stop for them. It's smart to look both ways before stepping down from a curb, even if the street is one-way—bicyclists often pedal against traffic (even if it's against the law) and may be unable to avoid striking you. If you're going to jaywalk (a misdemeanor which is actually ticketed in cities such as Los Angeles), don't tempt fate by running across without applying extra precaution.

3. If you need to make time, use the edges of the sidewalks, which are a kind of no-man's land in that traffic moves both ways. The slowest lane is the extreme right or left, which is peopled with window-shoppers.

Polluted Air

Months before moving to New York City, I had hung a poster of the skyline on the wall of the kitchen of my college apartment. The photograph of Manhattan's East River Side was taken at night when the lights in the United Nations, Chrysler and Empire State Buildings illuminated the sky with a golden glow. I had always thought the glow was a special filter the photographer had used; I've since learned that it is the reflection of light off the dust particles in the air. While New York's air is hardly acceptable, other U.S. cities have worse air pollution problems. Boise, Salt Lake City and San Jose are among the twelve most severely polluted cities, according to ratings done in *Places Rated Almanac.*

In his book, *So Human an Animal,* René Dubos writes, "Since people can function effectively despite the almost constant presence of irritating substances in the air they breathe, one might assume that human beings can make adequate adjustments to massive air pollution . . . but the respiratory tract continuously registers the insult."

Short of donning an air tank scuba-diver style, there's not much you can do to avoid breathing polluted air if you're living in a city. But to some extent, you can control the circumstances under which you exercise, when breathing is intensified.

1. Exercise in the early morning, before offensive rush-hour fumes and other pollutants have a chance to accumulate.

2. Hold back on days when the PSI (pollution standards index) exceeds a reasonable number.

3. Run in parks or other green areas where obnoxious vehicle exhaust fumes are less concentrated (photosynthesis also creates more breathable air).

4. If your access to parks is limited or nonexistent, consider exercising indoors, whether it's calisthenics in your apartment, an aerobic dance class at a local Y, or a racquet sport or swimming at a health club.

Where to Exercise

Contrary to popular belief, cities offer a variety of places where you can keep in shape. Here are the most popular options, ranging from the least to the most expensive:

City Parks. Facilities may include: Tennis courts; bicycle, jogging and bridle paths; ice and roller skating rinks; swimming pools and baseball diamonds. Costs: Use of most facilities is free, although those in high demand (tennis courts, baseball diamonds) often require an inexpensive permit which you can get from the Parks and Recreation Department. There may be nominal admission fees to rinks and pools. Philadelphia, Los Angeles, New York City, Washington, D.C., and San Diego have the largest in-city parks.

Y's. Facilities may include: Swimming pool; body-building equipment; squash and racquetball courts; indoor track. Reasonably priced classes in all kinds of athletic skills—sports, exercise and dance—are available. Most Y's are now co-ed, although single sex swim times and classes are available. Some facilities suffer from overuse and crowding; locker rooms and showers are "no frills" facilities.

School Facilities. High schools, prep schools and colleges often open their pools to community residents during off-peak hours. Costs: Some use a system of inexpensively priced passes; others operate on a pay-when-you-come basis.

Alumni Clubs. Facilities: Squash courts; weight room; saunas and steambaths. In clubs of formerly all-male schools, women's locker rooms are new and well kept. Extras like shampoo and towels are provided free. Membership: Primarily for graduates of the school, but associate memberships are often sometimes available for non-graduates. If your school doesn't have a reciprocal agreement with the club, you'll have to be nominated by one or more members. Check with the club's admissions office for details. All potential members must go through an interviewing process, which is usually just a formality for graduates. Costs: Often under $100 for recent graduates (up to five years after graduation); several hundred dollars thereafter.

Apartment Building Health Clubs. Facilities: Swimming pool; exercise machines and weights; saunas, steambaths and whirlpools. While intended primarily for building residents, underused or undersubscribed clubs sometimes take "outside" members. Well-equipped locker rooms and showers. Since these clubs rarely advertise, you'll have to learn of them on your own—by signs posted in the lobby or glass-bubble roofs on building tops. Check with the club manager for more information.

Racquet Clubs. Facilities: Tennis/racquetball and squash or paddle tennis courts; exercise machines and weights; saunas, steambaths and whirlpools. Individual and group lessons available. Well-equipped shower and

locker rooms. Towels and toiletries provided. Costs: In addition to a membership fee, you pay for court time. Lowest prices are weekday late mornings, afternoons and late evening and weekend nights. Tennis court time usually commands the highest hourly rate.
Health Clubs and Spas. Facilities: Swimming pools (some are small); state-of-the-art exercise machines such as Universal and Nautilus; saunas and whirlpools. Locker rooms and showers are among the most luxurious to be found anywhere. Dance and exercise classes free for members.

Dirt and Litter

Dubos's observation that "Most of us become oblivious to the filth, visual confusion, dirt, and outright ugliness that we encounter morning and night on our way to and from the office," is one that most city dwellers would agree with. Even if we've grown up in areas of the country where constellations are visible on starry nights and backyard gardens meant fresh vegetables and flowers on the table several months a year, most of us who move to cities shelve memories of nature and find ourselves confronted with overflowing garbage cans, dog droppings on the sidewalk and fellow citizens who think littering is acceptable social behavior.

Most people believe there is little an individual can do to make a dent in visual urban blight. While it's true that many eyesores can't be remedied by an individual, it is possible to eradicate small ones and even beautify neighborhood areas. Sometimes all that's needed is to raise the consciousness of the offender. Since the passage of the "pooper-scooper" law in New York City in 1979, dog owners have begun cleaning up after their pets, and when they've been derelict in their duty, passersby have been quick to remind them of it. Confrontations can erupt if the admonition is delivered in the wrong way, but it's been my experience that when the comment is friendly rather than threatening—"Do you have something to clean up after your dog with?"—most offenders are embarrassed into looking for a piece of paper.

Block and neighborhood associations have been instrumental in planting trees, flowers and shrubbery to dress up the often impersonal facades of buildings. And in some neighborhoods, a community garden takes root in unused park or building space, where local residents can plant their own flowers and vegetables.

How to Get in on a Summer Share

Come Memorial Day, many city residents escape to weekend retreats. Manhattanites head for the Hamptons or the Berkshires. Those who live in Philadelphia go to the Jersey shore. Bostonians set their sights on Cape Cod. And residents of the nation's capital flock to the beaches of Delaware.

Because summer rentals in these popular vacation spots are expensive, a group of people often share the cost of a house. While friends frequently rent a place together, co-tenants often haven't met more than a few times before they begin living under the same roof on weekends. If you're new in town and aren't just scraping by financially, taking a share (as the practice is commonly referred to) can be a good way to make friends and cope with the heat and humidity of the summer.

Where to Learn About Available Shares. As soon as winter settles in, people start talking about their plans for summer—at work, at their health clubs, over lunch, at parties. It's a good idea to ask veterans of the summer share scene what they've liked and didn't like about houses they've been in and whether they know of house organizers who are looking for subtenants. Other good places to look: bulletin boards at work, professional organization or club newsletters, and the newspaper classifieds under real estate listings. In Manhattan, summer share parties, which are open to the public, are given in February in the auditorium of Marymount Manhattan College.

What Kind of House to Get Into. A lot depends on your idea of a pleasant summer weekend. If you want peace and privacy, you will want to avoid getting into a house with more than a handful of people. If an active social scene excites you, on the other hand, a large co-ed house comes highly recommended.

How to Choose the Right Place for You. Becoming a part of any summer share group is a two-way street: the person (or people) who are organizing the house will be judging whether you'll fit in, and you'll be sizing up whether the total package meets your needs. Here's what you should consider:

• How well you'll get along with your co-renters—What to look for: Do you come from similar backgrounds, enjoy the same sports or leisure-time activities, or share other common interests? Be wary of groups with mixed age groups or couples and singles. Find out, too, whether the house organizer will be living there or whether he's putting it together strictly as a business proposition (in which case, you'll definitely want to meet the other house members ahead of time).

• The location and size of the house—If you can't get out to see it in person, ask to see pictures. And be sure to ask: How far from the city is it? Is there a way to get there if you don't have a car? Do other members of the house have cars? How far away is the beach, tennis courts, center of town? How many bedrooms and bathrooms are there? How many roommates to a bedroom? How are roommates chosen (one compelling reason why it's smart to get a share with a friend)? How many people will be sharing the house? Are there only full shares (meaning you can use it whenever you want), or are half shares (the every-other-weekend alternative) also available? If so, how are holiday weekends divvied up, and how difficult will it be to switch weekends?

• The policy on guests—Find out: Whether there's a separate guest room, how often you'll be able to invite guests, how much advance notice is needed.

• How expenses will be divided—Aside from the rent (which in most cases must be paid in full before the summer begins), it's important to know: Who is responsible for purchasing the food (and whether you're expected to dine regularly with your fellow shareholders); whether the cost of housecleaning services and yard work are included in the cost of your share; whether a security deposit is required.

The Behavior of City Folks

If there is one word that captures most newcomers' perception of people who live in cities, it's "impersonal." The people you meet in the course of going about daily routines—taxi and bus drivers, post office employees, store clerks, delicatessen sandwich makers—often seem to be brusque, uncaring and sometimes downright rude. It's not uncommon for an unpleasant early-morning encounter to ruin one's entire day, even if you woke up feeling ready to tackle life in the city.

The best explanation for this kind of behavior is that it is an adaptive mechanism to "overload"—one simply comes into contact with too many people to be able to give them the attention and time that is considered normal in less congested places. Stop to consider, for example, the sheer numbers of people one can encounter in the heart of the most densely populated U.S. city—in midtown Manhattan, you can be in the midst of 220,000 people within a 10-minute radius from your office by foot or by car. Still, sheer numbers don't excuse obnoxious behavior from those who serve the public or from strangers on a crowded sidewalk or street.

How you choose to respond depends on the seriousness of the offense and whether you can actually gain anything by making an issue out of it. Certainly if the behavior was annoying but resulted in no lasting harm or inconvenience, it's worth ignoring—and venting your frustration in a more positive way.

If, however, the treatment you received was undeserved and you stand to gain something by sticking up for your rights or complaining to someone in authority, you shouldn't be afraid to do so. The calmer and more in control you come across in such situations, the more likely it is that you'll get the results you want.

A woman friend of mine once refused to pay a cabbie a 50-cent surcharge he felt she owed him. (In New York, some cabs still charge an extra fee between 8 P.M. and 6 A.M.) She told him that since she had gotten in the cab before that time, she didn't legally owe him the money. When she tried to leave, he locked the doors and walked over menacingly to her window. A passerby heard them arguing, walked over and began arguing on her behalf. Even though she felt like sticking the situation out on principle, she finally decided to pay up—the aggravation and threat of physical violence simply wasn't worth it.

Dealing with Strangers

Most women who grow up outside major metropolitan areas are inclined to be helpful and polite when a stranger stops to ask a question. But in large cities, it's not always a good idea to let a person engage you in conversation—he or she may simply be looking for an opening to take advantage of you in some way. I learned that lesson in a most unusual way.

Six months after I began working at a major women's magazine, I was kidnapped while on my lunch break and held for ransom—or so my boss and the personnel department thought when they received a frantic phone call from my roommate. The incident began innocently enough.

After getting a bite to eat at a nearby restaurant with a friend, I had gone to an ice-cream store in Grand Central Station, which was adjacent to the building where the magazine's offices were located. The young man who approached me seemed normal enough. He was doing a study on young women's feelings about their jobs and wondered if he might interview me, if not then, at some more convenient time after work. To my undiscerning ears, he was a convincing enough graduate student in psychology, and I gave him my home phone number. He thanked me and left.

I continued eating my ice cream cone, slowly making my way back to my office. When, some ten minutes later, I reached the entrance to the building, I was surrounded by no fewer than seven people from my office, who were about to comb through the station to search for me. I couldn't understand their relief at my appearing unharmed until they told me about the threatening phone call.

The "graduate student" had immediately called the number I had given him, reached my roommate (who worked at home), described to her what I was wearing and told her he was holding me for ransom in a phone booth in Grand Central. She in turn had called my office, and upon finding that I was not at my desk, told my boss about the call. In a city where anything is possible, the immediate reaction was to take the call seriously. I was, of course, embarrassed beyond description. I couldn't have felt more like a farm-girl on her first visit to a city than had I been wearing overalls and a straw hat. The incident made such an impression on me that I never again talked to a man (unless he was accompanied by a woman who appeared to be a relative or girl friend) on the streets again.

Over 60 percent of all newcomers are cautious around strangers, according to the results of the Urban Experience Survey. Keep in mind that certain behaviors encourage strangers to approach you, whether to ask a legitimate question or to bother you in some way. These behaviors include: looking as if you're not sure where you're going, not acting as if you're in any hurry to get to your destination, gazing at street scenes as if it's all very novel (also a telltale tourist trademark), smiling or making eye contact with people you pass by. You may at first think you don't want to develop a glazed, unfriendly look, push by people who are blocking your path or ignore the pleas of those who implore your assistance. Once you realize that people will try to take advantage of you if you let them, however, you'll begin developing these defense mechanisms.

It takes most newcomers months to develop the nerve to act in what they would consider a rude manner when confronted with someone who violates their privacy. But it took Bekah Herring only one day to learn how to say "get lost"—in the appropriate vernacular and with the right amount of indignation. She was 20 years old when she came to New York City to start a modeling career, having spent two successful previous summers working for a top New York modeling agency. On her first day of "go-sees" (a term which refers to taking one's portfolio around for various clients to see), she was accosted by two men, both of whom quickly identified her as being someone not wise in the ways of the city.

The first was Ugly George, who hosts what may be the first late-night all-nude talk show. With portable camera in hand, he stalks city streets looking for attractive women who are willing to bare their bodies in front of his lenses. "He came up to me and said he was filming women's breasts and would I like to be a guest on his cable TV show," remembers Bekah. "My first mistake was bothering even to respond to him by saying I really didn't have all that much to film. My second mistake was being sweet and nice about it, rather than expressing how outraged I was that he would even ask a woman he didn't know that kind of question."

Later that same day, Bekah walked into the lobby of a building and saw a well-dressed man who told her that she had to go down to the basement to catch the elevator. Not being all that familiar with city buildings, Bekah believed him. He followed her down, and when she became suspicious and began retracing her steps, he pushed her against the wall and grabbed her between the legs. She screamed so loudly that he ran away. "That night I called my daddy and told him what happened and that I wanted to come home. He reassured me that things would be all right and that I ought to stick it out, although he'd come and get me if I wanted him to," says Bekah, who took his advice and thereafter became much more cautious about how she dealt with strangers.

Bystander Apathy

It's one thing to know how to act when accosted by someone on a street; it's quite another to witness a stranger in need and know how to respond. Cities are infamous for the alleged lack of concern of their citizens for each other.

The most poignant example of bystander apathy in this half of the twentieth century is probably the 1964 murder of New Yorker Kitty Genovese. Her cries of terror brought 38 of her neighbors to their windows to witness her murder, and although it lasted 30 minutes, no one called the police. Their reaction—and lack of action—has been analyzed by many social scientists. Writing in *American Scientist* five years after the incident, Bibb Latane and John M. Darley concluded, "Caught, fascinated, distressed, unwilling to act but unable to turn away, their behavior was neither helpful nor heroic; but it was not indifferent or apathetic either."

Latane and Darley have conducted experiments to determine what causes individuals to intervene in an emergency and how they make the series of decisions that any rescue involves. What they discovered was that the reactions of other bystanders and their relationship to each other was an important determinant in intervention. First, if other bystanders feel the situation is a serious one, as a fellow observer you're more likely to as well. And if you're among people you know who are also witnessing the emergency, chances are higher you—or one of your group—will intervene. A victim may be more likely to get help (or an emergency get reported) if there are only a few bystanders available to take action. The reason that city people seem to be more callous, explain Latane and Darley, is that when an emergency occurs in an urban setting, a crowd is likely to gather, most of whom are strangers to one another as well as to the victim.

Having been both a victim and an intervener in pickpocket incidents, I can appreciate why bystanders often seem slow to respond. Before you can act, your mind goes through a rapid series of observations and decisions, which have been broken down into five steps by Latane and Darley. First, you have to notice that something unusual is happening. Second, you have to interpret the event and figure out that something is wrong. Third, you must decide that you have a responsibility to act— that is that you're qualified to do so and that no one else has done anything. Fourth, you have to figure out what kind of assistance you can offer and last, how to implement your choice (i.e., where is the nearest telephone, police officer or hospital?).

Perhaps the single biggest deterrent to intervening is fear for one's own safety. In most large cities, that is a legitimate fear, since there are numerous incidents of bystanders intervening on behalf of a victim to their own detriment. For most women, the question of physically coming to the aid of a stranger in trouble is not a good idea unless you have a black belt in karate or see a way to foil the assailant without putting yourself in jeopardy.

Helping Those Who Don't Ask

A second variety of bystander apathy that troubles many newcomers to the city is the indifference of most passersby to street people, many of whom are alcoholics, homeless or mentally disturbed. In smaller communities, these faceless people seem to be more cared for, if only because they have a roof over their head or because people know who they are and talk to them.

Soon after Penny Farthing moved to Washington, D.C., she spotted a man lying unconscious on the sidewalk on her way to work. Everyone was rushing by, oblivious to the man's predicament or the fact that they had to step over him to continue on their way. Penny was the only person who stopped to find out what was wrong. "He might have been a bum, but he could have been a guy on his way to work who dropped over from a heart attack for all I could tell," says Penny. She went in search of a policeman, who came back to take care of the situation. "What bothers me is that I'd probably no longer go out of my way to make sure that someone like that got help," says Penny. "Life in the city doesn't always allow you to be very considerate of other people, while life in a small town does—in fact, it even obligates you to do so."

It is impossible to deal with every altruistic impulse you have because there are so many people who visibly need help in a big city. Whether you decide to act—and how—depends on your conscience and whether there is something worthwhile you can do for someone. Once again, to guard against those who might take advantage of your generosity, it's best only to take the risk of getting involved if you're in a public place where there are others nearby who can come to your assistance should that be necessary.

Learning to Live with Lines

Waiting in line is a fact of life in a big city. It's not always a disagreeable experience; social scientists who have studied the psychology of line behavior have discovered that under some circumstances, it's a way to meet people and part of the ritual of attending the event.

But waiting in line to conduct the transactions of everyday life is often frustrating and boring. Learning which lines are avoidable—and how to cut down on your waiting time—is a skill worth learning.

In most circumstances, timing is everything. You can count on lines being the longest when nine-to-fivers are on their way to or from work and during their lunch break. Even if you're in that group yourself, try to schedule your visits to the most line-filled stops—the bank, post office, the grocery store—at non-peak times. That may mean changing habits you've developed, such as cashing a paycheck immediately, but if your time is important to you or the experience of waiting your turn stressful, it may be worth rearranging your schedule.

Using the phone rather than doing transactions in person is another way to avoid waiting in lines. An increasing number of businesses—from airlines to theaters to universities—are offering their customers the option of making reservations or other transactions over the phone. If payment is required, it's necessary, of course, to have a credit card. Likewise, electronic banking services, with their personal identification cards, can virtually eliminate your having to set foot inside a bank.

Even technological advances and well-designed line feeding systems don't always eliminate waiting, which is why New Yorkers, who live in what has been called the "uncrowned queue of the U.S.," are rarely spotted without something to read.

Developing Sophistication

During my first year in the city, I was invited to a party at the celebrity-studded Dakota Apartments. It was a party unlike any I'd ever attended in college; perhaps it was the air of formality created by well-dressed men and women who seemed to know just how to hold their drinks and hors d'ouevres while engaging in complicated discussions about the state of society, culture and the arts.

Tennessee Williams was there. So was Elia Kazan and critic Rex Reed. What does one say when introduced to one of the noted playwrights of the century—"I really enjoyed the third scene of the second act of *The Glass Menagerie*"? All of my comments and conversation starters sounded so artificial as I rehearsed them in my mind that I decided the less said the better.

Neither did I feel prepared to answer the inevitable city cocktail part question, "What do you do?" At the time I was a lowly editorial assistant who answered phones and sharpened my boss's pencils. Working at a national women's magazine did carry a certain status (which I was unaware of at the time), but it also caused people to scrutinize your looks and clothes more closely, as if you were supposed to look like the models featured in the magazine. I didn't. In fact, my wardrobe at the time consisted of many pairs of jeans and more than a few self-made dresses, one of which I was wearing that night. It took more than a year for me to realize that my clothes were woefully out of place in a fashion-conscious city like New York, and that the long hair that I'd had all through college wasn't consistent with a sophisticated image.

When people asked where I was from originally (my voice was also a dead giveaway that I hailed from West of the Hudson), and I told them Ohio, they always assumed I must have grown up on a farm, when in fact, I was very much a product of suburbia. In those early years, I desperately wanted to come across as someone for whom city living had become second nature. It took years to merge my straightforward Midwestern ways with the self-assured suaveness that more experienced city women exuded. According to the results of the Urban

Experience Survey, the majority of women who move to a city don't begin feeling more sophisticated until they've been there at least two years. As a newcomer to the city, you may well go through that "feeling out of step" phase, particularly if you're moving to the East or West Coasts where how you look, speak and act are critically judged by the people with whom you come into contact. For the first time in your life, being a nice person won't be enough to win friends or more than a five-minute conversation. There are, quite simply, many talented, attractive and entertaining people around with whom one can choose to spend time.

The word "sophisticated" has two meanings: the one people most often associate with it is, "supremely cultured, intellectually appealing, finely experienced." But the second speaks to the psychological issue of divorcing oneself from one's roots—"deprived of a native or original simplicity." It is possible, however, to retain the "essential you" aspects of your personality while altering aspects of your appearance, voice or manner.

Five Ways to Make a Splash at a Cocktail Party

Few situations are more intimidating than finding yourself in a room with 25 strangers with whom you're expected to make small talk for two hours. Even if you go with a friend, it's smart to develop the skill of circulating so that you can maximize your enjoyment of cocktail parties, which are held just as often for business as for personal reasons. Here's how:

1. *Introduce yourself to others.* If your host or hostess isn't making introductions, take it upon yourself to meet people. Look for someone who is standing alone; that person will be flattered that you've singled him or her out. All you have to say is, "Hello. My name is —————. I don't believe we've met."

2. *Wear something unusual.* That doesn't mean you shouldn't dress for the occasion, but adding a piece of

jewelry or item of clothing that is out of the ordinary gives people a reason to approach you—to ask what it is or where you got it.

3. *Know some good conversation openers.* Initiating conversations at the bar or hors d'oeuvres table is not only appropriate but usually appreciated by others. The best way to start one is to ask an innocuous question, such as, "Are you a business associate or friend of the (host/hostess)?" "Wonderful place to have a party, isn't it?" or "Have you had a chance to see the view (or the rest of the apartment)?" Avoid making negative comments such as, "Dull party, isn't it?" (you may be speaking to the hostess's boyfriend) or tired one-liners such as, "Don't I know you from somewhere?"

4. *Ask people questions about themselves.* Most people warm up right away if you seem to have a genuine interest in learning something about them. Make your queries non-threatening—where they work, what their job involves, how long they've lived in the city, where they live. Avoid asking questions that may put them off—whether they're married, how old they are, how much rent they pay.

5. *Be a little outrageous.* The least memorable people at parties are those who hold back. You don't have to be a gregarious sort in order to be noticed—just don't hesitate to use a special talent you have when the setting or mood is right (or when the party needs picking up). It might be playing the piano, telling a joke or story, directing charades or demonstrating a new dance step.

How You Speak

Bekah Herring, who moved to New York City from Goldsboro, North Carolina, decided to take speech lessons to get rid of her nasal voice. "As early as the seventh grade, I became aware of my Southern accent and began altering it then because I was going to a school with the sons and daughters of

Air Force personnel, who didn't speak the way I did," explains Bekah. "When I arrived in New York, I wasn't embarrassed about the way I spoke, but I was aware that once again, it was different from the people around me. And I wanted the flexibility to speak any way I want to—for professional and social reasons."

"Although . . . there is no 'best' form of speech or manner of communicating, the preferred sound in this country—the so-called 'General American' that has been adopted by media and stage professionals—is free of regional characteristics. It is the voice of the person 'who comes from nowhere,'" says Dr. Morton Cooper, a speech pathologist, in a *New York Times Magazine* article. Speech can be improved by correcting functional inabilities, according to him. It is possible to alter one's pitch, tone focus (a nasal or throaty sound), quality, volume and rate of speaking.

If you feel that changing aspects of your speaking style would help you professionally or make you feel more comfortable, it's worthwhile to investigate the many courses offered by learning networks, the continuing education divisions of colleges and universities or by private speech consultants who are usually listed in the Yellow Pages under "Speech Improvement, Voice and Diction," or "Speech Pathologists."

Even if you don't want to make changes in how you speak, you should pay attention to the language you use. If you've recently graduated from college, you probably still use slang expressions that sound sophomoric. Or you may find that exclamatory expressions that are commonly used where you came from are hopelessly out of date in the city you're now living in. In the movie, "Annie Hall," Alvie Singer (Woody Allen) accuses Wisconsin-bred Annie (Diane Keaton) of sounding like she's straight out of the 1950's when she uses the expression, "Neat." "What's next?" he asks, "Peachy keen?" Much of Annie Hall's charm, of course, came through in her use of old-fashioned expressions such as "La-di-dah." But, like many women who lack self-confidence, she frequently punctuated conversations with hedges such as, "Kind of" and "well, I mean," which began to disappear as she became more comfortable with herself and her singing career.

What's in a Name?

Performers, politicians and others in the public eye have long recognized the importance of a memorable and flattering name. Dyan Cannon would probably have made it just as big had she kept her real name, Samille Diane Friesen. But it would have clashed with her appealing image.

Your name is an important part of how people react to and think of you. In big cities where you're apt to meet dozens of new people in the course of a year, names that are unusual or interesting stand out. You may want to readopt a first name you discarded as a child because others thought it funny. Or if your nickname sounds frivolous or too youthful, you may want to have people know you by your more formal first or middle name. When you move to a city where few other people know you, you also have the option of choosing to go by a new first name altogether.

How You Dress

Many women moving to cities make the mistake of buying new clothes before they leave, partly because they know where they like to shop and where the best bargains can be found. It's a smarter idea, though, to wait until you arrive to determine just what changes you need to make in your wardrobe, particularly if you're moving to a different part of the country where regional styles or the weather may affect your choices.

If you're just graduating from school, you'll no doubt discover that your student wardrobe is woefully inadequate for the work world. But aside from the suit you may have purchased to go to interviews in, it's better to wait until you're on the job and can observe how women whose jobs you aspire to are dressing.

Probably the single biggest fashion mistake that newcomers to a city make is buying clothes that lack real quality, either because they're on a shoestring budget or have never before

been exposed to so many people sporting well-designed and
-made clothes. If you want to feel confident and project a
sophisticated image, it's better to buy a few wardrobe basics
of good quality (even if they do cost more) and build from
there.

5

Connecting with People

〜〜〜〜〜〜〜〜〜〜〜〜〜〜〜〜〜〜〜〜〜〜〜〜〜〜〜〜〜〜〜〜〜〜〜〜〜

DURING THE SUMMER of '71, when I first moved to New York, a popular Carole King tune was getting a great deal of airplay. I remember its lyrics well, for they spoke of my situation at that time.

> So far away,
> Doesn't anybody stay in one place any more?
> It would be so fine to see your face at my door.
> Doesn't help to know that you're so far away.

The "you" in the song was everyone in my life who I knew and loved. For several weeks, there was no one in the city I felt free to call up and chat with. There were many nights early in my stay when I gazed out the window of my dormitory, perched high on a bluff overlooking the eastern portion of the city, and realized how unconnected I was to the dramatic cityscape beyond.

The intense loneliness I experienced is common among newcomers to an area, whether they're married or single. Sociologists categorize this kind of loneliness as social isolation—dissatisfaction with available friends and relationships. It's not unusual for this feeling to last up to a year after you move to a city where you have few or no contacts. In fact, more than half of the respondents to the Urban Experience Survey reported that the most depressing time they experienced while living in the city was during the first six months to a year after arriving because they knew so few people.

We need to be around people we know, whether they're familiar faces, acquaintances, friends, relatives or lovers, to survive emotionally. Without the support of such a network, we lose the mirror which reflects the validity and importance of our thoughts, actions and being. And it's not unusual to feel bored, restless and depressed when deprived of regular encounters with people whom we know and trust. For the person who is accustomed to belonging, being socially isolated for more than a few months can lead to severe depression.

When Nancy Kelley talks about New Year's Eve, 1979, tears well up in her eyes. "It was the lowest point in my life. The closest I ever came to ending it. I was alone, absolutely alone. I had no one to call, no one to visit. I don't think anything could be as bad as that was," says Nancy, dabbing at her eyes. Although she had been in New York for six months, she had no friends. For an outgoing 35-year-old woman who had never had problems finding people to share her life with, it was confusing.

Back in Binghamton, a college town in upstate New York, she had had a close circle of women friends, several of whom, like her, had been faculty wives who were now divorced.

When her teenage son moved to Rochester to live with his father, Nancy decided it was time for a change. Eight months earlier she had left her job as an art teacher at an elementary school to try selling insurance. She didn't enjoy the work, and she made less money than she had as a teacher. "I knew that if I was going to make it in this world, I would have to go back to New York," says Nancy, who grew up in a small middle-class neighborhood in Queens.

The idea of moving to Manhattan, away from her "family" of the past eight years terrified Nancy; nonetheless, she contacted several personnel agencies specializing in sales and was hired by a firm that sold store fixtures, such as display counters and dressing rooms. Feeling proud of herself for having convinced a manufacturing firm with no female sales representatives to hire her (and having gotten a $6,000 raise from her previous sales job), Nancy felt ready to tackle the world outside academia.

It didn't take long for her to realize how desperately she missed her 14-year-old son and her women friends. "I found that women were not nearly as open in the city as they were in the smaller places I had lived. They all seemed to keep to themselves. And I was unable to meet any women through work—there simply weren't any women in my industry," remembers Nancy.

She turned to her mother. They had always had a good, if not close, relationship. Their weekly phone calls became daily phone calls. The knowledge that although she was alone, but not unloved, pulled Nancy through that shaky New Year's Eve.

Soon thereafter, on a snowy Saturday, Nancy bundled up and walked ten blocks to Bloomingdale's. It was in the lingerie department that she spotted a woman who had sat next to her on a recent flight. "There's nothing worse than seeing someone who appeals to you, whether it's a man or a woman, and feeling a spark of mutual attraction, and then walking away knowing you'll probably never see that person again," says Nancy. "It's so sad, and it happens to all of us regularly. I finally decided not to let another opportunity like it go by."

Nancy walked up to her and said, "Weren't you on a flight from Phoenix to New York about a month ago?"

"Oh, yes, I remember you," the woman, whose name was Shari, said. "When I saw your parents meeting you at the airport, I wished we had talked more and gotten each other's card."

Nancy and Shari had lunch, and Shari, who was a native New Yorker, taught Nancy how to shop Bloomingdale's ("for which I'll be forever grateful," says Nancy). The two women subsequently became good friends.

For some women who move to cities, loneliness becomes so acute that they seek out professional help. Dr. Dale Hill, a psychotherapist in Houston, sees many working women in their mid-twenties to late-thirties, many of whom come to her within the first year of their arrival. "Most of them have been emotionally healthy throughout their lives, but they're not prepared for the isolation that moving to a different city involves," says Dr. Hill, who understands the problem professionally and personally, because she herself relocated to Houston from Michigan. Dr. Hill does both individual and group counseling, and has found that her clients often strike up friendships as a result of having met one another.

Many women moving to cities today are the first women in their families to do so. There are no caveats for coping that mother (or father) can share with daughter, no rules of behavior that can speed up the process of assimilating. Pioneers in a new sociocultural landscape, women have to rely upon their own resources in dealing with situations of loneliness and unconnectedness that they'll inevitably encounter.

How to Curb Loneliness

There are many times when making a phone call, reading a good book or watching TV doesn't alleviate feelings of loneliness. When you're new to a city, it's important to seek out the company of others, even if it means developing nerve you don't think you have. The four ideas that follow come highly recommended by newcomers who met business contacts, men they later dated and even long-time friends by implementing them.

1. *Become a regular patron.* Weekly or even more frequent visits to a nearby bar/restaurant whose atmosphere, food and patrons are to your liking are a good investment. That way, if you get an unexpected attack of loneliness some night, you can drop in for a bite or a drink. Make it a point to get to know one or more of the bartenders— they're listeners by profession (a plus if you just need a sympathetic ear), can ward off men who bother you and occasionally provide a drink on the house. If you become good buddies, you may even get escorted home on nights you stay late. Developing a rapport with the maître d' and a waiter or two is advisable, since they'll give you special attention and make sure you're seated even on crowded nights.

2. *Make plans for Sunday night.* It can be the loneliest night of the week, since it's not a traditional date night, but is still part of the weekend. If you have difficulty talking people you know into going out because they've already spent too much over the weekend, offer to make a casual dinner, an invitation few can resist taking you up on.

3. *Get involved in an activity that meets regularly.* Run with fellow members of a local road runners club on the weekends. Take a course at a college, museum or learning network. Volunteer to work behind the scenes for a community theater or dance group. Any situation which guarantees you'll be seeing a group of people who share one of your interests is a goood loneliness preventive.

4. *Go to places conducive to starting conversations.* Museums, art galleries and college campuses are ideal for meeting people. Force yourself to speak to at least one person (the more you do it, the easier it gets). You can comment on something you're both observing, ask for directions or talk about the weather, for starters.

The Special Case of Single Mothers

When Alice Jamison* moved to Washington, D.C., in 1969 with her two-year-old son, she faced the prospect of having to care for him completely on her own. But she felt the extra responsibility was worth it; her prospects as a government lawyer working for the Internal Revenue Service in Indianapolis were not exciting. During a training session in Washington, she asked about the possibility of being transferred to the offices there. The "yes" was all she needed to make the decision to go, even though it meant leaving her parents and friends.

"I felt I had an advantage that single women new to a city

*A pseudonym.

did not," says Alice, who was 26 years old when she relocated. "I had someone to come home to each night, who couldn't wait to see me. I never knew what it was like to face an empty apartment."

According to the results of the Urban Experience Survey, women with children are less lonely than those without them, but factoring in one's marital status can change the picture. Women who are separated or divorced are lonelier than either single or married women. As Dr. Robert Weiss, author of *Going It Alone: Family Life and Social Situation of the Single Parent*, notes, "Even though children can fulfill many of one's emotional needs, they are not substitutes for adult company. But through them, single mothers can begin connecting to other adults in the community—through school, day-care or church-related activities."

As is the case with other single mothers who work, Alice's time to cultivate new friends was limited. There was no time to meet with colleagues or acquaintances over drinks after work. And Alice chose to live in a single-family-home type of suburb which further isolated her from other singles her age. "It wasn't easy. And I did get lonely. But for awhile, just being able to talk to my mother on the phone was enough to relieve it. Perhaps it was the sense of purpose I had at that time that kept me going. I had to prove myself in my new job. And I felt my son deserved to get the majority of my free time," remembers Alice.

There's no question that having children gives one's life the kind of emotional stability that no other relationship can. And children are a daily reminder of what's important in life, which one can lose sight of easily in the competitive, fast-track pace of a city like Washington.

Still, there is the pressure to be a "supermom," especially if the move has put a large physical distance between the child and important others in his or her life—grandparents and other relatives, one's "ex," neighbors and friends. When Sherry Richardson moved from Ohio to Miami with her five-year-old son, she had the advantage of having a favorite cousin nearby. That family relationship helped when she finally began dating a year or two after having arrived. "I was very sensitive about my son's reactions to men who I started seeing.

Whenever I could, I included him in the date. But when I wanted to go out for an evening of adult entertainment, I would explain why he was going to spend the night with my cousin and her children."

How to Begin Building a New Network

How hard is it to find a social niche in a big city? Despite the widespread belief that cities destroy personal relationships because of their size and complexity, one major study has recently concluded that city dwellers actually have more supportive personal networks than do residents of suburban and rural areas. Sociologist Claude S. Fischer theorizes that that is the case because city dwellers have access to a wider variety of possible friends and often become a part of a flourishing subculture (because of their professional or recreational interests, ethnicity, religious or sexual preferences) which usually don't exist in less populated places.

The two factors which made the biggest difference in the richness and intimacy of people's social life were education and income. The higher the level, the larger and more secure one's network of friends is. To the extent that cities attract well-educated people and provide high-paying jobs, Fischer says, they can be said to indirectly promote friendship.

Most of us, even those of us who aren't particularly shy, find it difficult to initiate conversations with people we've never spoken to before, even if we've seen each other in a socially acceptable context, such as a classroom or at a party. The hesitance stems in part from being unsure of how people will react to our friendly overture. And for those who never had to make a conscious effort to make friends because we were continually meeting new people through our already established network, the idea of cultivating contacts is foreign. (People who have made previous moves, even as children, are usually more skilled at initiating encounters and are less hesitant to do so.)

The result is that many newcomers take a passive role in

making connections in a new place. They wait for others to notice and acknowledge their presence or make the first move, and consequently end up feeling extremely lonely. Many Urban Experience Survey respondents felt their transition to a new place would have been easier had they made the effort to meet more people sooner.

When Suzanne Lasky moved with her husband to Miami in the early seventies, she didn't even know how to make friends. "When you grow up in one area and go to school there, friendships develop naturally over the years," says Suzanne, who lived in Oceanside, Long Island.

Now, some ten years after her arrival, Suzanne's face is familiar to thousands of people in that city—she hosts a TV talk show, *Kaleidoscope*. As if to remind herself that life in the city wasn't always as exciting and filled with interesting friends as it is now, Suzanne has hung on her office wall a painting she did during her first few months in Miami. It portrays a young woman sitting alone in a room, bare except for the chair against which she is leaning. She is staring distractedly at the floor, looking for all the world as if she'd been abandoned by those who cared for her.

"I was terribly depressed for months after I arrived. Neither my husband nor I knew anyone and I didn't work for the first three or four months we were here, which made meeting people even more difficult. We were staying in an apartment in South Beach, a section of Miami which has an incredible number of elderly people, and we didn't even see any people our age. I remember looking out the window one day and spotting a young couple. 'Hurry and get dressed—I see some potential friends walking by,' I called to my husband. We ran out of our apartment and chased after them. When we caught up, we nonchalantly asked them if they lived in the neighborhood. They were the only couple we saw regularly during our first year here," says Suzanne.

Moving to a new place with a husband or boyfriend (or to join one) eliminates the loneliness of not having an intimate relationship (what sociologists call "emotional isolation"), but the problem of social isolation can be just as difficult as it is for the single person. Establishing a network often takes longer for married couples, because one or both people are reluctant to seek out individuals, rather than couples, as friends. That was true of the Laskys. "I was reluctant to look for women who might become my friends because I saw myself as being part of a couple, perhaps because I was in my early twenties and because I had only been married a year," explains Suzanne.

Since, during their first year in Miami, the Laskys had a hard time meeting couples they both liked, they put a lot of effort into getting to know couples who were "good friend" candidates. "If, for example, we met a couple at a cocktail party, we'd ask them what they were doing afterwards and find out if they wanted to go out for dinner. Or we'd invite people we'd met over to our home for dinner," says Suzanne. Their tactic worked—people, even those who already have plenty of friends, enjoy being sought out and are apt to reciprocate if they've enjoyed their time with you.

Eventually, Suzanne and her husband began developing their own individual networks of friends, because it wasn't easy finding couples where everyone liked one another, and if the couples split up, as happened to a number of their friends, it often meant the end of the friendship for everyone. Having friends of your own if you're married or having a steady boyfriend provides opportunities to spend time away from one another and to bring back tales and experiences.

How to Launch a Friendship

Getting to know someone beyond the "Hello, how are you?" stage is difficult in the city because so many activities compete for people's time and attention. If you meet someone whom you would like to have as a friend, it's a good idea to take the initiative to find out whether the attraction is mutual. Here's how:

1. *Ask for advice.* It might be as simple as asking for a restaurant recommendation or as serious as soliciting an opinion about how you should handle a problem with your boss. The point is, most people are flattered that you would think to come to them for help and respect their advice enough to give it a try.

2. *Suggest that the two of you do something together.* Even if you both work for the same employer or have some other basis for getting to know one another casually, you can speed up the process of becoming friends by doing something outside the context in which you see one another. It might be having lunch, playing a sport you both enjoy or going to a movie. If you're unsure of the other person's interest, make it a casual inquiry and don't pin the other person down to a date or time. You'll be able to tell from her response how interested she is in accepting your offer.

3. *Go out of your way to be thoughtful.* The gesture doesn't have to be a grand one—just remembering to call when you know she's waiting to hear some important news in her life, for example, tells her that you were thinking of her.

4. *Keep in touch.* The more often you communicate with one another, the greater the chances of your sharing more confidences and activities in your life. That's easy if you run into one another frequently, but if that's not the case, you might call to report on the restaurant you tried at her suggestion or how your problem at work was resolved. If your friendship hasn't yet gotten to the point where you feel comfortable calling just to say "Hello," you can stay in touch by sending an article you clipped from the newspaper that you know she would be interested in reading, for example.

Getting to Know Neighbors

Neighborliness is not a quality associated with living in the city. Indeed, city people often say that one of the qualities they like about their life-style is the absence of nosy neighbors who monitor their comings and goings.

In interviewing more than 1,000 adults in 50 communities in Northern California for his study of personal networks, Claude Fischer discovered that those who lived in cities were less involved with their neighbors than were those who lived outside cities. The reason, he says, is that city people turn to neighbors only if they find them compatible and of interest as potential friends. The only exception to this finding is new-comers to the city (particularly long-distance movers), who often looked to neighbors as potential replacements for the support network they left behind.

Whether or not your neighbors do, in fact, become friends is less important than developing a rapport with them. You both have a stake in the safety of your homes and the mutual need of having someone close by upon whom you can rely for small things, such as getting your mail when you're away for a few days or borrowing the proverbial cup of sugar. In fact, in Fischer's study, many city dwellers noted the absence of any-one nearby on whom they could depend for such things. The reason: they failed to cultivate neighbors as neighbors.

The best time to develop a neighborly relationship is when you're moving in. Most city dwellers are curious about who their immediate neighbors are (although most won't make the effort to find out). So take advantage of the fact that you're a new face in the building or on the block. Ask questions about the best places in the neighborhood to eat, shop or have a drink—most people are flattered when asked for their opinions or advice. A friendly gesture on your part—sending over brownies that you've made, or offering to help out a neighbor in some way—can go a long way toward establishing a mutu-ally beneficial relationship that may span your stay in the neighborhood.

If you live in an area of the country where you and your neighbors share recreational facilities, you will come into con-tact with even more people, many of whom you may not see regularly in your building or hallway. Unless you have the personality of a politician running for office, you'll undoubtedly find it awkward simply to go up to people and introduce your-self.

Taking the initiative can, however, be done in creative ways. The Laskys, for instance, wanted to get to know the other people in their 16-story Miami high rise. So they brought a cooler of drinks to the pool on Sunday and offered them to the other sunbathers. Their gesture got people talking to one another, and someone else offered to bring drinks the following weekend. Soon thereafter, the Laskys invited a group of poolside neighbors to their top-floor apartment for a barbecue, which became a weekend event, with each guest contributing a dish.

Sometimes just putting yourself in a position to be noticed by your neighbors can be a way to meet people. If you're a jogger, for example, you might do some of your exercises in front of your home or apartment building rather than inside, which gives a fellow runner who may pass by an opportunity to ask something about your involvement with the sport.

One of the easiest ways to meet people beyond your next-door neighbors is to become a dog owner. A study that was conducted in London's Hyde Park showed that pet owners spoke to more people and had longer conversations when they were walking their dogs than when walking alone. In another study, people who walked dogs were viewed by others as being more intelligent, confident, sympathetic and friendly than those who were petless. Canines, it seems, promote social encounters—they're a non-threatening conversation starter.

Follow Up on Contacts

Don't hesitate to look up people you knew from school, previous jobs or other settings from your past, even if you haven't seen or spoken to them for a long time. Most people would be flattered that you bothered to look them up and interested in what's happened in your life (or telling you about theirs). Even if you discover after one meeting that the two of you aren't destined to become great pals, you may find that they know a person who would be worth meeting because you share a passion for the same sport or hobby, work in the same field or have some other interest in common.

If you haven't already asked people you know who they know in the city to which you're moving, do it now. It's best to have your friend call to say that you'll be in touch. Whenever you call (particularly if you're making it cold), it's a good idea to feel out the other person by asking questions (about where some good weekend entertainment spots are, for example) to get a sense of whether he or she seems to have the time and inclination to get together.

Socializing with Co-Workers and Business Contacts

Unless you work in a small office or one in which there aren't others at your level, you'll probably find work a natural place to find people with whom to do things in your free time. Once again, you'll have to let others know that you're interested in spending time with them.

You can avoid putting someone on the spot by casually mentioning your interest in something they do (i.e., taking exercise classes) or would like to do (i.e., checking out a new Mexican restaurant), or by asking whether they'd like to get together at some point (and making your follow-up dependent on the enthusiasm of their response).

According to Fischer's study, people who work long hours or unusual shifts are more likely to fraternize with co-workers off the job. News broadcaster Natalie Windsor, who has often worked the radio drive-time shift (5 A.M. to noon), often socialized with her colleagues because they were the ones free during the day.

If you're new to the work world and unsure of what's kosher in terms of after-work socializing, know that, generally speaking, it's best to *avoid* socializing with:

—Members of the opposite sex unless you work for a large company and in different departments

—Clients or customers of either sex if your chumminess might be misunderstood by the powers that be at your company or the other person's

—Colleagues whose job level is much higher or lower than yours; you may be seen as trying to curry favor (in the case of socializing with a superior) or unsure of your status and authority (in the case of socializing with an underling).

If you've moved to a different region of the country, whose culture is unfamiliar to you, you may feel like an outsider, a situation that is exacerbated in a work situation, where local rituals, customs and the modus operandi are dramatized daily.

For almost a year after her arrival in New York, Mary Alice Kellogg, whose hometown was Tucson, kept a cartoon on the bulletin board above her desk at the *Newsweek* offices. It pictured a wild-haired country bumpkin kind of woman chewing on a weed beside a sophisticated gentleman in top hat and spats puffing on his cigarette holder. The caption reads, "Tell me, my dear, what brings you to the sophisticated East?"

"I very much identified with the woman in that cartoon," says Mary Alice, who found herself surrounded by co-workers who had gone to Ivy League or Seven Sisters schools, and who seemed to know the "acceptable" places to shop and be seen at. "It was as if they all belonged to some secret society and shared the same language, style and way of seeing the world," says Mary Alice.

Despite her feelings of being an outsider, she didn't let them stand in the way of her approaching people or making friends. "If you see a city as being intimidating and filled with people who are cold or who don't think you're worth knowing, it may become a self-fulfilling prophecy," she says. "But if you make an effort to reach out to people, it usually pays off." Later, as a correspondent for *Newsweek*, Mary Alice moved to Chicago and San Francisco. Several months after her arrival on the West Coast, she decided to give a party. Many of those invited were business contacts she had met only once and liked, and she asked each person to bring along a friend. The party turned out to be one of the most successful she has ever given; in fact, that night she met the man she later married.

Get Involved in Organized Activities

Even if you've never been much of a joiner, it's to your advantage to plug into organizations, meeting places or special events sponsored by people who share one or more of your interests.

* * *

Elizabeth Haas had never been to Cleveland before coming to interview with McKinsey & Co., a prestigious management consulting firm. She accepted the job in September of 1979 because it was just the opportunity she was looking for after graduating from the Massachusetts Institute of Technology with an MBA and a doctorate in operations management. While McKinsey's Cleveland office was the best geographic location for her work (her specialty is advising factory management on ways to cut costs and increase production), it was the last location she would have chosen for social reasons.

Nonetheless, Elizabeth feels that making friends in a city filled with more native Clevelanders than out-of-towners wasn't difficult. She soon became a member of the racquet club and she joined a bridge group and the Sierra Club, a national outdoor recreational organization. "I pour a lot of energy into my job and am frequently out of town on business, so naturally I found myself socializing with colleagues. But in order to expand my group of friends, I decided to participate in activities I already knew I enjoyed," says Elizabeth, who also became a Big Sister since she enjoys working with young people.

It's not always necessary to become a card-carrying member of a club in order to meet people with similar interests. There are plenty of other situations which provide opportunities to get to know other people.

Adult education classes may be one of the best alternatives. You're more likely to develop friendships over the course of a semester's time, particularly in classes where students are taking it for credit. But there are many less expensive and shorter-length courses given by a variety of educational institutions. Learning networks and Y's offer many courses that are especially useful for newcomers to a city—how to find an apartment, a bargain finder's guided walking tour, the best cheap restaurants, how to get a credit card and how to start a conversation. You'll be able to find catalogs of current course offerings from a variety of schools at the public library.

Although city dwellers are less likely to be involved in organized religion, according to the Fischer study, many women who describe themselves as religious say they were able to meet people—particularly men—who shared their values and outlook on life by attending church services. Some churches in downtown areas make a deliberate attempt to reach young adults. St. Bartholomew's, an Episcopal church in midtown Manhattan, for example, has a community club and center, whose interdenominational membership is composed largely of men and women in their twenties and thirties. Activities in the club range from weekend socials to volunteer work to sports outings. Members frequently see one another in the club's dining and recreational facilities.

Still another way to expand professional and social contacts is through alumni clubs and organizations. A recent *New York Times* article stated, "Today's young college graduates, new New Yorkers who come to the city to seek their fortunes, have revived one of the city's oldest traditions—its university clubs." While membership dropped throughout the seventies, there has been a turnaround in the last few years. Most clubs offer good deals on food, drink, and sports and meeting facilities, and many offer reduced rates to recent graduates. Even more valuable are some of the new services provided—career counseling, networking cocktail parties and seminars on how to adjust to big city living.

Even if you didn't attend a university with a club located in your city, you may find that there is a functioning alumni group which periodically schedules luncheons with speakers or social events. Your college alumni association can tell you who to contact.

Meeting Interesting Men

How easy is it to meet the right kind of men soon after your arrival in a city? The results of the Urban Experience Survey indicate that most newcomers have a difficult time meeting men. Knowing few people, male and female, reduces the chances of your being with people or in situations where you might normally get introduced.

*   *   *

"When I first moved from Boston to New York, I thought I'd meet a lot of new people and be going out every night. It didn't happen. I ended up going out with relatives and friends I'd known for years who had also moved here," says Angela Fowler, who moved to Manhattan when she was 23. "The problem with meeting people, particularly men, in big cities is that you rarely bump into them on a regular basis the way you do on a college campus. When your paths don't cross frequently, you can't slowly develop a friendly relationship, which certainly makes it easier to determine if you want to go out on a romantic basis. On occasion, I would meet a nice guy at a party and we'd spend the whole evening talking or dancing. But that was often the end of it—there wasn't any follow-up situation where we might have met again without the pressure of having to go out on a date."

The Best Places to Meet Men

Unlike the suburban dating scene where connecting with eligible and interesting men is largely confined to weekend night parties, bars and clubs, the dynamics of the city make it possible to meet men you would like to see more of in a wide variety of situations. They include:

Blind Dates or Fix-ups. Even if they've never panned out before, don't hesitate to take a friend up on his or her offer to introduce you to someone they think you might like. Unless your friend has bad judgment, you'll end up at the very least with a pleasant night on the town. And if he or she has great intuition, you may be in for a brief romance or even a longer-term relationship. In fact, more city women meet men through friends (53 percent) than any other way, according to the results of the Urban Experience Survey.

Church Organizations. Worth becoming active in if you're interested in meeting men whose values and background are very similar to yours.

Classes. Once you've decided what you want to take, choose your school carefully. Those located in downtown areas are the most likely to draw professionals who work nearby. Courses that cater to the "single and looking" crowd turn up all kinds, many of whom won't appeal to you in the least.

Classified Ads. For the adventurous who feel that all options are worth a try. Expect plenty of interview-type dates, but don't get your hopes up for many (if any) going beyond that stage.

Health or Sports Clubs. The odds are in your favor (unless it's an exercise class or a predominantly female organization). One of the few opportunities to get to know someone casually before making a decision about whether you want to date him.

Introductions Through the Parent Network. Most bomb out. But every so often, the guy who calls and says he's the brother of your mother's best friend's son can turn out to be someone worth knowing. Ergo, if there are no exciting men in your life, why not meet for a drink?

On the Job. Office romances usually aren't worth it if the man is: (1) your boss—or someone who has power over your job; (2) a co-worker with whom you must interact daily; (3) a client with whom your job forces you to have a continuing working relationship. Those exclusions leave plenty of other possibilities. Forty-four percent of city women say they meet men through work.

Parties. Prime meeting spots. Social gatherings are even more promising than business affairs because introductions are easier and guests are more often looking for a chance for romance.

Political Campaigns. The perfect environment for romances to bud and bloom. Major races—gubernatorial, congressional and especially presidential—draw the most volunteers. Be sure to work in some sort of group or committee situation—publicity or fund-raising, for example. Don't get stuck in a backroom licking envelopes with less action-oriented campaign workers.

Public Places. Easy-to-connect places include museums, art galleries and city parks (particularly on weekends). Recommended for those with dating experience who can easily tell the difference between a smooth-talking jerk and a witty, gregarious gentleman.

Singles Bars. Few long-standing relationships start here, but they're fine for a night of fun and flirting if you're with a friend or two.

Video Dating Services. The latest twist in the electronic matchmaker business. Pricey but legitimate way of meeting men to whom you're attracted and with whom you have something in common. Good for those who can't find the time (or don't have the patience) to meet men in more conventional ways.

Most young professionals who have lived in a big city for a year or less meet the men they date through friends or work.

If you come into a city with few or no contacts, knowing where it's socially acceptable to meet men can be confusing. Singles bars are unquestionably a popular meeting spot, and newcomers are far more likely to frequent them than are women who have lived in the city for several years, according to the Urban Experience Survey.

Coming from a college or smaller town environment, you may have frequented the local watering holes and felt quite comfortable meeting new men there, either because they were part of a homogeneous group with which you were familiar—students, natives of the area or young professionals—or you got introduced through acquaintances or friends. While there are local bars with a regular clientele in large cities, many bar scenes attract a wide variety of people, which makes them exciting but sometimes dangerous places to meet people.

Within a year of my arrival in New York City, a murder took place which rattled the psyche of every young woman like me who had ever ventured into a big city bar alone. A twenty-eight-year-old schoolteacher met an attractive stranger in a West Side bar and invited him back to her apartment. What started out as a casual sexual encounter ended in her brutal murder.

Unpleasant encounters are not all that rare. Forty percent of single women who were surveyed by Jacqueline Simenauer and David Carroll in *Singles* said they suffered some kind of physical or mental abuse at a singles bar, ranging from the unpleasant to the life-threatening. The type of woman most likely to encounter some type of demeaning incident is the educated, high-wage-earning career woman. Why? Psychologist Elayne Kahn is quoted in the book as saying, ". . . [these women] have very high expectations when they go to bars. They feel they're the cream of the crop and expect men to treat them accordingly. But at a bar, men mostly view women as sex objects, while women are there to meet men."

Many young women think they're good judges of character and can handle themselves in difficult situations, but most of the time their experience is limited to men whose background is similar to theirs and whose behavior doesn't go beyond certain understood limits. The only way to protect yourself against unwanted advances or behavior is to get to know someone over the course of several dates before you spend time alone together.

The same adage applies to men you meet in public places. More city women (21 percent) than small town and suburban women (15 percent) say they date men they meet in museums, stores and parks.

Finding People Like Ourselves

Although city dwellers say that one of the best things about living in a city is the variety of people—the mixture of classes and ethnic groups—by and large, their networks are peopled with men and women like themselves. In particular, young, unmarried adults in cities tend to socialize with people who share their lot and interests.

In his book, *The Nine Nations of North America,* author Joel

Garreau documents the distinctions among the various areas, each of which has its own values, customs, view of the relationship between the sexes, among other things. Sociologists have yet to come up with hard evidence that people who move from one cultural region to another have more trouble fitting in than do those who move within their area. But loneliness expert Robert Weiss believes the former to be a tougher transition, particularly if there are few other people from your hometown region living in the city.

Moving from One Cultural Zone to Another

Washington, D.C., is a unique city in that newcomers from every state in the Union are well represented as are citizens of other countries. Most of the women interviewed for this book who moved there from elsewhere say that people who grew up in the same area of the country they did comprise a disproportionate number of their friends and acquaintances. That was certainly true of Connie LaPointe, who moved to the District in 1980.

Connie spent most of her childhood and adolescent years in Westbrook, Maine, a town of 15,000. Her decision to come to Boston to attend Emmanuel College, a private Catholic women's college, was her first big step away from home. She figured it would be a way of easing into city life, and it was. After graduation, she worked in a series of jobs in Boston's City Hall, where she got to know politicians and love politics.

Then she spent several years in the governor's office in Maine, during which time she managed Kennedy's Presidential campaign for four months.

On the basis of her reputation and her administrative abilities, Connie was able to get hired as a member of the Washington, D.C., staff of Maine Senator George Mitchell. It was 1980, and even though she had been out of college for six years, her move to the nation's capital was more a cutting of the umbilical cord than her previous moves had been. "It was a combination of factors—living outside of New England for the first time ever, being a long distance away from my family and close friends, and having an important political job in a city where many people held important posts," Connie explains.

She took advantage of her relatively regular office hours to explore the area, often with colleagues from her office. And she frequently visited the restaurant owned by a college friend's husband. "What was interesting was that even the new people I met were New Englanders. There was an attraction, almost a bond among us. It was easy to meet people from there. As soon as the conversation began it was, 'Oh, you're from Boston. I went to school there, too. Did you know so and so?'" explains Connie, who has a distinctive New England accent.

Connie's experiences are very similar to those of women from Texas and Kansas and Alabama who come to Washington to stay for a term of office or end up permanently relocated because they can't bear to leave the magic that is Washington's. Associating with people who share the same frame of reference makes adjusting to a new city easier—one doesn't always have to explain the context of a story or experience and they're more likely to sympathize and understand problems you encounter. Friends and acquaintances who talk, think, look or behave in ways familiar to you are not only connections in your new world but connections with a world you've left behind.

6

Learning to Live on Your Own

xxxxxxxxxxxxxxxxxxxxxxxxxxxxxxxxxxxxxxxxxxxxxxxxxxxxxxxxxxxx

FOR MANY NEWCOMERS to the city, the move is a declaration of independence—from their parents, ex-husband, hometown or adolescence (which isn't limited to one's teenage years). Adjusting to life in the city, possibly in a different region of the country, while trying to develop wings of one's own is usually a trying time, filled with the exhilaration of being the mistress of one's own fate and the apprehension of being a stranger in a strange place.

Keeping Your Fantasies in Line

It's normal to think that getting a fresh start, shedding an old routine or leaving behind stale relationships will bring relief, excitement or both to your life. Fantasies are important because they help shape dreams. But unless you have stopped to consider how realistic they are in view of your personality, background and education, you may be disappointed.

If, for example, you've always been a shy person but imagine you'll be much more daring and adventuresome once you're on your own, you'll be surprised to discover that there won't be any overnight changes in your way of approaching people. It is likely, however, that if you put yourself in a situation that forces you to be more outgoing and questioning to survive, you will begin to feel more comfortable about relying on yourself than had you stayed where you didn't have to worry about basics such as how to get around or where to shop.

Your daydreams about what living on your own in a city will be like may center around finding the perfect job or meeting exciting people and interesting men. But these projections rarely withstand the test of reality.

Several months before moving to New York City, I had met an actor from there who visited my campus and encouraged me to go ahead with my tentative plan to try living in the Big Apple. I imagined that he would show me around town and introduce me to the theater world. I saw myself on his arm— attending theater openings, meeting actors and actresses, and having a wonderful love affair—experiencing the city on a level I could not hope to as a newcomer without connections.

I was temporarily crushed to discover upon my arrival that he had a girl friend and that aside from seeing me occasionally for drinks, he had no intention of helping me adjust to city life. Had I not made plans of my own—to take graduate courses and find a job—those first few months may have been a disaster rather than the positive experiences they turned out to be.

Unless you are excited about the prospects of what life in a new place will be like, you wouldn't be motivated to move in the first place. It's important, however, to consider how you can help make them happen and how long it may take for your dreams to materialize, and be flexible enough to accept different results from those you had anticipated.

Making the Break from Home

Moving away from your family or a place in which you've grown comfortable isn't always an easy transition. Women who have lived in a city less than a year say they suffer from physical and mental symptoms of depression. A third of the respondents to the Urban Experience Survey say they have frequent headaches and nights of restless sleep; three-fourths report high levels of worry and anxiety.

"One of the symptoms of acute newcomeritis is homesickness," says psychologist Lawrence Balter. "No matter what your chronological age is, it's not uncommon to think about the situation you have left behind—school, your job, your friends and family—and wish you were back there during the first few months in a new place."

Jill Cochrane was 29 when she moved to New York City from the college town of Amherst, Massachusetts, which had been her home for twelve years. She had landed a terrific job organizing world-wide conferences for an association of company presidents.

"I was so happy about the prospect of starting a new life after my divorce that the possibility of missing my old life didn't occur to me before I left," explains Jill.

Many of her contemporaries envied her early success. After graduating with a degree in recreation administration in 1969, Jill married her college sweetheart. Six months later, she landed a job as program advisor in her alma mater's student activities office. Her husband found a position in the dean's office. Despite the overlap in their professional and personal lives, the marriage began to disintegrate—their hectic schedules allowed for little time alone together. They were divorced in 1974, sold their house and bought individual condominiums.

Living in a small community became increasingly confining. When Jill learned of a job opening in New York from a colleague on campus, she interviewed for it right away, and was hired soon thereafter. Within fourteen days of accepting, she was in Hong Kong, organizing her first educational program for them. From that point on, she was out of the city an average of ten days a month. "It was almost impossible to make friends when you don't have a routine and you're not around enough to make plans ahead of time," explains Jill.

So she headed back to New England—a five-hour drive—almost once a month during her first year in New York. Being around the people whom she had known for over a decade restored the feeling of connectedness that her new job, with its demanding schedule and limited number of new colleagues, robbed her of.

"There's nothing wrong with weaning yourself away from an old situation in order to better adjust to a new one," says Lawrence Balter. "People often think they have to make transitions completely on their own so that they won't be thought of as weak or dependent. But there's nothing to be gained by saying, 'I did it alone,' if you're suffering in the meantime. Healthy independence means knowing when you need support and reaching out for it."

When Your Parents Disapprove

Despite the growing acceptance of women holding important jobs, living alone and delaying marriage, there are still parents who try to persuade their daughters to stay close to home for selfish or protective reasons. While almost half of the respondents to the Urban Experience Survey said their parents encouraged them to try city living, 20 percent of the women said their parents wished they hadn't moved so far away. Eighteen percent said their parents' reaction to their first move to a city was fear for their safety; four percent of the women said their parents actively discouraged them from going.

If your parents try to influence your decision to go by disapproving in blatant or subtle ways, you'll no doubt feel guilty or resentful or both if you go anyway. And you'll certainly feel more pressure to succeed since you'll have to contend with their "I told you so's," if you don't. The best you can hope to do under those circumstances is to reassure them in as many ways as you can—by living in a safe neighborhood, checking in with them frequently and by fending for yourself financially so that they know you're serious about making it on your own.

Staying in Touch with Family and Friends

Once you move to a city, your schedule and finances may not permit you to get home as often as you did in college or when you were living closer. You can keep up your ties with people you care about without running up an astronomical phone bill. Here's how:

1. Subscribe to your hometown newspaper or encourage a family member to send clippings you'd enjoy reading.

2. Make sure your high school and college have your name and current address so that you'll receive their newsletters.

3. If you're an infrequent letter writer, compose an occasional newsletter about what you've been up to and news you've heard about. Make copies and jot a personal note at the bottom to each family member or friend you send it to.

4. Send pictures. Take pictures of your apartment, your neighborhood, your friends, where you work, famous sights in your city (preferably with you in the foreground). Since your parents and friends can't be there, they can at least live your experiences vicariously.

5. Subscribe to a nationwide long-distance phone service. If your long-distance phone bill comes to more than $25 a month, you can reduce the cost of each call by paying a monthly subscription fee of $5–$10 to a long-distance service (MCI and Sprint are the two largest services). Both services require that you have a push-button phone (for which you'll pay a slightly higher monthly rental to your local phone company).

The Freedom of Being Your Own Person

Moving to a city can be a tremendously liberating experience if you grew up in a small community where your place was defined by who your family is or in one in which convention strongly influences the behavior and expectations of its residents. The people you meet in a city have no preconceived notions about who you are; you can invent an image that reflects how you want to be known.

*   *   *

Souris is a potato-farming community on Prince Edward Island in the Gulf of St. Lawrence in the Canadian maritimes. In postcard pictures, it looks like one of those corners of the world that is frozen in time with its white-shingled churches and acres of green rolling gently toward the sea. It was Ellen MacDonald's universe for 20 years. One of two girls in a family of six children, she grew up a farmer's daughter. The women in the family tended to all the domestic chores.

After graduating from the small Roman Catholic college on PEI, as it is often referred to, Ellen won a full scholarship at McGill University's law school, some 1200 miles away in Montreal. Moving there to compete with the brightest students in Canada was the most traumatic period in her life. She had been the first woman president of her college's student council. She had had her own university radio show. She had aced her undergraduate courses with little effort. Now all that was changed. She was one of two women in her law school class (it was 1970, one of the first years that women began enrolling in professional schools in greater numbers than ever before). Her early papers came back with so much red ink on them that she began to wonder if she truly belonged there. But Ellen never let on just how difficult her adjustment was or how painful the first term had been when she had failed three of her six exams.

The Importance of Self-Esteem

Ellen is the first to admit that had she not believed in herself, her dream of becoming a lawyer may not have gone further than six months of law school. "A high level of self-esteem can pull you through the most difficult of transitions, even when you're faced with circumstances or events you couldn't have foreseen," says psychotherapist Loretta Walder, who is also a lawyer.

One of the major determinants of how comfortable you'll feel being independent is your level of self-esteem. If you're a person who has had small successes throughout your life—in school, in personal relationships, in previous jobs—your ego is probably healthy. You know how to set goals for yourself and achieve them—and are willing to take credit for what you've done. But if you've been trying to fulfill someone else's prescription for your life and satisfying their dreams for you rather than your own, you probably have doubts about your ability to pursue your own ideas of happiness. Making a move to a city to find your own way is undoubtedly going to be more of a psychological hurdle for you than for the woman who goes with her parents' support.

One's sense of self-esteem, of course, has its roots in childhood. Whether or not your parents approved of and rewarded your efforts beginning at a young age makes a big difference in how secure you feel with yourself as an adult. And once in school, the feedback you received from teachers likewise went a long way in forming a strong self-image. Without a high level of self-esteem, it's easy to be unsure of one's choices and once made, whether they're attainable.

If your parents support your decision to move to a city, you'll probably be more comfortable with your independence. And your chances for career success increase, too. According to the Urban Experience Survey, 57 percent of the parents of the most successful women encouraged them to try city living compared to 45 percent of the parents of women who hadn't gone as far in their careers.

Being the First to Leave Home

The oldest child is usually the biggest risk-taker in a family. She (or he) is often the least traditional of the children in her thinking and often feels the urge to forge her own path in the world, which others in her family sometimes end up following.

"I am the most independent-minded of five daughters," admits Judsen Culbreth, an "oldest" who grew up in the South. She always had her nose buried in a book; she played weird (that is, classical) music; she enjoyed trying out new words she'd learned in everyday conversations. Although Judsen is soft-spoken, she often found herself arguing with her friends at college. She didn't find their sexist or racist jokes funny;

they thought she had no sense of humor. And the prospect of living her life in an area of the country where women's roles were rigidly defined made Judsen uncomfortable.

The revelation that she was not the only one who thought that way came when she was selected as one of the top college women in the country by *Glamour* magazine and came to New York to meet her fellow winners. "I met and got to know nine other women who were bright, ambitious and politically active on campus. So I'm not the crazy one after all, I thought to myself," recalls Judsen.

She found it somewhat ironic that she felt more normal in a big Northeastern city whose frantic pace and idea of hospitality were much different from those of the folks back home. Even though she was close to her family, she made the decision to return, knowing that she could pursue her dreams without regard to what those around her thought was "right."

Even though the sensibilities of New Yorkers were closer to her own than were those of the people with whom she'd grown up, Judsen discovered that some Northerners suspected her of the very prejudices that she disliked in some of the people with whom she'd grown up. When she was being interviewed for a job as an editorial assistant with a women's magazine, the managing editor warned her, "We don't tolerate any kind of prejudice in these offices. If we discover that someone has acted in a discriminatory way, she'll be fired. Do you understand?" Judsen was so astounded at the editor's presumption of her bias simply because she grew up in the South that the only thing she could manage to say in her own defense was that one of her roommates was black.

While living with Sheila and Kate (both of whom were also *Glamour* magazine college winners) helped ease the transition from going to college in Mobile to working as an editorial assistant at a national women's magazine in New York City, Judsen very much missed the camaraderie of her sisters. The five were particularly close and dependent on one another because their family had moved frequently when they were growing up.

The first time her younger sister Jennifer had come to visit her, Judsen felt more comfortable with the city than she ever had. She had someone to cook for, someone to clean house for, someone to take care of. When Jennifer left for the airport, Judsen couldn't stop crying.

Four years after Judsen left Mobile another sister, Jeffry, came North to be with her. "I had been living in an apartment by myself for eight lonely months. It was the first time in my life I didn't have someone to come home and talk to. So when Jeffry said she was coming, I was ecstatic," remembers Judsen. Five years later, another member of the Culbreth clan, 22-year-old Jennifer, joined her sisters.

Even before her two sisters came North, Judsen was beginning to think of herself more as a New Yorker than a Southern expatriate. She took pleasure in walking the city streets and discovering shops and galleries that one would never have chanced upon in a city the size of Mobile.

Phasing out an attachment to the place you leave is often necessary in order to develop a strong identification with a new one. In other words, you have to start thinking of yourself as a native before your ties with your hometown begin to dissipate. If you're infatuated with the way of life in your adopted city, as Judsen was with New York, you're much more likely to want to be a part of it.

How to Establish Financial Independence

You don't need an M.B.A. to learn how to manage your personal finances. But if you want to become financially self-sufficient, practicing good fiscal habits is essential.

Establish a Credit Track Record. Start by applying for credit cards. Department store credit cards are the easiest to obtain, but if you're earning a decent salary, you may be able to qualify for a major credit card (such as American Express, Visa or Mastercard) through your bank. So long as you pay in full at the time of billing, you'll incur no interest charges. But in most states, you'll have to pay an annual card user's fee. If and when you need a loan, your chances of obtaining one are much better if you've proved you're a good credit risk.

Keep Track of Your Income and Expenses. Figure out your fixed monthly expenses (rent, utilities, basic phone charges, parking, loan payments) and keep a running tab of your variable expenses (groceries, eating out, entertainment, clothes and other purchases). Until you know where your paycheck is going, you won't know where you can cut back.

Establish Money-Saving Habits. Even if you've never watched your pennies before, now is a good time to start. Make your long-distance phone calls when rates are least expensive, take public transportation rather than cabs, shop sales, brown bag your lunch, buy your food at grocery rather than convenience stores.

Begin a Forced Savings Plan. No matter how small your paycheck, set aside a certain amount from it each week, even if it means giving up something you'd like to buy or do. If you can spare more, you might check into an automatic payroll deduction plan at work. The point of setting aside money is to get into the habit so that when you make more, you can begin investing the money.

Plan Trips Home and Vacations in Advance. It's the best way to take advantage of bargain air fares and other low-cost transportation and lodging costs.

Many women who leave behind the sheltered lives they led in their college or hometown are aware of their vulnerability, and unless they are moving into some kind of structured environment such as school or a prearranged job situation, they often seek out the company of a protector, someone who can show them the ropes and who cares for their well-being, if only for a short while.

"Women who have no connections in a new place to which they're moving are much more likely to find men who fulfill this role than they are women," says psychotherapist Loretta Walder. "It's a fact of life that most of us—men or women—are too busy or uninterested in reaching out to a newcomer who suddenly appears in our life at work or elsewhere. When there's a sexual attraction it's more likely that someone will take the time and make the effort to be a Good Samaritan. Whether the sexual desires are ever satisfied depends on whether there's a mutual attraction and the relationship is give-and-take on both sides."

What many women, particularly young women in their early twenties, don't take into account is that finding a man who interests you soon after you arrive in a city is a mixed blessing. It certainly helps relieve the loneliness pangs one experiences in leaving behind a group of friends or family because one can replace it to a certain extent with the friends or family of the man. It also alleviates one's fear of crime, because many evenings are spent in the company of a man, which automatically discourages potentially bothersome people from picking you out as a victim.

But it is indeed a borrowed world, and the likelihood of the relationship developing into a serious one is not great. "In times of great emotional need, we're all less discriminating about the people we choose to spend time with," comments psychotherapist Walder. And if you've made the move in order to establish your independence and build a career, at some point the relationship may prove suffocating.

Several months after moving to New York in the fall of 1976, Jeffry Culbreth thought she'd found the man of her dreams. Introduced to him by a friend of her sister, Jeffry fell in love on their first date. Tom was nine years older than she, a boyishly handsome Irishman whose family lived in Vermont. He had recently set up his own law practice in New York and had high ambitions for where his business would eventually take him. He was the most educated man she'd ever dated up until then, and he was also the most charming. He cooked. He did woodworking. He seemed to appreciate women the way Southern men did.

Jeffry began spending most of her free time with him. "I had no motivation to go out and develop other relationships. I was comfortable operating in the social world of my sister and my boyfriend," explains Jeffry.

Her world fell apart 18 months later when Judsen got married and moved out at a time when she and Tom were beginning to have problems in their relationship. Tom wanted to cool things down and he decided he needed more time alone. Jeffry felt rejected.

"Those two events forced me to grow up very fast," says Jeffry now. "Until that happened in 1978, everything—my job, my apartment, my social life—had conveniently been arranged for me. For a time, I felt like a child abandoned by her parents. But I knew going home wasn't the answer, so I stuck it out and learned to live for myself." It took Jeffry the better part of a year to get on her feet emotionally. (Five years later, she and Tom got married.) Still, the moral of the story is not to become so entrenched in a relationship that you do not concurrently seek out the friendship of others.

There's another caveat to keep in mind from the beginning—you may want to leave the protection of the man whose company you initially found comforting. "Some women can live very contentedly for a long period in someone else's world—it really depends on how far along she is in the developmental stage of forming her own identity," says psychotherapist Phoebe Prosky.

The man can be a mentor and role model if he has professional contacts to share with you and is living the kind of lifestyle you someday hope to attain yourself. Or he may play the more traditional function of a father/provider if he's older and well-established professionally. Such a man can make your life more comfortable because he picks up the bill at dinner or you spend time at his place, which may be a major improvement over your own more humble quarters.

"There's nothing wrong with getting into such a relationship, but be aware of what's going on. You may think it feels like true love when it's not," says psychotherapist Prosky.

If you are concerned about your emotional and professional development, it's better to understand the limitation of a relationship established early on. Leaving the very person who was responsible for providing for you in your time of need is not easy. If you're serious about establishing your own identity and place in a city, however, it's better to put aside any feelings of guilt about the way things did or didn't turn out. If you view each relationship as an experience that will contribute to your self-development rather than a potential life-long commitment, you'll avoid getting tangled up in a relationship whose benefits have run their course.

STAGE THREE

Making a Go of It

~~~~~~

CITIES ATTRACT special people, intellectual, gregarious, talented and motivated. Being among the best and the brightest is both a stimulation and a challenge. For those who have consistently excelled in school or their work, the opportunity to find out how well they measure up against the top people in their field will give them a perspective on whether they have what it takes—and how long it will take them to achieve similar success.

If you haven't come to the city to pursue a particular career interest, you will probably feel somewhat lost among the throngs of upwardly mobile women who know what they want. That's not to say that you won't find professional success if you don't have a grand scheme in mind when you first arrive; in fact, some of the most successful women I interviewed for this book didn't figure out what they wanted or were best at until their late twenties.

Perhaps the most important realization about career success is that while there is pressure to do your best, you don't have to be the best to have a satisfying job. There are many ways to live out some facet of your career dream even if the clothes you design aren't featured in the windows of Saks or you don't become the evening television news anchor. Cities are filled with jobs you've never heard of, and unless you're there looking for work and intensely pursuing your dream, you aren't likely to find these hidden jobs. The first chapter of this section talks about the problems of putting your heart and soul into your work and how to survive the inevitable letdowns.

Work, of course, is an important factor in feeling things are all right in your world. But love is the other half of the happiness equation. It's not an easy time, historically speaking, to strike an easy balance between the two. City women are more demanding of themselves and the men in their lives than are more traditional women. They complain more about men and relationships because they expect more. They stay single longer than women living elsewhere because there's less pressure for them to conform to conventional life-styles, and they have the financial independence to make it on their own.

Emotionally, we are probably still very much the same; most of us, however, consider the state of being in love a highly desirable one. Sometimes the quest for a steady relationship becomes an obsession; the first few dates are often interview sessions, during which time we determine what the chances for falling in love with the man are. If they're not good, most women don't see the point of dating. That's where single men have an edge over single women; if they enjoy a woman's company, they'll see her again, regardless of the long-term prognosis for the relationship. If city women were able to relax and enjoy the company of the men they date (cities *are* packed with eligible, interesting men), they would probably be a happier group even though there wasn't anyone special in their life. The differences between being open to love and actively searching for it are elaborated on in the chapter, "Looking for Love."

Making a go of it in the city would be much less stressful if it wasn't for a third factor which is an unpleasant fact of city life: crime. It had touched the lives of many of the women I interviewed and forever changed their basic faith in human nature. And, having grown up during a time when the idea that a woman could be as free-spirited as a man, most women who come to cities are disappointed to find that the fear of crime compromises their life-style in small and big ways. While the threat of crime is real, it's a risk that can be minimized if you understand where and how it happens and develop an awareness rather than a fear—issues that are discussed in the third chapter of this section.

7

Pursuing Your Career Dream

〜〜〜〜〜〜〜〜〜〜〜〜〜〜〜〜〜〜〜〜〜〜〜〜〜〜〜〜〜〜

ON MANHATTAN'S West 72nd Street is a restaurant called Palsson's, whose upstairs room is a cabaret. In late 1981, a troupe of five exceptionally talented and virtually unknown actors and actresses began appearing in a musical comedy revue which spoofs Broadway show tunes and the perils of the acting profession itself.

One of the songs featured in the show is "Tradition," from *Fiddler on the Roof.* In the *Forbidden Broadway* show, however, it has been retitled "Ambition." The opening lyrics are half-sung/half-talked:

"An actor in New York. Sounds crazy, no? But on this little island of Manhattan there are over 50,000 actors trying their best not to end up in Baltimore. It isn't easy. You may ask why do we stay here if it's so competitive? We stay because everyone else is here. And what keeps us from going to Baltimore? That I can tell you in one word: AMBITION!"

It was ambition and rejection that motivated Gerard Alessandini, the show's lyricist, and his partner, Nora Mae Lyng, to create their own production. After almost seven years in the acting profession, they decided not to wait any longer to be singled out for stardom in a cattle-call audition. If they were going to get a break, they'd have to create the circumstances for it to happen. Encouraged by the reaction of their friends, who donated their living room for the first performance, Gerard and Nora Mae got a booking at Palsson's and added two more members to the cast. After three-months of well-received weekend performances, the critic Rex Reed came to see it and gave it a rave review in the New York *Daily News*. The show began playing six nights a week and is often sold out weeks in advance.

Pursuing your career dream in a city where there is a concentration of professions in your field is the surest route to finding it. Sure there's more competition. But there are also more opportunities and an active grapevine through which names and recommendations continually circulate, increasing your chances for exposure in a relatively short time.

Top Cities for Ambitious Women

The chart below shows the percentage of women employed and working as managers, professionials and technicians in the service sector, which includes such professions as accounting, marketing, education, health, communications, law, management consulting, hotel and restaurant work. (For example, 67 percent of those employed in the service sector in Minneapolis/St. Paul are women and 42 percent of the managers are women.) Cities are ranked (high to low) by the percentage of women employed in service industries.

City	Total Employment	Managers	Professionals	Technicians
Minneapolis/ St. Paul	67	42	70	68
Seattle	64	39	66	70
Denver	60	37	58	57
Philadelphia	60	35	57	65
Cleveland	59	38	63	72
Chicago	57	34	54	53
Miami	56	30	62	67
Boston	54	28	50	52
Los Angeles	53	31	55	56
San Francisco	53	30	55	52

Washington, D.C.	53	26	43	50
New York City	52	30	53	53
Atlanta	51	27	44	42
Houston	45	19	46	49

Source: Equal Employment Opportunity Commission

The Attraction—and Pitfalls—of Being Dedicated to Your Job

Being good at what you do isn't enough to propel you down the road to success. Hard work, that is, making a commitment to developing your talents, is ultimately even more important. Your work habits also have to reflect your dedication and ambition so that important others—your boss and the powers that be—are aware that you're serious about getting ahead. In corporate environments, that means putting in hours (whether or not your work actually requires more than eight hours a day of effort) because time spent in the office connotes dedication. If you work on your own or in a more independent setting, the number of projects (or tryouts or calls) you take on is evidence of ambition.

If you're a recent graduate or are accustomed to working in a more relaxed work setting, you may be surprised at the intensity with which upwardly mobile city folk attack their work. For many, particularly those who are single and in their twenties and thirties, work is the focus of their lives. It is a time of high energy, few obligations and unlimited possibilities. It's what the hustle-bustle of cities is all about.

Whether you've relocated to take a promotion, find your first "professional" job or start over in a new field, you'll no doubt feel the pressure to prove to your boss—and yourself—that you can handle your new responsibilities. Successful women, particularly those in male-dominated fields, maintain that they had to work twice as hard as men who were their colleagues to get to where they are. But if doing so becomes an obsession, you are becoming a classic candidate for one of the most common addictions of the ambitious: workaholism.

The National Press Club in Washington, D.C., is a busy place. The President often comes there to make a bipartisan announcement. Many V.I.P. out-of-town visitors are toasted there. Working as the banquet manager is like being in a pressure cooker, since luncheons and dinners at conferences must come off without a hitch.

Mia Taylor took her job as manager very seriously. It was her first "real" job after graduating from the University of North Carolina. A political science major, she came to Washington, D.C., in 1973, with absolutely no idea of what she wanted to do. After working several months as a temporary secretary for a number of companies, including the National Press Club, she did a brief stint as a receptionist for an investment counseling firm. When the National Press Club asked her if she wanted to come back and work as a reservations clerk, she left her $6,000-a-year position without hesitation. Soon after starting her new job, she was promoted to banquet manager, a position that had been vacated by her boss.

"It was the most unbelievably demanding job I've ever had," says Mia, who was 24 years old at the time. She often worked 14 hours a day during her two-year tenure. Mia felt it was necessary since she had never before managed a food service operation. "If I had been a more experienced manager, I would have delegated responsibility better and once the setup for the meal was complete, left it in the hands of the people who worked for me," explains Mia. Instead, she stayed through the events to make sure that things ran smoothly.

While the tension she was feeling wasn't visible to her boss or the public, it was taking its toll on her physically—she began experiencing severe stomach cramps.

Her excessive dedication to a job she truly enjoyed finally caused her to loathe it. "I made the mistake early on in the job of setting a precedent for always being available. After a year, I started feeling as if I were being taken advantage of. I didn't think I could hack the schedule anymore, but it took another year for me to rally the energy to get out of the job," explains Mia.

People whose work involves frequent contact with others under tense and stressful situations are classic candidates for burnout. The work in itself is emotionally exhausting, and when long hours are part of the scenario, the stress one feels is exacerbated.

Experts who have studied on-the-job stress say that how you cope is more important than the frequency or severity of stress. If you suspect that the time and effort you're putting into the job is pushing you to the edge of your limits, paying more attention to your physical needs can help. Regular meals, sleep and exercise will make your body less susceptible to a break-down. Compartmentalizing your work and leisure time provides mental relief from problems. The worst coping strategy is to spend even more time working. Even if your body doesn't rebel now, it may in the long term. Already, studies indicate that more women are developing stress-related health problems, including heart disease.

The hours Mia devoted to her work had a secondary negative effect: no social life. Mia was too exhausted from her job to make arrangements to go out with friends, nor did she have any time or energy for a romantic relationship. Instead, she spent most of her free time with her sister, with whom she lived. "It was a period of too much togetherness. With both of us so involved in our work, it was easier to depend on one another for companionship. Being with other people who had different perspectives on life might have helped both of us get a better handle on ours," says Mia.

Newcomers to a city often spend inordinately long hours at work to substitute for their lack of social world outside it. "Workaholism is a mechanism for coping with loneliness," says psychologist Dale Hill. "It's fine to spend a lot of time at work when you first arrive because it may be the only place you feel you belong. But newcomers should simultaneously begin forming a network of acquaintances and friends."

Working hard can distract you from feeling lonely, but it can't replace time spent with friends. Keep in mind, too, that unless you get involved in interests outside work, the only people you're likely to socialize with are co-workers.

Learning to Compete

Competition is endemic to big cities. People vie for parking places, bus seats, tickets to popular events, tennis courts, and the attention of sales clerks, among other things. Whether they succeed in getting what they're after depends on luck, an understanding of the system and sometimes downright aggressiveness.

Nowhere does competition take on higher stakes than in the work world. And never has it been as difficult for newcomers to the city to pursue their career dream. The numbers of baby boomers flocking to big cities in search of fame and fortune have been increasing. Between 1970 and 1980, the single biggest generation ever born in America came into their twenties. "Many members of this first generation of suburban children decided to give city living a try," says Larry Long, head of the analysis staff at the Census Bureau's Center for Demographic Studies. "The result is that the number of 22-to-29-year-olds in many U.S. cities has increased even though the cities as a whole were often losing population."

Even though the basis of the economy of many cities is shifting from manufacturing goods to providing services and generating ideas, the number of skilled, white-collar occupations hasn't risen as quickly as the number of college-educated applicants who seek them. Until 1985, when the last of the baby boomers will be in the job market, one in four college graduates will have to settle for a job that has traditionally been filled by someone without a college degree.

What these numbers add up to is plenty of competition.

Many city newcomers from areas of the country in which people are used to waiting patiently to get what they deserve are
unprepared to be calculating in their career strategy.

When one first meets Susan Hattan, it's somewhat difficult
to believe that this soft-spoken, low-key 32-year-old native of
Concordia, Kansas (population: 7500), is the senior legislative
assistant to Senator Nancy Kassebaum.

"My personality does put people off guard," says Susan,
laughing. "But I've been able to use that to my advantage." Her
first job was working in the basement office of Senator Robert
Dole, typing names and addresses. She stuck it out and one-
and-a-half years later, was promoted to answering constitu-
ents' mail. In two years, she made it to the not quite full-
fledged legislative aid level. Then, having earned a master's
degree in American politics by going to school part-time in the
evenings, she worked as a policy analyst at the Department of
Agriculture. When Nancy Kassebaum was elected one of the
Senators from Kansas in 1978, Susan asked several of her
contacts from Dole's office in Kansas to put in a good word for
her. She was subsequently hired as a legislative aide.

Earlier in her career, Susan was confronted with what she
regarded as an ethical dilemma. A position she had very much
wanted was given to another woman who she didn't feel deserved it or was capable of doing the job. Susan's competitor
was later demoted for being incompetent; Susan was to be her
new supervisor, unless, their mutual boss asked, Susan preferred they fire her. "I decided that saying yes would be vindic-
tive," explains Susan. "A true competitor might have tried to
hasten her downfall, but I've often found that you save yourself
a lot of trouble if you're patient enough to let a competitor hang
him- or herself with the ropes of their own incompetence."

Unless you are as sure as Susan was about the field you're
working in, you may be beat out by talented people whose
career dreams are their first love and priority.

Competing in a "Glamour" Profession

On any given day, there are some 24,000 members of Actors Equity without work in the theater—an unemployment rate of 80 percent. Those who do get hired for parts make very little money. Two-thirds earn about $2,500 a year from stage jobs. It was against these odds that Wanda Urbanska decided to try to make it as an actress.

Five months after her arrival in New York City, Wanda landed the lead female role in an Off-Off-Broadway production, which had a three-performance run. "Even though I was encouraged by the reaction of friends and others who saw the show, I realized then how strong a commitment I'd have to make to the profession and how limited my chances for success would be even if I struggled for years," remembers Wanda.

Still, she wasn't quite willing to give up her dream so readily. Through a friend of her mother's, Wanda met the casting director of the soap opera *Love of Life,* and she appeared as a nurse on several episodes. "Even though you have to constantly look for work as an actress, I minded that competition less than I did the hustle all my classmates from Harvard were going through to get nine-to-five jobs," explains Wanda. A year after she arrived, Wanda's dream of acting fell prey to financial realities. She couldn't afford to do things with her friends who had regular jobs, and she had enough of a competitive edge that she felt she was falling behind. "I kept thinking about how much effort I'd already put into learning how to write, and I realized that maybe my chances for success were better in a field where I'd already received some recognition and positive feedback."

When she moved to Los Angeles 18 months later to join her screenwriter boyfriend, Wanda got back on her original career track. She became an assistant editor at *California Living,* the Los Angeles *Herald-Examiner*'s Sunday magazine supplement. And she returned to her early love—writing fiction—in her free time.

How to Compete Effectively

Even if you've always been your own best competition, understanding the ground rules for competing in the work world is essential to achieving personal goals.

1. *Know what you want.* That doesn't mean it's essential for you to have your five- and ten-year career game plans laid out if you're just starting out in your first job or in a new field. But unless you have a general sense of your career direction, it will be virtually impossible for you to recognize and take advantages of opportunities that come your way—and which you may have to compete for.

2. *Identify people or circumstances that may block your progress.* Even if you have a pleasant, nonthreatening personality, you can become the object of someone else's frustration or wrath if that person feels you're a threat to his or her success. It's smart to be sensitive to the feelings of those who may have designs on the assignments or job you have or want so that you know who your competition is. Likewise, situations that may initially be beyond your control (i.e., a reorganization of the office) can best be dealt with if you're quick to recognize them.

3. *Develop a plan for circumventing or confronting the obstacle.* While a "wait and see" position is fine if no negative effects are immediately likely, it's a good idea to come up with a plan of action that will turn things in your favor. Passively waiting for the situation to change may work to your detriment.

4. *Understand the rules of acceptable competitive behavior.* Aside from your own values of what falls into the realm of fair play, it's important to tune into how things are done in your particular field or office. You may find that being aggressively upfront in your request to those with decision-making power is the only way to get seriously considered or, on the other hand, that subtle behind-the-scenes lobbying is your best bet.

5. *Prepare your reaction to the outcome of a competi-*

tive situation. It's important to think through how an eventual negative outcome will affect your career. If there are plenty of opportunities for you to try again for what you wanted, there's less reason to let a temporary loss bother you. On the other hand, if you're going to have to live without something you wanted, you can constructively vent your disappointment by developing new goals or considering a change in your immediate job situation.

Surviving—and Making the Best of—Career Letdowns

The first five years of your career are truly the "building" years, a time when dissatisfaction with the kind of work you're doing or its progress is likely to run high. Only one in five of the survey respondents who had been working five years or less felt she was successful. Almost half reported that while they were working in the field of their choice, they were not yet doing what they wanted, although many had what they considered to be a good job.

Women who work in cities are more likely to be bigger risk-takers since many are single or married and childless, which increases the likelihood of their zooming up the career pyramid or falling flat on their face.

Eighty-five percent of the survey respondents indicated that their biggest career letdown occurred during the first five years of working full-time in their field. Their letdowns varied in intensity and type. During the first year in the job market, a common problem is being unable to find an entry-level job in one's field. Not being given enough responsibility and status shock—the clash of expectations and reality—are two other frequent complaints. For those who have worked two to five years, becoming disillusioned with their career choice is often the source of the letdown. Too few chances for advancement, or getting fired, can also trigger career problems.

A career failure, disappointment or crisis can strike any time in your career. Some come up unexpectedly, like a thunderstorm on a clear summer day; others build over time, giving plenty of warning about their eventuality, like a swelling tropical depression. The fact that working women in their twenties report as much work-related unhappiness as do their male colleagues (25 years ago, women's dissatisfaction with their work was much lower than men's) points to two developments: women take their careers as seriously as do men, and they are no longer willing to passively accept whatever career ups and downs may come their way.

In the stories of the three women featured in this section, the quality they share is essential to coping with career letdowns. And that is their ability to see them as learning experiences rather than as disasters which may cripple their progress.

Handling Personal Rejection

For those in the performing arts and other fields, where youth is an asset, success can come at an early age. But it does not come overnight, as many people think, nor does it come without failure and frustration. For actress Sheryl Ralph, what seemed at first to be a setback occurred about 18 months after she'd graduated from college. A theater major, she'd won the prestigious Irene O'Ryan acting award for a performance she gave in a student production at the Washington, D.C., Kennedy Center for the Performing Arts in 1975. Two USO tours (Sheryl is a singer and dancer, too) to Europe and the Far East followed, then a part in the Sidney Poitier movie *A Piece of the Action*.

On her last day of filming the movie, Sheryl got word from her agent that she'd been chosen for a major part in a TV series, *Sanford Arms*, a sequel to the long-running *Sanford and Son*. She would be playing the role of the daughter of the new owner of Fred's junkyard. "This is IT, I told myself. This is my big break. I went bananas. I called my father, who usually stays calm even when I get excited, and he went bananas, too."

Sheryl taped one episode of the show before she was fired. The reason: "They told me I wasn't 'black' enough. What they meant was that I didn't project the image of my character in what they considered a black enough way. I cried and cried and cried. It wasn't just the hurt of being replaced by someone else—it was insulting."

What made the rejection especially difficult for Sheryl was the fact that she had packed her bags and moved out of her Long Island home to live in Los Angeles, where the series was being taped. Everyone from back home knew about her being in the series. "I didn't want to go home because I felt like a failure," remembers Sheryl, "but ultimately it strengthened my resolve to succeed."

One positive outcome of her being fired was getting a large lump sum of cash in fulfillment of her contract. Sheryl bought $2,000 worth of savings bonds, a new car and moved into her first apartment on her own. She found an agent who sent her on calls for commercials. Sheryl did several soon thereafter, including ones for Eastern Airlines and Pepsi. "Commercials were my bread and butter income for a long time," explains Sheryl. "They're the only reason why I've never had to do anything but what I do best—singing, acting and dancing."

California was a lonely place for Sheryl. She made only one good friend, a musician, who was a neighbor. And of the several men she dated, the one she really liked turned out to be gay. But she was determined to stay and make it as a TV actress. Her first appearance was guest-starring with Peter Frampton in the Robert Conrad series, *Black Sheep Squadron*. She subsequently appeared in a number of others including *Good Times, The Jeffersons* and *Wonder Woman*.

"I always knew that things would turn out all right, even if I didn't get a part I wanted. And I never let my disappointment show. It was always, 'Okay, Sheryl, on to the next audition,' and I'd be there all smiles, like everything was going my way. If you're not happy and secure, no one is going to want to hire you," says Sheryl.

On one of her trips back home to visit her family, she heard about a Joseph Papp workshop called *Dreamgirls* that was being cast. She landed a small role and worked with the group developing the musical for six weeks. For about a year, she went back and forth between the East and West Coast, working on *Dreamgirls* in between other projects. Her role expanded, and when the musical opened on Broadway in late 1981, Sheryl Lee Ralph was one of the female leads. The critics and the audiences loved it. Sheryl was nominated for a Tony Award. By 1982, *Dreamgirls* was one of Broadway's smash-hit musicals.

While Sheryl's dismissal after taping only one segment of her first TV series was devastating, learning to live with rejection is one of the facts of life of being a performing artist whose work is a "series" of jobs. Even if one director or producer doesn't like you, another is bound to see your talents differently.

Getting Fired

It's not the same, of course, in academia or the business world where most jobs last years, and getting fired is traumatic. Even if getting your walking papers has nothing to do with your performance, it's difficult to avoid feeling responsible. A letdown as serious as getting fired is often more than just something to get over; it can be a real turning point in your career.

Jill Cochrane had been working in New York City as a conference organizer for only one year before she was fired. She had not known that turnover among management level employees in the organization at that time was high.

"Most people in my position would have immediately gone out and looked for another job. But I wasn't sure at that point if I should stay in the city. With all the traveling and hours I'd put into my job, I hadn't really had time to develop a network of friends or even get to know the city," explains Jill, who was 30 at the time. It's not easy to survive—financially or psychologically—without a job in New York, because of the expense and work-oriented nature of the city. Jill managed to do both.

She went on unemployment and received food stamps (both of which were foreign to her work ethic upbringing) and walked everywhere to save money. She got to know the city intimately. And she finally had the time to track down alumni from the University of Massachusetts who had settled in the metropolitan area and got to know her neighbors.

"It was much harder on my parents than it was on me," remembers Jill. "At times, they could barely say hello to me on the phone. They'd just ask, 'Have you got another job yet?' They could no longer talk about where their successful daughter was traveling or who she had met." When her unemployment ran out, Jill still wasn't sure what her next professional step should be.

She decided to support herself by doing what she'd done during her college summers—waitressing. It provided the income to live on and the time to look for a "real" job. "I loved it. I worked 38 hours a week, which seemed like a cinch compared to the hours I'd worked before," says Jill, who deliberately chose to work in a World Trade Center restaurant, where she might meet business people who might prove to be useful contacts. Her "time out" from a professional position was not only a needed breather from her breakneck work pace, but it gave her the time she needed to put her life in perspective. New York, she decided, was her city after all, and it was there that she wanted to continue to build her career and her life. Fourteen months after she began waitressing, Jill heard about an opening. After a series of interviews with the American Management Associations, Jill was offered—and accepted—a job as director of conference development.

Coping with a "Victim of Circumstance" Crisis

Getting caught up in events that are beyond your control can produce yet another kind of career letdown.

In 1974, five years after relocating from Columbus, Ohio, to Miami, Sherry Richardson was riding high in her job as an administrative assistant at a pipeline construction company. She had learned to speak Spanish so that she could assist the foremen supervising field-workers. She'd taken engineering courses at night school so that she could read charts and keep records. "When I first started working for my boss, who ran his business out of a rundown warehouse, I really lacked self-confidence. I'd never worked full-time before. I wasn't sure what my skills were. Within five years' time, I had taken on much more than my secretarial responsibilities," remembers Sherry.

She was on the brink of being named a vice-president, a position which would have provided her with a secretary of her own and a company car, when two disasters struck: the recession (a result of the Arab oil embargo), which cut seriously into the business, followed by the sudden death of her boss.

"I was 31, unemployed and ready for adventure. When my career future disintegrated, I thought, 'Why not look for a job that will allow me to travel?' What I really loved about Miami was its cosmopolitan atmosphere. I was especially excited about using my language skills in countries where Spanish was the primary language," explains Sherry.

After several weeks of intensive job-hunting, she went to work for a cargo airline which transported goods between Central America and the U.S. "I was able to arrange several trips for my son and myself. We flew in two of the three seats that were 'first class'; the coach seats were reserved for the chickens," says Sherry, who worked for the airline for six months. Although the travel benefit was exciting, the job itself was a step down in Sherry's career. In her former position, she had been dispatching crews and attending meetings with officials from major oil companies; in this job, she was putting stamps on envelopes and clocking in.

Sherry began scanning the help-wanted ads and came across a position that very much appealed to her: working as the executive secretary to the president of a public relations firm. A good conversationalist with plenty of enthusiasm (who had also majored in English in college), Sherry got the job at Hank Meyer, one of Miami's biggest public relations firms. It further prepared her for an even bigger career leap—becoming marketing vice-president at a large Miami bank.

8

Looking for Love

^^^

WE BABY BOOM WOMEN were born in the worst and best of times. We were the first generation of women who were not expected to go straight from our parents' home to one we shared with a husband. Living on our own in college and in cities became an acceptable stage of young adulthood. Many more of us got jobs that had traditionally been held by men. We could support ourselves. Traditional sexual taboos went out of style. Little did we dream that these newly available goodies came with strings attached. The confusion inherent in the dramatic sociocultural changes that included the women's movement, the sexual revolution and the baby boom generation's prolonged adolescence has surfaced in relationships between men and women.

Many of us have delayed getting married because we don't have the time (too busy with our careers), the interest (too busy having a good time) or the right man. In fact, after 1970, the proportion of unmarried 25–29-year-old women doubled. City women in that age group are 20 percent less likely to be married than their peers in suburbs and small towns, according to the Urban Experience Survey.

But just because marriage isn't on our minds at age 22 (the average age at which women marry) doesn't mean we don't want relationships. The trouble is, we aren't sure what we do want from men, nor are they sure what to expect from us. The baby-boom generation has spawned men and women who journey through deserts of emotional isolation in their quest for Mr. or Ms. Right.

The Loneliness of Emotional Isolation

The morning light has found its way through the slats in the blinds. She awakens to the muffled sounds of a Sunday morning. In her half-drowsy state of consciousness, she verifies who and where she is. Yes, she's alone. And this is her bedroom. Peering across the room, she can see the clothes she wore to last night's party draped over the chair. They are a painful reminder of a realization that has begun to possess her. There is no one special in her life. The absence of love yet to come makes her anxious. When will he appear? It isn't as if she hasn't tried; it's just that nothing has come of her efforts. The sinking feeling that perhaps something is wrong with her— just what she's not sure—begins to eat away at her self-confidence. The warmth of her bed and the darkness of the room are womb-like, safe. It's another one of those mornings when she's not at all sure of the purpose of going through the motions of living.

Most single women experience the emptiness of being unattached from time to time; the intensity and frequency of this variety of loneliness varies depending on one's circumstances. And although women admit to being lonely more often than men, it's an emotion common to both sexes. Those in their teens and early twenties are more vulnerable to experiencing emotional isolation because they're often obsessed with finding "true love," according to social psychologists Carin Rubinstein and Phillip Shaver in their book *In Search of Intimacy*. But loneliness can strike the unattached at any age. Most of us fend off the feeling by filling our time with work, the company of family and friends and activities we enjoy. But nothing short of an intimate relationship can satiate the emptiness its absence imposes.

Single women who move to a city where they have few or no contacts are particularly vulnerable to intense periods of loneliness. Not only are they without an important other in their life, but they have left behind any network of support that may have taken the edge off their isolation. It's small wonder, then, that these newcomers are willing to plunge headlong into relationships with men they meet early on. A relationship is an insulation against the pain of loneliness, even if it's not an ideal one.

Survey Finding

Have you experienced feelings of loneliness in the last year?

Women who are divorced or separated	62%
Single women	48%
Married women	27%

The Pain of Losing Someone You Love

Studies indicate that the loneliest of the lonely are the recently divorced and separated. The loss of someone with whom one is or once was in love with can put a person into a psychological tailspin. If the breakup comes on the heels of a move to a new place, the isolation can be extremely traumatic.

Nicole Cunningham* was devastated when her husband told her he wanted a divorce. They had been married for two and a half years, and from her point of view, things had been working out well. They had met at Northeastern University in Boston, where they were both physical education majors, and like many of their friends, had gotten married during their senior year of college.

After graduation, the couple moved to Stony Brook, Long Island—Tim had been accepted to medical school at the state university there. Coincidentally, it was Nicole's hometown, which made it easy for her to find a teaching job at a local high school. A year later, Tim dropped out of medical school and suggested they move back to Boston. Although Tim quickly found a job, it took Nicole several months to find work. She

*A pseudonym.

found a position as director of a local university's women's athletic program, a part-time job, and also did substitute teaching to bring in more money.

Six months after their arrival back in Boston, Tim came home one night and announced he felt trapped and was going to move out (which he did several weeks later).

The first thing she did was to move out of the singles complex where she and her husband had been living to a one-room apartment in a nearby working-class, Hispanic neighborhood. It was the first time in her life she'd ever lived alone. Had it not been for the fact that Nicole's job was going well (it became a full-time position) and that her master's degree program provided a constructive framework for her days, the loneliness that flooded into her life might have swept away any positive self-image that remained.

Nicole eventually found a charming one-bedroom apartment in the historic Back Bay section of Boston. She also decided to become more involved in the counseling program that she had begun on a one-class-per-semester basis when she'd first moved back to Boston. It proved to be as helpful personally as it later did professionally. Soon after her divorce, she took advantage of group therapy that was available to students at the university. "At the time, I told myself it would be a good idea to get a first-hand exposure to a counseling situation, but I soon discovered that it was probably instrumental in bringing me through my post-divorce depression," says Nicole. Several of her classmates had gone or were going through divorces. "I was very much encouraged by the people who had survived the breakup of their marriage and who had become happy, satisfied individuals again. It gave me hope that I could make it, too," explains Nicole.

In addition, going to school two nights a week and preparing assignments made weekend nights and Sunday afternoons less threatening. "Knowing that I had good reason to stay in made me think less about the reality that I no longer had close friends with whom to socialize," says Nicole. Nicole subsequently became very close to other graduate students in the counseling program, several of whom became long-time friends.

When she began dating again, she deliberately went out with a number of men. "It was a needed psychological boost. Having just had a man reject me, I needed to know that it wasn't my fault and that I was attractive to other men," says Nicole. But now, ten years after her divorce and several relationships later, a new problem has surfaced. Nicole, who is 32, feels the pressure of the biological timeline that women in her age group face. That is, if children are a part of their future plans, they must begin casting about more seriously for a partner.

The Dilemma of Women Over 30

City women marry significantly later than most women in America. The ages at which they're most likely to be married are between 29 and 32, according to the results of the Urban Experience Survey, which is seven to ten years later than the national average.

"Most women who are not in a serious relationship by age 32 become more calculating in their dealings with the opposite sex because they feel 34 is a cutoff point for having their first child," says Houston psychotherapist Dr. Dale Hill, many of whose clients are in their twenties and thirties. "Every man they date is subjected to the suitability test, and no matter how subtly it's done, most men resent it, and their response is to flee before they've ever given the woman a chance."

For the unmarried woman in her mid- to late thirties, the concern she may have felt several years before can evolve into panic. The idea of going through life without the love of one man and/or having children is particularly hard for a successful career woman to accept. She has learned the value of planning ahead in order to achieve her goals; she is at a stage in her life when she knows what she wants and what's required to get it. When her pursuit of a desirable man (or series of men) ends in failure, she may begin questioning her own desirability. Her self-esteem may plummet (despite her professional success, attractiveness and network of friends and business associates). She may begin avoiding social situations, or unconsciously project her uncertainties in her dealings with the opposite sex.

"The more negative experiences a woman has, the more defenses she builds to protect herself from further pain or rejection," says psychotherapist Muriel Goldfarb. "If a woman has had more than her fair share of bad luck with men, she may unconsciously close herself off to any emotional involvement."

In addition to the emotional baggage that women in their mid- to late thirties can develop, there is another problem: a diminishing pool of eligible men. Women typically marry men who are several years older than themselves. For women who are at the top of the baby boom (those born in 1946 and 1947), there are fewer older men available—the generation born before the end of World War II was 35 percent smaller than the one that came after it.

Why Looking for Love So Often Backfires

Trying to find a man with whom to build a relationship isn't the same as looking for a job with growth potential. Still, some women who are desperate to get involved operate on the premise that the getting hired strategy of uncovering and following up on every possible lead will get results. Unfortunately, lasting relationships rarely evolve from encounters in situations where singles are actively seeking one another out. Relationships that stand the best chance of working out are those that start with meeting someone through friends, relatives, coworkers or neighbors, says Dr. Robert Weiss in his book *Loneliness: The Experience of Social and Emotional Isolation.* They're much more likely to share our values and priorities; the likelihood of that being the case with someone we meet by chance, particularly in a big city, is not good.

There are things that people who feel emotionally isolated can do to get a better handle on their loneliness. "Directing one's energy to projects, friendships or groups one cares about isn't simply a time-filler," says Dr. Weiss, "It's far more likely that you'll encounter someone with whom you can develop an intimate relationship in a situation in which the focus is not on finding someone but working toward a shared goal or enjoying the same activity."

Where Have All the "Good" Men Gone?

If an extra-terrestrial anthropologist surveyed single women in cities about their feelings toward men, it might come to the conclusion that urban populations are doomed to extinction. Why? Because many unattached women say they'd rather stay home and read a good book than go out with a guy who is emotionally immature, unromantic, too wrapped up in himself (or his work), or one of a dozen other negative "types."

Survey Finding

How many of the men you date would you consider the right kind of men for you?

All	3%
Most	18%
Some	25%
Few	43%
None	11%

Given the number of men who flock to cities for the same reasons women do, both sexes ought to be in singles heaven. But the dating scene is anything but celestial from most single women's point of view. One of the biggest perceived problems is the ratio of eligible men to women. The majority of city women (64 percent) feel that the odds favor men. *In actuality, there is one man for every woman in the 22–34-year-old age group in the fifteen largest U.S. cities.* The only city in which this one-to-one ratio is not as promising as it looks is San Francisco, where 25 percent of the male population is estimated to be homosexual.

Survey Finding

What is your impression concerning the number of eligible women and men in your city?

Many more women than men	35%
Slightly more women than men	29%
Equal numbers of eligible men and women	28%
Slightly more men than women	5%

"The myth puts men in a power position. Many women, in turn, panic, feeling lost among that mythical herd, all competing for those supposedly very few available men. So some single women seem to value themselves less, are afraid of appearing desperate or pushy, don't stand up for themselves when they are mistreated or don't hold men accountable for their behavior," concludes a *Washington Post Magazine* article entitled "Hard Hearts."

Having played the field myself throughout much of my twenties and having heard as many discouraging tales as I have love stories with happy endings from the women interviewed for this book, my conclusion about the dating scene is that we women are as much a part of the problem as the men are. Those of us who are ambitious, independent and earning our own livings are not only demanding of ourselves but of the men we date.

Respondents of the Urban Experience Survey confirm that the standards for modern-day Prince Charmings are indeed high. Many of the traditional qualities that women have prized in men are still very important, in particular his sense of humor and a positive outlook on life. But equally and sometimes more important to women today are qualities we've never evaluated so carefully before. The top-rated one is an ability to sustain an intimate relationship (very important, said 67% of the respondents). A man's supportiveness of a woman's career was more important to city women (59 percent called it very important) compared to 41 percent of their suburban and small-town sisters.

How much a man makes (something which upwardly mobile women have traditionally considered essential) isn't as important to city women as what he does professionally. Only a third felt a man's income was very or quite important, while 59 percent said they very much cared about what he did for a living. The fact that a man's work matters more to city women than does his paycheck reveals two things: They are looking for a partner who is as ambitious and interested in his work as they are, and they're less concerned about money because they no longer have to depend on a man to get the material things they want.

City women's expectations of men go beyond personality and career. How good he is in bed was very or quite important to half the survey respondents. Never before has the pressure to perform been openly admitted to by women. Having come of age in the wake of the sexual revolution, today's city women aren't afraid to admit they want a satisfying sexual partner.

Despite their high standards, 44 percent of those who aren't involved in a steady relationship go out once a week or more, which is one-third more often than their counterparts living outside the city. Still, women who date frequently aren't notably happier than those who go out less regularly.

Seven out of ten women who date one or more times a week said they were very or moderately happy. The numbers were not much different, however, for those who dated once every few weeks. What that says about today's single women is that they derive a great amount of satisfaction from their work; their sense of well-being isn't rooted in their social life. It's only when men are noticeably absent that a woman's level of happiness takes a nose dive. Fewer of those who dated infrequently—once every few months or several times a year—say they're very happy.

Connecting with Compatible Men

The longer you live in a city, the easier it should be to meet up with your type of men. After a year or two of getting established, you're more likely to date men you meet through friends or at parties than through chance encounters. That, of course, increases the probability that the relationship will go beyond an enjoyable evening or a several-month fling.

Survey Finding

How do you usually meet men? (check as many as apply)

Through friends	53%
Through work	44%
At parties	29%
In public places	21%
Through clubs and organizations	17%
At singles bars	14%
At school	11%
At church (or related activities)	8%

Networks for Professional and Personal Contacts

Contrary to popular opinion, men in big cities have just as difficult a time ferreting out desirable dates (and partners) as women do. That is why the Potomac Bachelor's Club came into existence some ten years ago in Washington, D.C. As the federal government began expanding in size in the '70s, the first wave of baby-boom college graduates rolled into town, and the dating scene increased exponentially. Soon, the idea of a club consisting of the most eligible of the eligibles—doctors, lawyers, legislative aides—for the express purpose of meeting women was born. Every Thursday, a well-orchestrated cocktail party is held in an elegant setting such as Georgetown's 1789 Club. Just how does one get invited to this crème de la crème bachelor scene? According to Gerald Stoltz, a former officer of the club, you must be asked by a member, although women come unescorted and are greeted by female hostesses.

How do women feel about going? "When one of my neighbors first asked me if I'd like to come, I was a bit put off because it sounded like just another organized singles scene," says the former Carri Coggins, who had recently moved to the Washington area from Cincinnati. "But when the day came, I thought, 'Why not?' I didn't have anything to do that evening and I wasn't going out with anyone special." Carri found the evening to be tremendously ego-gratifying. "Every time I turned around, there was a new man at my elbow, being introduced to me by the man I'd just finished talking to." Carri subsequently dated a number of the men she met through the club. One of them was Jerry Stoltz. She is now Carri Coggins Stoltz.

The key to the success of the Potomac Bachelor's Club is that it makes organized use of personal networking for social reasons. That concept has found acceptance among a group of women professionals in Washington, D.C., as well. Three years ago, they formed the Circle and Avenue Club to promote professional and social contacts. Their co-ed cocktail parties are held every other month, again in fashionable restaurants and clubs. On alternating months, the group convenes without men to hear guest speakers talk about investments, wardrobe planning and staying organized. For the members, most of whom are in their late twenties and early thirties, the club is a viable way to meet people whose life-styles and interests are the same as their own.

Both clubs are exclusive (that is, you become a member by invitation only), dues-paying organizations with elected officers. Non-exclusive singles organizations, both profit and non-profit, are much more common in big cities.

Relationship Roadblocks

The chance-for-romance scene in cities is bewildering enough because of its size. But for all the talented and interesting men and women who congregate in cities to find others like themselves, relationships between the sexes appear to be more on the rocks than on the rise. Why such discontent?

Those of us in the under-35 generation may be the victims of our own causes. Better educated and more mobile than any previous generation, we rallied against overly restrictive sexual standards, rebelled against institutionalizing relationships, and believed that change justified moving on (even when it meant dissolving a commitment).

The most telling statistics are marriage and divorce rates. It's highly likely that there will be more never-married men and women in the remaining years of this century than ever before, predicts Landon Y. Jones in his book about the baby-boom generation, *Great Expectations*. That comment seems to be particularly accurate as far as cities are concerned. The numbers of people walking down the aisle are lower in the 15 biggest cities in this country than they are elsewhere. Conversely, divorce rates are higher in cities than elsewhere. Both trends suggest that cities may not be conducive to making relationships work. There are many reasons why.

Clashing Expectations

What do women want from men? What do men want from women? There is mounting evidence that the gulf between the sexes is deeper than any of us may have guessed. Role confusion is the label many psychotherapists use to describe it. But basically, the problem is that new expectations about dating, sex and relationships have encroached upon the old.

The lineups look something like this:

Traditional Expectations	*New Expectations*
1. The woman waits for the man to initiate the date.	1. She doesn't mind calling him (so long as it's not the first date).
2. The woman expects to be picked up (for a date) and dropped off at her doorstep.	2. She's willing to meet him and get her own way home.
3. The man picks up the tab.	3. She doesn't mind paying her own way.
4. The woman wants a strong man.	4. She prefers a sensitive man.

Traditional Expectations	*New Expectations*
5. The woman feels uncomfortable about sex without love.	5. She finds sexual intimacy without emotional commitment acceptable.
6. The right man is more important to her than a successful career.	6. Career achievement may take precedence over her social life during "building" years.

The trouble is, women's behavior is often predicated on a combination of expectations from each column. And the men they date, who are often unsure themselves as to whether they prefer independent or more traditional acting women, are confused by the mixed signals.

It's not surprising, then, that intimacy frequently surfaces as an "issue." In fact, three of the most frequently mentioned complaints about men in the Urban Experience Survey addressed this difference between the sexes. The biggest complaint, mentioned by 28 percent of the respondents, is that men are too noncommittal about relationships.

Survey Finding

What is your biggest complaint about the men you have dated?

Too noncommittal about relationships	30%
Too immature	16%
Expects too much too soon sexually	14%
Avoids emotional confrontations	10%
Not romantic enough	8%
Lack of ambition	7%
Too wrapped up in work	3%
Other	13%

Most women find a steady relationship more satisfying than playing the field. Most men in their twenties, on the other hand, prefer the flexibility of dating around to being tied down to a particular woman. That's because throughout much of their young adult lives, men see intimacy as dangerous either because they might be caught in a smothering relationship or humiliated by rejection or deceit, contends developmental psychologist Carol Gilligan. It's not until men reach their early thirties and have their careers firmly under control that settling down becomes an appealing idea. Women, on the other hand, put a high priority on relationships (of all kinds), and fear isolation.

The fact that women see men as lagging behind in their emotional development is an accurate assessment, for which the only remedy is to find those men who are exceptions to the rule or who are older and less threatened by the idea of emotional involvement.

In our eagerness to establish a relationship, we often short-circuit dating possibilities, simply because we decide rather quickly whether or not we might be able to fall in love with a man. Without that potential, many women opt out of any continuing association with a man. And that can be a mistake. A reporter I once dated explained his plans to go to graduate school (in another city) and then get assigned to Africa as a political correspondent. Although I very much liked him, I was not a fan of long-distance relationships, nor could I see myself in khakis and safari hat, and quickly let him know that I was not going to play Jane to his Tarzan. Since his departure was still several months distant, we continued to see one another, knowing full well that the end was in sight. Learning how to enjoy the frequent company of a man without becoming emotionally entangled can get you through those bleak times when romance seems as distant as a warm spring day in mid-January.

Closing the Communication Gap

Ultimately, of course, most "healthy" men and women want the same thing: a person who is understanding, giving and loving with whom to try to make a go of it. Having listened to the complaints of men and women, the psychotherapist team Muriel Goldfarb and Dan Rubinstein began doing something about the stalemate in 1980. They invited a group of clients to participate in a three-session workshop to try to put aside male and female differences and concentrate on what they had in common. "People initially came in feeling distrustful and even hostile toward the opposite sex and sometimes even toward their own," explains Muriel Goldfarb. "After splitting into separate groups (male and female) for two sessions during which both get a chance to work with Dan and me, we brought them together. What a change! They're amazed to find that they really like each other." Those who had participated in the workshops—both patients and friends to whom they'd recommended it—wanted to continue their association with others in the group. So the two psychotherapists began holding periodic socials and publishing a newsletter so that participants could become part of one another's support network and keep up with personal news (there have been several marriages among those who met in the workshops). The initial group of 40 has grown to a community of 200 people.

Dealing with the Walking Wounded

In the aftermath of the sexual revolution, the women's movement and the "me" generation are plenty of bruised egos and hardened hearts. They are the walking wounded, who have not fully recovered from the shock and personal hurt of being the victims of marriages or relationships gone sour or of having had more than their fair share of bad luck with the opposite sex. There seems to be a concentration of men and women who fit this description living in cities, very possibly because these baby boomers had the most exposure and opportunities to take advantage of the freedom to experiment with sex, love and relationships. They also incurred the greatest psychological risks, and many lost out.

One of Muriel Goldfarb's patients, an attractive, successful cable television producer in her mid-thirties, is a prime example of the walking wounded. Stephanie* came to New York

*Not her real name.

from a small California city after graduating from college in the early seventies. She felt a tremendous sense of euphoria; she had a good job and the freedom to live her life as she wanted it. During her twenties, she went to many singles bars and enjoyed the sexual freedom that had so recently become acceptable for women. Why the men she slept with didn't want to get romantically involved was a great mystery to her. In order to make up for what her social life didn't provide, she threw herself into her work. Stephanie had several good women friends, but men were largely absent from her life. She was miserably lonely when she began seeing Dr. Goldfarb, having had yet another affair end disastrously.

"Stephanie's problem is not unusual among people who feel rejected—she is unable to give. The defenses she's built up over time are so well entrenched that she thinks she can't get out; the reality is that no one can get in," says Dr. Goldfarb. "Until she learns how to share, the chances of her being able to sustain a relationship are practically nil."

Those men and women who have healthy self-confidence and a desire to get involved are often frustrated by the seeming lack of people like themselves. One Urban Experience Survey participant, a 33-year-old computer programmer in Dallas, summarizes the feelings of many women: "I became alone and lonely in the city. I have many friends, male and female, but rarely date. I'm very attractive and physically fit—I teach an exercise class. I'm outgoing, intelligent and funny, yet it seems men rarely ask me out. Perhaps it's my age, though everyone I've dated since my divorce says I look five years younger than I am. Men seem to be contained in themselves, unwilling to jump in and enjoy someone in the city. It's as if they have been abused a bit too much and won't let it happen again."

What's a woman to do? Going about the business of her life and being open to expanding one's relationships with men is the most reasonable path. If one's dealings with men are not confined to working with or dating them, you're much more likely to expand your understanding of the male mind. And having men as friends increases the potential of coming into contact with men with whom you can develop serious romantic relationships.

Ambition That Interferes

Ambitious career plans are not inherently dangerous to relationships. It's more a question of how much time and effort an individual thinks he (or she) needs to devote to achieving professional goals relative to personal goals that matters.

Upwardly mobile men usually follow one of two patterns in regard to commitment: they either marry young or put off getting seriously involved with a woman until they're comfortable with their career achievements. That leaves a sizable contingent of bachelors between the ages of 24 and 34 in the urban dating scene. But if you happen to fall in love with one of these fast-track men, plan on shouldering most of the responsibility for making the relationship work.

If you've never had experience dating an ambitious man who is in the building stages of his career, beware early deceptive appearances about what he's able to give to a relationship. "Men on the road to success are often extremely attentive, generous and affectionate partners during courtship. They are used to getting what they want and will go to extraordinary lengths to captivate and capture the woman who appeals to them. But once real intimacy is established and the relationship becomes secure, some of those attentions that were so attractive may disappear," writes Jane Adams, author of *Making Good: Conversations with Successful Men.*

Regardless of what stage the relationship is in, men whose jobs take first priority often make unreasonable requests:

"Can I come by about ten (P.M., that is) when I finish up at the office?"

"Can you find someone else to use my ticket? I won't be able to finish up my work in time after all."

"Do you mind if I bring along some papers to go over when we go away this weekend?"

To say no is to invite dissension or departure—his.

Ambition and its adverse effects on relationships are not confined to men's careers, however. As more and more women graduate from professional and graduate schools, a growing number of them are following the male prescription for success: hard work. The toll that women's workaholism takes on their social lives is hard to assess, but there's no question that it has become a problem for them and/or the men in their life.

Melissa Howard admits to being addicted to politics. Her earliest political "contribution" was handing a bouquet of flowers to John Kennedy during his presidential campaign when she was four years old. The daughter of politically active parents, she grew up attending fund-raising dinners and running errands for volunteers in campaign headquarters. When, some 21 years later, her boyfriend of five years left her, it was no surprise that her involvement in politics was the wedge that split their relationship apart.

After graduating from college in 1976, Melissa landed a job as coordinator of field communications for Common Cause, a lobbying organization in Washington, D.C. On free weekends, she flew down to visit her college boyfriend, who had moved to Houston to start his career. After carrying on a long-distance romance for two and a half years, Melissa and her boyfriend decided it was time to give their relationship a chance to work out. They decided to move to a "neutral" city, Boston, where they'd spent a short time together in 1977, when Melissa was doing field organizing work.

Getting a politics-related job in Boston proved to be impossible for an outsider, so Melissa went to work for a management consulting firm, and funneled her interest in politics to working in campaigns. "As soon as I got out of work at five, I'd head over to the campaign office and not get home until after eleven. As Ted Kennedy's presidential campaign accelerated, I began leaving on weekends to do field organizing in other New England states," explains Melissa. "I was used to working crazy hours and the experience was exhilarating." From her boyfriend's point of view, however, the situation was anything but acceptable. He was putting in long hours on his job, too, but his idea of having fun in his free time was not stuffing envelopes or handing out leaflets. Her boyfriend finally issued an ultimatum: "It's either Ted Kennedy or me." Melissa's response had the familiar ring of the "take me as I am or leave me" mentality of the traditional ambitious man: "You know

I've always been a political animal. I'm not about to give up what I love doing." After the March 1980 primary, John moved out.

Melissa is philosophical about the fact that her double-faceted professional life doesn't appeal to many men who may otherwise be interested in her. A number of the men she has subsequently dated and been in relationships with have been men she's met through campaigns. "They're a breeding ground for romances and relationships. The energy and excitement of working together for a cause creates tight bonds among volunteers," she explains.

The other scenario involving ambitious women who are devoted to their work is this: There is a limited amount of time in their lives to meet men, and the men they are most attracted to (who, like themselves, are well-educated and upwardly mobile) are no more flexible than they are about accommodating the other's schedule. This stalemate isn't often resolved until one person (usually the woman) decides that her personal and emotional needs deserve more attention than she's given them.

Thirty-three-year-old Ellen MacDonald, a partner in a prestigious Toronto law firm, feels that baby boom women who have reaped the benefits of expanding career opportunities for women are caught in a peculiar time warp when it comes to their relationships with men. "Whenever I get together with my female friends, we talk about the wonderful things that success has brought us—a sense of achievement, financial independence, the respect of others in our field. But invariably we get back to the same subject: Why are we in our thirties and still single? A lot of us think it's because of our work, but that's a smoke screen—you can make time for anything in your life that's important to you. I think it's a problem because most men aren't ready for us. They don't want partners who are as frazzled by work as they are at day's end, who make more money than they do and who are more successful than they are."

She speaks of the discrepancy in matter-of-fact terms, not so much angry or defensive as she is puzzled by the peculiar social dilemma in which she and other successful women who are single find themselves. One of her friends, Rosemary Mc-Carney, also a lawyer, joins in the conversation. "The only solution is to find a man who isn't intimidated by your ambition or success because he's got a healthy ego. I'm sure I wouldn't be married now if I hadn't met Barry," concedes Rosemary, who is 28 and has been married for two years.

Rosemary's story is an unusual one because the man in her life agreed to follow her not only to a different city, but a different country. The daughter of a banker and one of four children, Rosemary moved around frequently from one small town to another because of her father's career. She decided at age 11 that she wanted to be a lawyer because she wanted to help the Canadian Indians.

As a law student, she was one of the first Canadians to participate in an exchange program of the Canada-U.S. Law Institute located at Case Western Reserve Law School in Cleveland. When the Institute invited her to come back to direct the program and teach in the law school after graduation, she decided to postpone taking a job she'd already been offered by a Toronto law firm. "Barry and I had been dating a few years, but we hadn't considered getting married until then. Since we'd been in different places all along, we talked about continuing our commuting relationship for the two years that I planned to be at the Institute. But Barry said he was willing to move to Cleveland because he thought getting international law experience would be valuable," says Rosemary. They got married several months later.

Even though there were times during those two years that Rosemary spent only a handful of days each month with Barry (her position required her to frequently commute to Canada), the marriage survived the building years of their careers. Their original plan had been to return to Toronto when Rosemary's two-year commitment to the Institute ended, but they decided to stay. Barry was very satisfied with his position in an international law firm, and Rosemary was offered a job as an associate with one of the country's leading law firms.

Men who fit Barry's description—ambitious and successful in their own right, flexible enough to consider options that may emanate from their girl friend's or wife's career, and loving partners—may be a rare breed. Connecting with one at the right time in your life (and his) is a combination of fate and the ability to recognize a good partner. But realizing that all a good relationship (or marriage) requires is one such man can make waiting for him tolerable.

9

Living with the Fear and Threat of Crime

∼∼∼∼∼∼∼∼∼∼∼∼∼∼∼∼∼∼∼∼∼∼∼∼∼∼∼∼∼∼∼∼∼∼∼∼∼∼∼

IT WAS AN EVENING in late July in New York City. The hot summer day had fizzled into a balmy evening, although the buildings still radiated the heat they'd absorbed. The sun had not yet set, and the air was filled with the voices of children whose mothers had not yet summoned them inside.

She walked along the streets of Chelsea, an up-and-coming neighborhood below midtown, at her usual quick stride. Preoccupied with the thoughts about whether the co-op apartment she'd just seen was a good investment, she was oblivious to the people who passed by. Ahead of her was an entrance to the subway, a welcome sight since she was exhausted from a long day at work topped off by a squash game and co-op hunting.

As she approached the entrance, she saw people exiting—a sure sign that she'd just missed the train. She descended the steps leading to what she thought was a token booth and turnstiles. On reaching the bottom of the stairs, she saw she was mistaken. At that instant, a strong hand encircled her throat and squeezed hard. "My God, what's happening?" her mind screamed. The grip was so tight that she could utter no sound. She felt herself being dragged backwards toward a wall in the dark and empty station. The shock of the attack was so sudden that she couldn't believe that something very wrong was happening to her. Kick, scream, get away! Her mind tried to process the possibilities. But no, her arms were pinned behind her, her throat was aching from the pressure on it. Like a strong swimmer caught in a riptide, she felt herself helplessly pulled away from safety by an unseen force.

Two minutes passed, maybe three. Then suddenly, the fingers released their grip and he was gone. She sputtered and looked up. Another man had happened upon the attack and was walking down the stairs. She ran to him for protection and begged him to walk her back up to the street; she was afraid her attacker would be waiting for her at the top of the stairs. As the man accompanied her to the street, the terror of what had almost happened overcame her, and she began to sob hysterically. Spotting a cab, she ran into the street, narrowly avoiding oncoming traffic. She could not stop crying long enough to tell the cab where to go; she could only point in the direction in which she was headed. Over and over, she heard the cabbie ask, "Lady, are you all right? Are you hurt?" She could only shake her head "no."

Once she was safely inside her apartment, she tried to compose herself. The places where his fingers had gripped her throat were bright red marks. She called her best friend, Allen, with whom she'd gone to high school, and told him what had happened. He comforted her, suggested she report the incident to the police, then asked if she wanted him to come stay at her apartment for the night. She thanked him, but said she'd be all right.

It's easier for me to tell the story as if it happened to someone else because throughout and even after the incident, I felt as though I had watched it happen to someone else. That night as I lay in bed, I wondered whether living in the city was worth the threat of random violence. The attack was obviously a spur-of-the-moment decision. Seeing me walk alone into the subway entrance (it was in fact an entrance, but since there was no token booth below, few people ventured that way), one of the young men who had been coming out of the station turned around and stalked me like prey, knowing that I was walking into a trap. The motive was not robbery—he asked for no money, nor did he grab my purse—rape most likely was. My physique—I'm 5' 10"—was no deterrent. And the karate lessons I'd taken didn't exactly come in handy. Surprising a victim gives the assailant an unbelievable edge. I agonized over whether and what I would have done had the second man not interrupted the attack. And I was angry with myself for not having known better than to put myself in a potentially dangerous situation.

Newcomers to the city are more likely to become victims of crime, according to the results of the Urban Experience Survey (43 percent of the crimes reported by survey correspondents took place during their first two years in a new city). Still, becoming a crime victim years after you move into a city (when, presumably, you should know the risks and be able to avoid them) is not so unusual. The reason? Women let down their guard once they think they know what's safe and what's not. But it takes only one serious incident like mine to change your feelings about being vulnerable.

The Most Common City Crimes

Living in a city does, unfortunately, increase your chances of becoming a crime statistic. According to the results of the Urban Experience Survey, your chances of becoming a crime victim are one in two. Women who are financially successful are almost twice as likely to become crime victims as are those who earn less. Forty-one percent of those who earned $21,000 a year or more reported that they had been a victim of crime, compared to 21 percent of less successful women. There are two explanations of why. One is that you have more coveted belongings or wear expensive-looking clothing which makes you (or your possessions) more visible targets. The second is that successful women are risk-takers by nature and may put themselves in potentially harmful situations more frequently than they realize.

Survey Finding

Have you ever been the victim of any of the following crimes?

Having your car broken into	20%
Having your home burglarized	15%
Getting robbed	14%
Getting assaulted	8%
Having your home vandalized	7%
Getting raped	4%
Other	12%

The one piece of good news is that you're twice as likely to become the victim of a property crime than a violent one. The most common ones are larceny (theft of property from the possession of another—purse-snatching, pocket-picking, bicycle theft and theft from cars), burglary (unlawful entry and theft from premises) and car theft.

Unlike property crimes, which are committed in communities large and small, robbery, which the FBI considers a violent crime, is much more prevalent in cities. Seven of every ten robberies committed in 1981 occurred in cities with populations of 100,000 or more. According to the results of the Urban Experience Survey, city women are twice as likely to get mugged as women living outside cities. Getting robbed is much more frightening than being the victim of other types of theft because the criminal uses violence or the threat of it to get what he wants. You're far more likely to be robbed in New York than in any other city, but three smaller cities—New Orleans, Miami and Las Vegas—rank second, third and fourth on the list of places where you're most likely to become a victim.

The remainder of violent crimes—aggravated assault, forcible rape and murder—are not concentrated in the nation's fifteen largest cities. In 1979, for example, the places with the highest rape rates were: Pine Bluff, Arkansas; Memphis; Tallahassee; Savannah, Georgia; and Reno—all warm-climate places, where rape rates are often higher. In the same year, Houston, New Orleans and Las Vegas had the highest murder rates, and Miami, Pueblo, Colorado, and Savannah had the most instances of aggravated assault per 100,000 people. Nonetheless, it's still smart to be on guard against potentially dangerous situations since the incidence of serious crimes is, generally speaking, higher in cities with populations over 100,000.

Developing Street Smarts

If you've grown up in an area where you didn't have to think twice about where you went or going there alone, becoming aware of the real dangers that exist in a city will take time. It's especially hard to develop a healthy suspicion of strangers if you've been raised in an environment in which your basic trust in other human beings has never seriously been violated. It's easy to hide behind the "It won't happen to me" mentality, but the reality is that over two million women, most of whom are between the ages of 16 and 34, become the victims of violent crime each year. Sometimes, it's simply a case of being in the wrong place at the wrong time; but in many instances, victims could have avoided their fate or altered the consequences had they taken precautions or mentally rehearsed reactions to dangerous situations.

Caution: The Best Crime Preventive

Determining your vulnerability in new situations, particularly if you're not familiar with the neighborhoods you visit in a city, is difficult. But if you keep in mind that you should never put yourself in a situation where you're isolated from other passersby (the biggest insurance against becoming a victim of violent crime in a public place), you've already taken a major step in protecting yourself.

There are several other basics that will help you avoid
becoming a target:

- Avoiding dimly lit passageways and alleys
- Walking on the street rather than the building side of
  sidewalks
- "Dressing down" if you plan to take public transportation, or alternatively, taking a cab if you're wearing
  expensive clothes
- Keeping stealable items (cameras, jewelry, wallets)
  well concealed

Don't Take Unnecessary Risks

Even though most of us say we'd never walk alone through
areas that are obviously off limits after dark (parking garages,
parks, deserted blocks), there's bound to be a time when you
will be in a hurry or caught in inclement weather when taking
a shortcut through such an area seems like a good idea. Those
are inevitably the times when disaster strikes.

Traveling to your destination alone after dark can be risky if
you're walking or taking public transportation. It's not always
possible, of course, to go with someone. But rather than find
yourself in a situation where a crime could easily occur (should
your path cross a would-be attacker's), it's better to take a taxi
after non-rush hours. At least one study has shown that
women who rode public transportation between 6 and 9 P.M.
were nine times as likely to be a victim of a violent assault than
were women who traveled during rush hours.

Some city women are reluctant to accept offers from a date
or male friend to be picked up or dropped off after an evening
out, particularly if the man lives in a different part of town.
Unless it's just as convenient (and not prohibitively expensive)
for you to take a cab, you shouldn't turn down the offer. Any
man worth going out with will be concerned that you arrive
home safely. The only exception to accepting an offer is if you
anticipate problems saying good-bye to your date on the doorstep.

Keep in mind, too, that just because you are in the company of a man, the danger of becoming a crime victim doesn't disappear. The same rules about taking unecessary risks apply. Another Urban Experience Survey respondent, a Los Angeles woman, wrote about an incident which occurred while she was with a male companion:

"A friend of mine and I were coming from a club on Sunset Boulevard in West Hollywood when we were accosted by a couple. They put a knife to my throat and a gun to my male companion's head. We didn't struggle—I was scared to death. They were very violent, ripped open my dress and pulled off my jewelry. The girl with the knife turned on my friend and stabbed him repeatedly. When I came to visit him in the intensive care ward, he refused to see me because I was a reminder of the terror. Soon after the incident, I began seeing a psychiatrist because I was afraid to stay home alone or go out at night."

Develop a Sixth Sense

Folks who live outside major metropolitan areas call it paranoia, but veteran city dwellers know that being tuned into what's happening around you is a crime preventive. If you closely observe the behavior of women on city streets, it's easy to pick out those with a sixth sense. They are the ones who turn around when someone bumps into or walks too close to them; they watch the reflections of the passing scene in store and car windows to find out who is around them; they wait for other passengers before descending into subway entrances. Would-be attackers read the body language of potential victims, too, and they know that women who are aware of what's around them are usually not worth the trouble.

Being alert to potentially dangerous situations can give you the few extra moments you need to outwit them. If, for example, you suspect someone is following you, you can walk in the street, keeping parked cars between you and the person you suspect, or cross the street. If you spot some unsavory-looking character eyeing you in a train station, you can approach a trustworthy-looking stranger, explain your fear, and ask if he'd mind your staying near him.

Riding Mass Transit—Six Safety Rules

In most non-car cities, taking public transit is usually faster and more convenient, and is unquestionably less expensive than driving. It's smart to learn the rules for avoiding invasions of your privacy or safety right away, so that you won't become an easy target for a pickpocket, mugger or pervert.

1. If you're traveling alone, never put yourself in the situation of being the only person on a subway car, platform or stairway. Those who are bent on doing harm will take advantage of the fact that there's no one to come to your aid. It's the perfect opportunity not only to rob but to rape.

2. Avoid sitting near doors. One of the favorite tricks of thieves is to grab dangling purses and wristwatches from the platform just as the doors are about to close.

3. Make sure the contents of your purse or briefcase are not exposed. Open bags are like welcome signs to those with light fingers.

4. Hold your bag in front of you on a crowded bus or subway. Keeping it in sight at all times discourages pickpockets and can also be a protection from strangers rubbing up against you. If you're carrying other bags or parcels, don't put them between you and your purse; you'll never feel the nimble finger work of the thief who gets into your purse.

5. If you suspect a fellow passenger of "feeling you up," and there's no room to shift positions, say in a loud voice, "Get your hands away from me," to make the intruder and others aware that you're not going to stand for it. If he doesn't stop, give him an elbow or stomp on his foot. (Giving him an angry look is often not enough of a deterrent.)

6. Move away from someone who verbally harasses you, and sit or stand near a man who looks as if he could and would come to your aid if the harassment continues. If necessary, explain what's happening so that he feels comfortable intervening in the event the man who is bothering you won't leave you alone.

Don't Become an Easy or Foolish Victim

When the moment of realization that you may be in trouble strikes, it's smart to react quickly. The first best defense is to scream. "I used to be afraid that if I was ever in a threatening situation, I would open my mouth and nothing would come out, the way it happens in dreams," says Bekah Herring, who twice scared off would-be assailants by hollering at the top of her lungs. Most crime experts contend that the sound of a distressed human voice elicits more of a reaction from those who hear it (yelling "Fire!" is sometimes more effective) than does a whistle or siren device. The other disadvantage is the time it takes to locate those devices.

If you're being pursued on a street or in a parking lot and you're unable to outdistance your assailant, your best protection is to hit the pavement and roll under a parked car. Continue screaming and fend him off by kicking while hanging onto the underside of the car. The more difficult you make it for the assailant to get his hands on you, the more likely it is he'll abandon his plan and look for easier prey.

Trying to escape the situation is not viable if the attacker has a weapon and is close enough to use it. Consider yourself fortunate if all he wants is your money or valuables; many first-time victims resist. Most crime experts believe it's much smarter, though, to do whatever the robber asks, so long as it doesn't put you in further danger. When you're complying with his request, it's also a good idea to explain what you're doing ("I'm reaching for my wallet") so that he doesn't overreact to any movements you make. If your assailant doesn't seem too menacing and you have the presence of mind to ask to keep your credit cards and personal IDs, do so (most thieves just want cash). But you're tempting fate if you try to hold onto the diamind ring that is a family heirloom. Inexperienced and young robbers are particularly prone to getting rattled if the scenario doesn't unfold as they expect; your staying calm is some insurance for your safety. (One additional warning: It's a good idea to keep your keys separate from anything that has your address on it; if a thief gets both, have your locks changed immediately, or you may become the victim of a burglary as well.)

A different reaction may be called for if the assailant's intent is to rape you. While your first response may be to fight off a rapist, it's not a smart one: many rapists are turned on by a struggle with their victim. It's much better to try to outwit a rapist unless you've got a black belt in karate. (Some would-be victims have successfully talked themselves out of getting raped; several years ago, a woman jogger who was attacked by a man in New York's Central Park in the early hours of the morning told him she was an undercover cop and that her backup was close behind her; it was risky, but the rapist believed her and ran away.) You may want to give him the impression that you're not going to resist so that he begins concentrating on how to proceed rather than how to subdue you. He may release his grip long enough for you to give him a knee or otherwise disable him while you escape. If all else fails, you can pretend to faint by simply collapsing. Struggling to undress a totally passive victim is no easy proposition and penetration, while possible, is extremely difficult. Any tactic that buys you time—and the possibility someone else may happen by—is worth trying.

Any crime—attempted or committed—should be reported to the police immediately. Even if there appears to be no chance of apprehending the criminal, your description of him, the crime and the circumstances under which it occurred can alert police patrolling the area to be on the lookout for a second attempt (particularly if he wasn't successful with you). Your reporting it adds to the crime statistics in an area, which could affect the number of patrols dispatched there in the future. Finally, if you have off-premise theft insurance, it's necessary to file a report with the police in order to make a claim on your policy.

Protecting Yourself Inside Your Home

Like all Canadian cities, Toronto has a very low crime rate. The most dangerous thing about a low rate is that it can give you a false sense of security. But as Ellen MacDonald discovered, some neighborhoods are safer than others, and taking simple precautions can offer protection against those freak incidents.

Gentrification, the movement of affluent professionals into renovated buildings in what had been deteriorating neighborhoods, has spread into almost every section of downtown Toronto. Streets lined with red-brick Victorian town houses provide strollers a glimpse into the past. Ellen MacDonald moved to an apartment on such a street, in a neighborhood that was still transitional; that is, some of the unrenovated houses were occupied by previous tenants, among them drifters, alcoholics and those who simply could afford no better housing. Even though cabbies sometimes refused to drive into the area, Ellen wasn't particularly concerned about her safety.

On a mid-January night, Ellen arrived home very late, having just gotten off a flight. Feeling exhausted, she went directly to bed. Several hours later, she was awakened by the crash of glass; an intruder had broken in through a window. Ellen pulled a blanket around herself and ran out of her room, heading straight for the front door. Out in the street, she called for help, but no one heard her. She decided to risk sneaking back and telephoning the police. The intruder, who had seen her run out, didn't see her return. The police arrived within minutes and apprehended the man, who was very drunk. His intention was unclear, although he had slashed the mattress in Ellen's bedroom. "I appeared to be so calm that the police thought I was in shock and wanted me to go to the hospital. But aside from being very frightened, I was all right. The fact that the man was quite out of it gave me the advantage of thinking my way out of the situation," explains Ellen, who soon thereafter moved to a safer neighborhood.

Most intruders are burglars, who only want to make off with valuables. But if they inadvertently discover someone at home or are surprised by the occupant in the midst of their ransacking, they sometimes injure, rape or kill her. In fact, one out of every five violent crimes occurs inside people's homes. If you ever return home to find your door ajar or your belongings disturbed, get help before you go in to investigate further.

In a situation like Ellen's, the best course of action is to escape immediately rather than risk confronting the intruder as she did. (Planning several possible escape routes is a good idea.) If there's no possibility of getting out, try locking yourself in a room; it's possible the burglar will take what he can from the other rooms and leave, rather than confront you. Should you not even have the time to do that and the intruder seems bent on doing you harm, screaming may change his mind, especially if neighbors are nearby. On the other hand, if you become hysterical and he has a lethal weapon, he may try to silence you by using it.

Another possibility if you're concerned is to roll under a bed and keep the attacker at bay by kicking (similar to the under-the-car method if the attack is on the street). And, once again, you may be able to deter a would-be rapist by distracting him with a seeming surrender, and then quickly maneuver around or disable him to escape.

The best insurance against having to deal with an intruder face to face is to create a safe harbor in your home—a room or closet with a dead-bolt lock on the inside, suggests Hugh C. McDonald, a former law enforcement officer, in his book *Survival*. It's a particularly good idea if you live alone. Installing a telephone extension in the room enables you to call for help. So long as the door isn't hollow and opens out rather than in, the intruder won't be able to get inside.

Five Ways to Discourage a Burglar

You can reduce the chances of becoming a burglary victim by doing things that will discourage an intruder from choosing your apartment or house over others in the neighborhood. They include:

1. Locking glass sliding doors and accessible windows as well as entrances when you leave.

2. Installing window gates on fire-escape or ground-floor windows, which are the most vulnerable entry points. If a number of your neighbors use window gates, you should definitely install them as a deterrent.

3. Change the locks on the doors when you first move into a place. People besides the previous tenants may still have keys to the place and make use of them. The most burglar-resistant locks are dead-bolt or pin-tumbler locks; they require a key to open and close and cannot be forced open with a plastic card the way spring latches (the kind that lock automatically when you close the door) can. In more than half of all break-ins, the burglar gains entry by forcing inadequate door locks.

4. Keep lights and the radio on when you leave; it gives the illusion that someone is inside and may subsequently influence a burglar to look for an unoccupied home.

5.. Buy a watchdog. Its size isn't as important as its bark. Studies have found that homes with dogs are less frequently the targets of burglars.

The Entranceway "Trap"

Wedged into a category between street and home crimes are doorstep crimes—those that occur as victims are leaving or going into their apartment buildings. Most of us don't stop to think that danger might be lurking just around the corner from where we live, and that's why assailants can so easily take advantage of the situation.

If, however, you go through a short mental checklist each time you enter and leave your building, you can avoid finding yourself in the lobby with an unwanted visitor:

- Before entering or leaving, check to see who is around. If someone looks suspicious, don't go in (or leave) until they've gone a safe distance.
- Have your keys ready to unlock the door when you're coming in; the few extra minutes it takes to rummage through your bag can give an assailant the few moments he needs to accost you before you can get away. One study, "Crime, Women and the Quality of Urban Life," found that a majority of the women interviewed (81 percent) regularly had

their keys in hand when approaching their door. Only half of the men interviewed said they often used this precaution.

Another scenario is getting accosted by someone who has already gained access to the building. If rape is his motive, he'll no doubt want you to take him to your apartment, which will seal your fate. Knocking at the door of a male neighbor who is likely to be home or pretending to faint are the best ways out of the situation. In any situation in which your life is in danger, you'll have to make quick judgments about whether angering your assailant by deceiving him (and failing in your attempt) is a worthwhile risk.

Living with the Fear of Crime

Even though a small percentage of women become victims of violent crime (only four in 500 women who live in metropolitan areas are likely to be raped in any given year; the incidences of aggravated assault and murder are even lower), the fear of becoming a victim is particularly high, especially among women who are college-educated, young (18–29) and living in cities.

Women who move to a city are somewhat less likely to worry or think about crime than are those who have lived there all their lives, according to the Urban Experience Survey. But generally speaking, city women take more precautions against crime than do women who live elsewhere. They are more likely to install burglar alarms and anti-theft devices, own guns and live with others as a way of reducing their vulnerability.

Survey Finding

How have you dealt with your fear of becoming a crime victim?

I try to prevent an occurrence by avoiding unnecessary risks	86%
I have theft insurance for my home or car	56%
I don't worry or think about it too much	34%
I've had burglar alarms or anti-theft devices installed in my home or car	17%
I carry a Mace-like substance in my purse	14%
I sleep with something that can be used as a weapon near my bed when I'm home alone	11%
I carry a whistle or noise alarm	9%
I've marked my possessions with police identification numbers	9%
I've purchased a gun and know how to use it	7%
I've taken a self-defense course	6%
It's why I live with roommates	4%
It's why I live with my boyfriend	3%

Wanda Urbanska, who moved to Venice, California, after several years of living in New York City, found that her fear of crime escalated when she moved from the East to the West Coast. "I won't ever walk the streets of my neighborhood alone after dark. In fact, I often feel terrified when my boyfriend isn't here with me late at night," says Wanda.

Venice, a beach community which is within the Los Angeles city limits, has in the last decade been undergoing transformation from a lower-class community to a chic residential area for young professionals. Many expensive condominiums have sprung up among the aging single-family homes, whose occupants have elected to stay, giving the area a racially and economically mixed population. Wanda and Frank live next door to a family whose sons have criminal records. "One of them was once arrested on our roof. He was high on the drug PCP and was threatening to jump off; he also had a gun," says Wanda.

But that's not the only situation that has made Wanda apprehensive. The same year that she moved to Venice, a 23-year-old reporter for the *Los Angeles Herald-Examiner,* Sarai Ribicoff, was gunned down in cold blood as she and her date were leaving an expensive French restaurant in the neighborhood. After her date handed over his wallet, the robbers opened fire, apparently without provocation. One bullet lodged in Sarai's chest. It was the kind of senseless crime that leaves everyone asking, "Why?" "I was particularly shaken by it because I was the same age, working at the same newspaper, and like Sarai, I'd moved here from the East," says Wanda, who at the time lived two blocks from the murder scene.

While Sarai Ribicoff's murder was the most publicized crime that has occurred in recent years in that section of Los Angeles, instances of other violent crime are not uncommon there, judging by newspaper and magazine accounts. "The Figgie Report on Fear of Crime" concluded there is a high correlation between knowing a crime victim and being regularly exposed to reports of crime in the newspaper and on television and the fear of becoming a victim—which aptly describes Wanda's situation.

"When people ask me why I don't move out of this area if I'm so afraid, I tell them it's because I really like it here—being able to live near the beach and yet work downtown—and the rent is still a bargain," says Wanda. "Taking precautions is my way of dealing with my fear." After two years of living in Venice and never having had a skirmish with crime, Wanda and Frank moved to Westwood, which is one of the safest areas in Los Angeles.

Most women agree with Wanda in terms of handling their fear of crime; the majority of respondents to the Urban Experience Survey say they try to prevent an occurrence by not taking unnecessary risks such as walking home alone at night. Almost one in four said they carried a Mace-like substance, whistle or noise alarm. One in ten say they sleep with something that can be used as a weapon near their bed when they're home alone. A surprising six percent say they've purchased a gun and know how to use it. Only five percent say they've taken a self-defense course. ("The Crime, Women and Quality of Urban Life" study noted that many more men than women take self-defense courses.)

The Aftermath of Crime

The day after I was attacked in the subway station, I retold the story many times to my female colleagues. Doing so had a cathartic effect on my feelings of anger and helplessness; my message was: "Don't ever think you're not vulnerable; always keep your guard up." The reactions of sympathy and often empathy from women who had been or almost been victims was comforting. My male friends, too, were outraged, with the exception of one who commented, "At least the guy had good taste." I told him how thoughtless his comment was; he apologized.

Crime victims often blame themselves for what happened, which is why it's so important to have the support of those who are close to you. One crime victim who responded to the Urban Experience Survey described the devastating effect on her of having her apartment burglarized and then set on fire.

"Two other women in my building had the same thing happen to them. The police suspect it is a former maintenance man who has a thing against women. During my crisis, I found out who my friends were. A lot of people let me down, including my former boyfriend. That really hurt. I depended on myself and a few friends. Because of the way it happened, I had a lot of fear for a few months. Then I realized that I couldn't live that way and had to have faith that the Lord would protect me. I have seen how insignificant possessions are. Many of my clothes were destroyed, and I had to replace a lot of furniture. Luckily, I had insurance."

Many women who become victims of crime in their home decide to deal with their renewed fear by moving. That, of course, can be an expensive and difficult proposition (given

the low vacancy rates in some cities). Still, it's worth it if it's
what you need for peace of mind or you realize that even with
added protection, your living space is more vulnerable to being
hit than others (which is often true of ground-floor apartments). In the Urban Experience Survey, several burglary victims who reacted by reinforcing their doors and locks said they
did sometimes have dreams of being broken into again.

A newswoman in Los Angeles who participated in the Urban
Experience Survey had a traumatic ground-floor apartment
experience. "I was raped three and a half years ago by a man
who broke into my apartment in the middle of the night while I
was asleep and held a knife to my neck. I was very upset, but
relieved in a way because I wasn't killed. I immediately moved
out and stayed with my boyfriend until I found a new place. I
won't live in ground- or street-level apartments anymore, and
decided to have an unlisted telephone number. I consider myself lucky because I had no long-term psychological traumas,
but I am in general a bit more careful and paranoid."

Victims of crime are twice as likely as others to have irrational fears, according to the results of the Urban Experience
Survey. But most victims continue leading a normal life. Perhaps the most positive aftermath of having a brush with crime
that leaves you shaken but unharmed is that you will become
more sensitized to the realities of crime and avoid potentially
dangerous situations more than you have done in the past.

STAGE FOUR
Putting Down Roots

WHEN I ASKED the question, "At what point did you decide to stay?" of the dozens of women I interviewed around the country, few of them had ever analyzed when the feeling of being an outsider subsided and the sense of having become a resident settled in. It was less a dramatic turning point and more a recognition of small but symbolic changes in their lives—applying for a new driver's license; saying that they're from their adopted city when they're out of town; finding a local dentist rather than seeing the "old" one on visits home.

The process of putting down roots is partially dependent on your letting go of the world you've left behind. The younger you are and the greater the cultural differences between your hometown and adopted city, the tougher it is to feel that you belong in your new home. It's human nature to feel attached to the turf where you spent your childhood, even if you've since discovered that you feel much more comfortable in a different place. It takes time to acclimate your thinking, language and behavior to city life.

A crisis can be the catalyst in your making a commitment to stay. None of us thinks that fate will conspire against us and make our lives miserable, but it sometimes does. How we deal with circumstances beyond our control is the true test of character. Most of the women I interviewed had experienced at least one major crisis since moving to the city, which made them think twice about whether or not they should stay. The only way to come through bad times in good shape is to believe in yourself and take positive steps to get your life under control. The women featured in the chapter "Coping with Crisis" did so—but sometimes only after they first had gotten a perspective on their situation by leaving town temporarily.

Because women who move to cities today have serious career aspirations, work is often the most important reason for making a commitment to a city. The network of professional contacts you develop in your city during the building years of your career are critical to your future progress. Finally, the longer you work, the more specialized your expertise will become, which can decrease your marketability outside cities which are centers for your profession. "Consolidating Your Career," the second chapter in this section, discusses the relationship between career turning points and where you live.

A comfortable living situation is another anchor in the often uncertain seas of city life. It's not until you get a place of your own that you'll begin to feel like your home is your castle. Even if it's a rental, you can do what you want when you want to and furnish it to suit your own taste. Those two freedoms contribute greatly to feeling at home in a city, which is one strong argument for your planning to live alone at some point.

Buying your own place will make you feel even more rooted because the emotional attachment is strengthened by a financial commitment. Making the decision to buy on your own is a statement of self-confidence, independence and money-management abilities.

Aside from the emotional commitment to friends and the financial commitment to your own home, the personal commitment to get married often further entwines your future with that of your adopted city. And for many women, that is the point at which buying city real estate becomes a feasible financial option. If the city in which you're living isn't the place you plan to make your permanent home, be wary about getting too involved romantically with someone who does have roots there. Despite long-distance relationships being heralded as a solution for two-career couples, traveling between cities to keep love intact is not romantic at all. Better that the man you seriously become involved with has the same ideas as you as far as putting down roots in your adopted city.

The third chapter in this section, "Making Personal Commitments," discusses how your satisfaction with these three areas of your life outside of work affects your decision to stay in the city.

10

Coping with Crisis

ON A COLD, wintry January evening in 1974, the ringing of the phone in the house in Ohio could barely be heard above the din of teenage boys playing rock 'n' roll music on their guitars and drums.

"Schmidt residence," a woman's voice answered. It was my mother.

"Hi, Mom, it's Peg."

"It's a surprise to hear from you on a weekday night. (Would you boys turn those instruments down!) Sorry, I can't even hear myself, let alone you. Is anything wrong?" I could hear the concern in my mother's voice.

"No, nothing. Just thought I'd call."

For several minutes, my mother proceeded to bring me up to date on the news from home. Then she asked, "Well, how are things on the job front?"

"I had a few more interviews this week, but nothing looks very promising," I was trying my best to sound nonchalant. I heard my father pick up the second phone. "Hi, Peg, how's everything?" His cheeriness made me realize how depressed I must have sounded.

"Okay," I said, lying.

"What's Keith up to?" he asked, referring to my boyfriend. That did it. I burst into tears. The minutes it took to regain my composure seemed like hours. I'd never called my parents before to tell them about my problems. Having moved to New York two years earlier, I was relishing being on my own. I didn't want them to think that I couldn't handle my own affairs at age 23. But the frustration and unhappiness I'd been feeling rushed out as quickly as if someone had opened a floodgate. How were they to have known that Keith hadn't shown up (yet again) for a date, and that I'd been waiting around for the last few hours hoping to hear from him.

It wasn't just my relationship with him that was on the rocks. I had been unable to find a job in publishing for the last five months. To make ends meet, I did temporary secretarial work through an agency; it was a real comedown after having worked for a year at a national women's magazine, where I was writing a monthly column. I had left after a year, feeling that I wasn't moving up quickly enough, and had spent the summer doing free-lance writing on Cape Cod, which turned out to be a romantic but non-lucrative venture. Because of my three-month hiatus from the city and being unable to find another magazine job quickly, I had lost touch with many friends and acquaintances. And my closest friend, who had also been my roommate the previous year, had moved upstate to work on her first newspaper job. There was no one around to give me a pep talk, tell me things would work out, reassure me that I had what it takes to make it through a low period.

I'll never forget that conversation with my parents, who for the first time began lobbying for me to come home. "Why stay if you're so unhappy?" they wanted to know. The offer of home-cooked meals and the company of people I loved was very tempting at the moment, but I knew I had to stick out the situation.

The journal I kept reflected my state of mind:

"I don't quite know why I feel so utterly trapped by city life at this point. Perhaps it is because I have so little money in a place where it makes so much difference in my comfort and safety. I find myself daydreaming about the days of summer when I ran along the beach and everyday living was so effortless. I am tired of hassling with the world as it exists here. I feel so uneasy walking the five blocks to the laundromat, across the street from where a Columbia University professor was recently knifed to death by neighborhood thugs. I feel like I'm losing ground to the cockroaches in my apartment. I don't enjoy spending a lot of time there because it's so dark, even on the sunniest days.

"Most depressing of all is looking for work. It can be so humiliating. Although I have had articles published, I don't have enough experience to get the kind of job I'd like. What I must do, I think, is become very experienced in one thing, preferably by working for one employer, over the next few years. Keith is yet another exercise in frustration. I vacillate between wanting to be with him and away from him, to exist happily on my own until the time comes, if it ever will, for us to be together. I guess I'll try to make the best of things until my life begins to resolve itself."

As it turned out, it took months before my life got back on an even keel. Within a month of that conversation with my parents, I had been hired as an associate editor at a plastics magazine. Writing stories about injection plastic molding machinery and the prices of resin wasn't my idea of exciting reporting, but I was given my own office and frequently traveled to interview sources. A regular paycheck enabled me to pay off the credit card debts I had acquired (one of my ways of coping with depression had been to go on buying sprees). Having spending money also meant I didn't have to turn down invitations to go out with friends to bars and restaurants and shows.

Five months later, I moved to a nearby suburb and lived in a two-family house with five friends, including Keith. Not only was I paying less rent, but my living situation improved dramatically. The house was on a tree-lined street in a solid, middle-class neighborhood, where no one thought twice about walking the few blocks to town alone, even after dark. I began jogging and playing tennis regularly since a track and courts were located nearby. And my relationship with Keith improved dramatically, since he vastly preferred suburban to city living.

The nine months that it took for me to begin feeling satisfied with my life again was unquestionably one of the most depressing periods in my life. I felt like a forest firefighter who slowed down the acceleration of the flames in one area only to discover that while my back was turned, another wall of heat was coming up fast behind me. Handling one specific crisis is manageable, but when several erupt within a short time of one another, the psychological toll they exact can be overwhelming.

For newcomers to a city, the three major sources of stability in one's life are having a comfortable (and safe) place to live, a job that you can tolerate (if not enjoy) and a support network (which may include a spouse, boyfriend, friends and nearby family). If one of these beams of well-being gives way, you usually have enough structural strength to shore up your life; but if two or more go, the threat of your emotional floor giving way is great.

Survey Finding

What was the most depressing period you experienced while living in the city?

Less than six months after arriving	56%
About a year after arriving	13%
One to two years after arriving	9%
Three to five years after arriving	13%
Six to ten years after arriving	7%
More than ten years after arriving	2%

Developmental psychologist Erik Erikson contended that the stages of life are linked by crises. He defined the word as meaning times of increased vulnerability and heightened tension. A crisis also signals a turning point since it is a moment of decision. If you take risks and forge ahead into uncharted emotional territory, personal growth usually results. If, on the other hand, you choose to escape the crisis by retreating from it physically or psychologically, chances are you will regress and probably postpone having to deal with a problem that is likely to confront you again.

Most of the women interviewed for this book had experienced one or more crises since the time they arrived in the city.

Interestingly, major crises don't pop up during most women's first few years in a city, perhaps because they're still in the process of getting their new lives together. But once they become more established, the problems they experience are more complicated and seem to greatly affect their happiness. Of all the women surveyed in the Urban Experience Questionnaire, those who had lived in the city six to ten years were least likely to feel that all was well in their world. (Compared to women who had been living there less than six months and over ten years, almost 90 percent of whom were very or quite happy, only 56 percent of those who had been in town six to ten years felt the same way.) More of them reported symptoms of depression; specifically frequent headaches, crying and irrational fears as well.

When you're in the throes of a crisis, it's natural to think that you might be better off getting away from the problem and being in a less stressful environment. But as the stories of the three women in this chapter prove, leaving the scene of the crisis doesn't end it; only soul-searching and a decision to make positive changes restore and enhance self-satisfaction.

Going Home to Heal

At age 25, Bekah Herring has already done what many young women only dream of doing. During her six-year career as a model, she made more money than she knew what to do with and traveled abroad extensively on assignments. She knew the chic-est discothèques and got invitations to dinner in New York City's best restaurants and to Europe's finest hotels from model groupies, many of whom were wealthy foreigners.

"Modeling was a phase of my life, a time during which I did a lot of fast growing up," says Bekah, who first came to New York when she was 18. "Having grown up on a horse farm in North Carolina in a religious family, I was pretty shocked about some aspects of life in a big city," remarks Bekah. Dressed in a pink shirt, white cotton skirt and moccasins, she is sitting on a brocade couch in a regal apartment at one of New York's most prestigious addresses on Beekman Place. It is the apartment of her boyfriend, who is a successful business-man. The living-room window overlooks the East River, where tugboats churn through the waters of Hell Gate, the juncture at which two rivers converge, creating whirlpools and treach-erous currents.

Less than two years ago, Bekah was trying to keep her head above water in her own mental Hell Gate, torn by her feelings for the man in her life at the time, her love for her parents (who disapproved of him), and her own sanity.

She had met Lonnie at a party given for photographers and clients. When they were introduced, there was an immediate mutual attraction. He was 11 years older than she, a native New Yorker, whom Bekah describes as being neurotic, cre-ative and hyperactive—the type, she says, who is appealing to a sweet Southern girl because he is her opposite. Bekah promptly fell in love with him and began seeing him ex-clusively.

Once the seriousness of her relationship became apparent to her parents, they were quick to disapprove. Whether it was because he was her first steady boyfriend, from New York City, or from a background much different from their own Anglo-Saxon Protestant one—or all three reasons—was unclear at the time. But they singled out his being Jewish as the cause of their concern. "Will your children be going to Hebrew school?" her mother, who came from a Quaker background, wanted to know. "Mom, we're not even talking about marriage yet," Bekah would answer.

Bekah's relationship with her parents, which had always been a very close one, began deteriorating over the three years she dated Lonnie. Although Bekah and Lonnie got along well for awhile, he increasingly lost his temper and physically took out his anger on her. That brought Bekah to the breaking point. "I began losing interest in my work at a time when my career was doing really well. I was so emotionally drained from our fights that I didn't have much energy left over to put into my assignments. I finally realized that the only way to break off the relationship was to escape. When I called home and said,

'Mom and Dad, I'm on my way,' they were there for me."

The month Bekah spent back in Goldsboro was a time of relaxation and reassessment. She was finally able to discuss Lonnie with them, knowing that she had no intention of getting reinvolved with him. What made reconciliation feasible was her parents' basic trust in their daughter's judgment.

Bekah's month-long break from work also proved to be a time of soul-searching about her future. "Modeling is a profession in which you can make money when you're young, but you also have to deal with what your next career is going to be when your 'look' isn't in anymore or your face has been around too long," says Bekah. She decided to enroll in an undergraduate business program and possibly go on for an MBA. While she was home, she considered studying at the University of North Carolina in nearby Chapel Hill. "I discovered that I'd changed so much from the time I'd left North Carolina that I'd outgrown the place and the time and the people. To have stayed would have meant taking a step backward, so I made up my mind to come back to New York," explains Bekah.

When moving to a city comes at a time when you're establishing your independence from your parents, as it did with Bekah and her sister, there's likely to be friction between you and them. What makes understanding your new life-style all the more difficult is if your parents have nothing but media accounts of life in a city to go on. Bekah's family had lived on their North Carolina farm for several generations, and were understandably unaware of the pressures and new situations their daughter was likely to encounter in a city in an entirely different cultural region.

Deciding how much to tell your parents about your life depends on your relationship with them and how far you've come in terms of establishing your independence. Passing along too many details may cause them to worry or feel they're losing you (if what you're doing runs contrary to their values). Saying too little about the changes you're undergoing may deprive you of their support and them of feeling needed, particularly during a crisis. "Going home to mend fences and recharge your batteries is a positive way of dealing with crisis, so long as you don't overstay," says psychotherapist Loretta Walder. "It only becomes counterproductive if you lapse back into letting your parents take care of you and don't resolve to go back out and resolve your own problems."

How to Survive the First 48 Hours of a Personal Crisis

When something goes terribly wrong in your life—losing your job, having your relationship fall apart, finding out you have to move out of your apartment—it's hard to function normally, especially in the aftermath of the news. Unless the situation demands immediate action (e.g., a death or sickness in your family), it's a good idea to wait until the shock subsides and you're able to think more clearly before you act on it. In the meantime, you can:

1. Call or get together with a friend. Talking with someone who isn't directly involved can give you a perspective on the situation and help you to come up with ideas on what to do next.

2. Keep yourself busy with work, a personal project, a hobby—anything that will provide some distraction from the pain you're experiencing.

3. Ask a friend to spend a night or two at your place. Having company in the evening hours, when you're likely to feel particularly despondent, can be a big comfort.

4. Finances permitting, treat yourself to something special, especially if it's something that can keep you temporarily occupied.

5. Get plenty of exercise. Take long walks. Swim laps. Schedule several games of your favorite racquet sport. Physical exertion is a good way to get rid of pent-up stress and anger and is a virtual guarantee that you'll sleep better.

6. Go on a housecleaning binge. It's a constructive outlet for nervous energy.

7. Put your thoughts down on paper. Expressing your anger, frustration or confusion in words may actually help you sort out your thoughts and release your emotions.

Retreat to the Past

When too many things in your life go off kilter, the idea of escaping to a place or situation reminiscent of easier times is appealing. That's especially the case if you're removed from any support network of family or long-time friends who might otherwise provide the encouragement you need to see the crises through. For women who have gone further in their careers faster than they'd ever imagined possible or whose lives have otherwise undergone dramatic changes as a result of having moved to a city, the possibility of being overwhelmed by it all is great.

Gale Smith, the former schoolteacher who moved to Washington, D.C., as a marketing consultant for a graphic arts company at age 23, worked incredibly long hours to prove her competence to her boss and colleagues, all of whom were older and male. Her marriage to her college sweetheart six months after the move intensified the stress in her life. Her husband was willing to move from Massachusetts to the D.C. area; unfortunately, the only job he could find was in Delaware, which forced them into a commuting marriage.

When the Arab oil embargo occurred, the weekend commute by car became extremely difficult because of the lines for gasoline, so Gale decided to give up her job she'd had for nine months and find one closer to her husband. Three months after she convinced the Xerox Corporation to take her on as one of two saleswomen in their training program in Delaware, her husband was transferred to New Jersey. "It was obvious that the only way our marriage would work was if my husband and I both made compromises. He went to New Jersey and four months later was able to arrange a transfer back to Massachusetts, where I was also able to relocate with Xerox," remembers Gale. When she arrived, she was told she wouldn't be given a sales territory for six months because of a hiring freeze. Rather than wait around, Gale searched for another job.

She succeeded once again, landing a job which involved selling computer time-sharing to banks. Unfortunately, it required her spending three days a week in Boston and the other two in Rhode Island, which meant driving 400 miles a week.

Gale's husband was also in sales, so the two rarely saw each other until after the 11 o'clock news. "After a year, I couldn't stand it any longer. I had no free time. I felt like I was still in a commuting marriage. I was losing sight of what was important in life, and I thought that being around children might get me back to the basics. I returned to the school where I had taught earlier at a salary that was less than half of what I was making in sales," explains Gale.

She and her husband bought a home in the country. She raised her own flowers and vegetables and herbs. However, the more relaxed routine of teaching soon became boring to Gale, who began taking graduate courses and gourmet cooking classes to keep herself busy. The more restless she felt, the more resentful she became that she had derailed her career in order to save her marriage, which began to look as if it wasn't going to work out after all. "We had changed enormously since college, but we'd both been so busy since then that we hadn't noticed it," says Gale.

The turning point in her life occurred over a period of four months in late 1977 and early 1978. She was three months pregnant when the car in which she was a passenger was struck by another car. She lost her baby as a result of the accident. For the next three months, Gale was in and out of the hospital, and at one point required emergency surgery to stop a previously undetected infection. "My husband said he had gone to Las Vegas for a business sales meeting, and couldn't be reached when I came out of surgery," says Gale.

How to Be Your Own Nurse When Sickness Strikes

On a winter weekend in 1979, I went skiing with the man I'd been dating for seven months. On one of my first runs down the mountain, I took a nasty spill and landed in the hospital. When I left two days later, I was on crutches so as not to put any weight on my left leg which was entirely encased in plaster.

Everyday routines—getting dressed, taking a shower,

making a meal—became major productions. I had no choice but to temporarily leave my fourth-floor walk-up apartment and move into the elevator building where my boyfriend (whom I later married) lived. I took cabs to and from work. Having been on my own for eight years, I had to learn how to be dependent on others for the six weeks that I was in a cast.

Most accidents or illnesses that happen won't leave you as incapacitated as I was. Nonetheless, getting sick when you're far from family members and long-time friends whom you would feel comfortable turning to for help can be traumatic. But there are things you can do that will help you cope and speed your recovery.

1. Make sure that you get a good night's sleep throughout the duration of your illness. If you feel something coming on, sleeping an extra hour or two a night may prevent the onslaught or reduce its intensity.

2. Don't force yourself to go into work for appearance's sake. If you can't function at a level close to normal, stay home. Your co-workers will appreciate your keeping your germs to yourself, and the chances of a quick recovery are greater if you don't get overly tired.

3. If you're sick for more than a few days with a bad cold or the flu (or symptoms you've never had before), see a doctor. He or she may be able to prescribe medication that may ease your discomfort and prevent your condition from getting worse.

4. Don't hesitate to ask friends or neighbors for help. Most people don't mind playing a Florence Nightingale role if your request is reasonable—stopping by after work with chicken soup, making a trip to the drugstore, or even spending an evening cheering you up.

5. Phone home. You'll get plenty of sympathy and probably some good old-fashioned advice on remedies and reliefs.

As if two crises weren't enough, Gale found out that her teaching contract was not going to be renewed (the school board could hire two recent graduates for about the same amount as Gale's salary, which had gone up as a result of her earning a master's degree). "I was at ground zero. All I had was a hundred and twenty-one dollars in my checking account and a little blue suitcase when I went back to live with my parents. I vowed then that I would never become helpless and lose control over my life again." Gale speaks of this low point in her life in a detached way, without bitterness. But that is no doubt because in the five years since that has happened, she has scaled to new heights in her career.

She is an enormously successful stockbroker at a prestigious Boston firm. Gale began her comeback in the summer of 1978 when her teaching job ended and her divorce became final. Her piano teacher's husband, a stockbroker, told Gale she already had the skills needed for a position like his from her previous business experience. "It was the boost of confidence I needed to start investigating what I had to do to sharpen those skills," remembers Gale, who took courses at an institute of finance before applying for a position as a stockbroker. Two offers came through, and she took the one which provided the best training.

From the windows in her plush office, Gale has a view of historic Faneuil Hall and the Boston Harbor. Once her day starts at 9:00 A.M., she rarely has time to look out. Her phone begins ringing even before the market opens at 10:00, and she consults her computer terminal as freqently as she once did her lesson plan. "Women who move to cities can't afford to wait for some Prince Charming to come by with a glass slipper that's going to change their life," says Gale, who is now 34.

At this point, some 11 years after she first moved to a city and seven jobs later, Gale is living her life on her own terms. Like many women on the leading edge of the baby boom, she was torn between her responsibility to her marriage and her own goals. The early job changes she made to accommodate her marriage were carefully planned: Gale never made a move unless the new job offered a chance for advancement or an opportunity to learn. After two and a half years of job-hopping, however, burnout took its toll. It was the result of a combination of pressures, internal and external—wanting to impress new employers, making a drastic career change and the nature of the sales profession itself.

Gale's decision to return to teaching and to make her marriage work by resorting to a more traditional life-style was probably destined to backfire, even without the car accident. Confined by her commitment to her marriage, Gale was unable to pursue the plan she'd set out to accomplish when she first moved to Washington. Piece by piece, she gave up the very financial and emotional independence she'd established in her early twenties and ended up back where she'd started. Being a survivor and an optimist, Gale didn't wait long before setting out to accomplish her new goals.

It's human nature to wait until we've reached a breaking point to make a decision about what to do with our lives. But taking the radical surgery method—that is, cutting out the situation that seems to be a major source of our discontent—usually doesn't restore a healthy state of mind. The pressures of Gale's professional life were real, but rather than being the cause of her dissatisfaction, they simply aggravated and complicated her personal life, which is where the real problem existed.

When a series of crises threatens your sanity, it's far better to take time off to reassess (whether it's a vacation or a visit home to remind yourself of the circumstances you left behind) than to make major life choices whose repercussions you'll have to live with for months or even years.

Where to Go for Personal Counseling

You don't have to be in the middle of a major life crisis to feel confused, depressed or lonely. Sometimes those feelings work themselves out in a short time, but when they become severe or don't seem to be going away, it's a good idea to look into the possibility of professional help.

A therapist can help you solve a specific problem, get through a difficult transitional period brought on by a change in your living situation, the breakup of an important relationship or the loss of a job, or build self-confidence or rejuvenate interest in pursuing your goals.

Getting Referrals. Finding a good therapist is like searching for a competent physician—it's a trial-and-error

process, whose success often depends on getting recommendations from other clients. Start by asking friends
if they know of or have used someone they think is effective. You can also call local professional organizations
listed in the phone book, for example, the Association of
Practicing Psychotherapists or the Society of Clinical Psychologists. The local chapter of the National Organization
for Women can refer you to feminist counselors or clinics.
Finally, check the Yellow Pages under the headings
"Mental Health Services" or "Clinics." You'll find hot
lines, referral services, non-profit organizations and individual counselors listed there.

Financial Considerations. Check whether your health
insurance policy will cover some or all of the costs of your
therapy. If it doesn't, you might want to consider a clinic,
where rates are usually lower than those of private therapists.

Choosing a Therapist. Research has shown that a professional's credentials and the kind of therapy he or she
practices are less important than their experience. But the
bottom line is whether you feel comfortable with the
therapist and feel that he or she can help you.

Make appointments with several people whose names
have been referred to you. (Some therapists charge for a
preliminary interview; others don't.) Rather than talking
about your problem at that time, ask the therapist questions that will help you determine whether he or she is
right for you. For instance: What do you see as the goal of
therapy? What approaches or techniques do you use?
How do you feel about women's and men's roles, marriage, children/no children (or other attitudes about life-
style that can give you a clue about their biases)?

Trust your instincts in making the decision. If you felt
comfortable with a particular therapist and liked what he
or she had to say, that's a sound basis on which to choose
that individual. But unless you've seen several therapists,
you won't be able to make comparisons.

Getting a Perspective from a New City

Some newcomers to big cities seem to have a remarkably easy time with their transition. Often, they have harbored ambitions to come to the city since they were young because they see it as a place where they can pursue activities or academic subjects in the framework of real jobs. Partly because they know what they want and are resourceful in looking in the right places, they find a niche in their chosen field. They find satisfaction in their love life, not always, of course, but often enough to say that they're happy. And if they don't already have friends in their adopted city, they seem to make them easily enough.

Cindy Root was one of those people. Born in Houston, she grew up in El Paso and went to college in Tucson before heading East to Washington, D.C. She had fallen in love with the area when she came to Annapolis for her older brother's graduation from the naval academy there. So no one, including her twin sister, was surprised when, a month after graduation, Cindy packed her Volkswagen and drove East.

Six weeks after arriving, she was hired as a receptionist in a Senator's office. And for the next seven years, she worked her way up the ladder of positions on his staff, becoming his executive assistant in 1978.

Her love life was also on a fairly even keel; Cindy was involved in one relationship from the time she arrived, when she had met a man she thought she would eventually marry. Three years after Cindy came to Washington, her sister and brother-in-law moved there. She was elated, for now she would be able to re-establish a close relationship with her identical twin.

Cindy was coasting through her twenties when several yellow caution lights began blinking. The first one went off at work. The Senator for whom she worked had remarried, and his new wife got involved in staff hiring and firing decisions. "I survived for a year and a half before I had a falling out with her and was offered the option of heading up one of the Senator's homestate offices," says Cindy. It was a job offer she probably would not have considered were it not for two other imminent changes. "My long-standing romantic relationship seemed to be going nowhere. The two of us had different and irreconcilable ideas about what we wanted from it, so I could see the end was in sight. And then my sister and her family decided to move back to El Paso to be close to my parents," explains Cindy.

Feeling that the very foundation of the life she'd created in Washington was on the verge of collapsing, Cindy began entertaining thoughts of how much better it would be being closer to home. In fact, Dallas is a good 650 miles from El Paso, no weekend car trip home. But it was 650 Texan miles, which made the distance psychologically much shorter. "I never lost touch with my Southwestern identity while I was in Washington, so I thought that moving to a new city in my home state, where I'd often gone on business, would be a cinch," explains Cindy.

It took her only two months to realize that she'd made a mistake. Even though she knew a number of people from having worked in the Senator's office, Cindy no longer had the network of good friends and business acquaintances that she'd developed during her seven-year stay in the nation's capital. She found the two cities dramatically different. Washington was populated by a variety of ethnic and racial groups; in Dallas, people dressed, looked and talked the same. Conversation in Washington often focused on issues and political developments; the talk in Dallas was of family and fun.

After six months, Cindy told her boss that she was unhappy and planned to return to Washington and look for a different job. He offered her another position on his staff, dealing with legislation. The trip back to Washington was a tremendous joy. She was going home to a city she had truly come to love. Even without the key emotional supports she'd once had there, she felt confident about her decision: It was the place and the kind of work that she could do there that was the earlier basis of her happiness.

While Cindy's temporary move to another city brought her crises into focus and ultimately helped her renew her commitment, relocating to a new city isn't necessarily a good option to resolving crises. That's because financial and psychological disruptions are inherent in any move, which may outweigh the advantages of a new start. To the extent that Cindy wasn't making dramatic changes in her career but relocating to a place whose people and values she was familiar with, it was less stressful.

It's not unusual to develop a real attachment to a new city after living there for three or more years and not appreciate it until you spend time away from it. That's why a decision to leave town when nothing seems to be going your way can be a mistake. You may be leaving behind aspects of your life that can help pull you through a rough time at the same time you're saying good-bye to your problems. Once your state of mind improves, you may be sorry that you've yanked up your roots in a place where you might have found happiness. You can, of course, go back, as Cindy did, but there's no guarantee that your re-entry will be as smooth as hers, particularly if you left your job. If crisis strikes, it's best to shore up your defenses by asking for your friends' support and advice and stay put until the stormy period subsides.

11

Consolidating Your Career

⧓⧓

As SIGMUND FREUD OBSERVED, the combination of a satisfying love and work life is unbeatable. But for city women, career success is a bigger determinant of happiness than is getting married. (It's the reverse for women who do not live in cities.) Single women who felt they had accomplished more than they thought they would at their age or who felt they were among the most accomplished women in their field were significantly happier than were married women whose careers hadn't yet blossomed.

This finding and others in the Urban Experience Survey underscore the importance of getting your career act together—everything from deciding what you want to do to where you actually prove your commitment.

How quickly you consolidate your career will have a major influence on your decision to stay in your adopted city. More than half the city women surveyed said getting established in their careers was the reason they felt as if they had put down roots in their adopted home. The biggest leap in levels of career satisfaction occurred after three or more years of working full-time. Almost three-fourths of the women surveyed were quite or very satisfied with their work life after that time.

What does it take to pull together the pieces of your career dream and make it come true? In addition to talent, ambition and a willingness to work hard, you need ". . . plain old hustle, the ability to elbow yourself through the crowd to get close to the action, to turn a situation to your advantage, to manipulate and control the flow of events and people around you. . . ," wrote Chris Welles in an *Esquire* piece entitled, "Making It in New York: Career Secrets from the Success Capital of America." There's one more ingredient for women: The ability to see the impact of professional decisions on one's personal life and accept the consequences.

The Mid-Twenties Career Decision Crunch

Many of the women interviewed for this book came to their city unsure of their talents and what they could do with them. Their first, second and sometimes even third jobs were not always springboards for better-paying, more prestigious positions in a particular field. But neither were these work experiences a waste of time; in most cases, they did help women decide what they did and didn't like to do.

There comes a point in one's twenties when those who have been experimenting with different kinds of work have to make a commitment to channel their energy in one direction or resign themselves to career limbo, where there is little chance of finding satisfaction. That is where Deborah Rubin found herself at age 26.

She had been working as a waitress in Montreal for over a year and worrying that she might never do anything different unless she made a break soon. The money she earned allowed her to live comfortably, but she wanted something more from her work. "Some people decide what they want to do when at a young age, and once they're out of school, they go after it. But I floundered for years not knowing what I wanted to do," says Deborah.

Her first job after graduating from high school in Vancouver, where she grew up, was working as a secretary for a car-rental agency. At age 21, however, she became restless and applied for a job as a stewardess with Pacific Western Airlines because she wanted to travel, having only gone as far south as Seattle and as far east as Montreal. After three years in that job, she spent a year traveling through Europe and Africa, then studied and later taught yoga in Montreal and Chicago. But life in the ashram seemed to foreclose more options than it offered, so Deborah headed back to Montreal, where one of her sisters lived, and began waitressing.

When, some 18 months later, she was unable to find a promising sales job, Deborah decided to leave Montreal for Toronto, where she expected job opportunities to be better. Besides, a friend from Vancouver who had roomed with her in Montreal was already living in that city.

Not having stayed in Toronto for anything other than a visit, Deborah was amazed at the number of activities that were available—museums, theaters, movies, nightclubs, restaurants. She remembered having seen posters listing cultural attractions and events in major European cities. Why not do the same thing here? "City Nights," a weekly poster featuring entertainment listings and supported by advertising, was born. Working at the dining-room table in the apartment she shared with two other women, Deborah got her idea off the ground within several months.

"I really threw myself into a situation where I had to learn a lot in a very short period of time. But because I was young and enthusiastic, people were very generous with their time and would almost inevitably tell me someone else I ought to get in touch with," remembers Deborah. She got to know the city very well as she developed a distribution system; and she began making many business contacts as she tried to interest potential advertisers in buying space. Although she was just paying her bills between her meager income and unemployment benefits, Deborah soon hired two part-time people to work for her.

It took two and a half years of grueling work before the venture became truly profitable and accepted by the advertising community. "At that point, I finally felt my life had a direction. I had a goal. My business was my baby, and it needed care and nurturing if it was going to get any bigger," says Deborah, who was 29 at the time.

In the summer of 1980, five years after she started her business, Deborah added three new posters to her line, each one announcing events of interest to different audiences—cinema, children's activities and art. A year later, Deborah moved her company into smartly designed and renovated warehouse space, in the same building where her husband has his own public relations firm. At 34, she now employs 18 people, and found a working partner who handles the administration of the business, while Deborah does marketing and sales.

The turning point in her career came at a crucial time—when she was free of any responsibilities and had the energy and interest to make her business the focal point of her life for several years. (She met the man she later married after the rough initial two-year period.) In retrospect, starting her own business was a logical evolution. Throughout her early work history, Deborah had been developing sales skills which served her well when she finally had a project of her own to promote.

Matching a Job with Your Interests and Skills

Finding work that fits your interests and talents within the framework of an organization has its own unique set of frustrations. If you're unsure of what you want, you'll no doubt leave the job (and the company) once the initial excitement of the job wears off, unless you're fortunate enough to work for someone who is willing to help you develop your talents. Jessica Woods was lucky enough to have such a guardian angel.

She had come to Miami from the Northeast with her new husband right after graduating from college in 1969. It wasn't a move she particularly wanted to make, but she was willing to go because her husband very much wanted to live there. Jessica had no idea what she wanted to do, least of all what kind of job her art history major had prepared her for. In the first three years after college, she worked as a secretary to two stockbrokers, an administrative assistant at an ad agency and finally, and most happily, as a designer of needlepoint canvases.

"Even though I was able to use my painting skills in my work, I didn't feel that I was growing and learning after being there two years. My boss didn't want me to be creative; she would tell me what to design, based on her clients' requests. And, as is the case in most art jobs, the pay wasn't good."

She found her next job, which launched her into a success-ful public relations career, through the newspaper want ads. Once again, it was a secretarial job, but this time Jessica had serendipitously landed in an ideal job climate. Her boss was a New Yorker who was reorganizing a collection of small com-panies. When she started, there were only a half dozen em-ployees. Two years later, the company went public and had acquired several hundred employees in the process.

Impressed by her willingness and ability to learn, Jessica's boss had been grooming her all along for a more important position. When a public relations department was created, he asked her to head it up. "I knew as much about public relations as I did about being a secretary when I graduated from col-lege," remembers Jessica, who was nonetheless pleased that her mentor felt she could handle the responsibility.

At about the same time, her marriage, which had never quite lived up to her expectations, broke up. "Getting divorced was a positive event in my life because it was the first major decision I had ever really made on my own. For the first time, I had to take care of myself. At that point, I considered going back to the Northeast, but having had five jobs and lived in six dif-ferent places in the last four years, I knew that that would disrupt my life too much. Besides, I was finally in a position in which I enjoyed my work," explains Jessica.

Her company hired an outside public relations agency, one of the best in town, to assist her—a common practice. When she decided she was ready for a change a year later, she asked her contact at the agency if they might have lunch. "Finally, at age 27, I knew what I wanted to do next; what I needed to find out was what my options in public relations in Miami were," says Jessica. She ended up going to work for that very agency. Having found a true "career home," Jessica worked there for the next eight years and regularly got promoted. In 1982, she became executive vice-president of the 25-person agency, sec-ond in command only to its president and founder.

Even though Jessica landed in public relations by accident, she eventually recognized that it was something she enjoyed and could do well in. Taking advantage of opportunities that come your way is a critical success skill. And there will come a time when taking a positive career leap, as Jessica did when she left the security of a company where she had been given the opportunities to develop her talents, is necessary for career momentum.

Once they determined what exactly they wanted to do, both Deborah and Jessica spent the next five to eight years proving that they could not only do it but do it well. If, like Deborah, you don't have a college education as a credential, you may find your search more of an obstacle course, unless, like her, you decide to go into a profession which doesn't require that credential. Jessica, on the other hand, who had gone to a Seven Sisters school, found that employers in Miami weren't impressed that she'd gone to an academically prestigious college. Although her degree was no doubt an entrée to most of her jobs, it was her job performance, not where she went to school, that was responsible for her being recognized as a bright and competent employee.

While the timing of everyone's career discovery is different, the earlier you choose a particular direction, the more quickly you'll be able to acquire both general and specific skills related to that industry. One of the biggest drawbacks of not knowing what you want to do is that you'll end up in a series of entry-level positions—which translates into depressed earning power.

Relocating to Move Up

When career opportunities in your field are limited in the city in which you live, and you've gone as far as you can in your current company, sometimes the only way to move up is by moving out. Depending on why you chose that city in the first place (and what kind of personal commitments you've established), leaving may or may not be a difficult decision. Assuming you've already laid the groundwork for your career, it's better to line up the job before you leave. Job-hunting long-distance isn't easy, but you stand a better chance of connecting with an opportunity than the undirected or just-out-of-college job seeker simply because you've got a network of contacts.

The media—television, newspapers and radio—is one of the best examples of a field in which starting in a small city (or sometimes in a small town) and making career jumps to larger ones is the traditional path to landing a coveted position for a prestigious station or newspaper. Morning news radio anchor Natalie Windsor wasn't totally aware of this pattern when she applied for her first radio job in Cleveland, which is considered a major market, in 1976.

Armed with tapes from her radio broadcasting days at Kent State University, Natalie contacted a number of stations in nearby Cleveland. She was hired as a receptionist at a disco station and after several months was promoted to office manager. The new job came with the benefit Natalie had been waiting for; she was given air time. "From six A.M. to nine A.M., I did the morning drive news. For the rest of the day I got out the computer billings to advertisers," explains Natalie. She subsequently anchored the news at two bigger Cleveland stations.

In 1980, Natalie was contacted by a station in Rochester, New York, whose new management was interested in hiring talent from major market stations. Natalie had been in Cleveland for over four years and had been thinking of moving on. "I needed to leave because most people in my business remembered where I had started, which can be a disadvantage to moving up. It's the same situation that secretaries who are promoted into management jobs at their companies have; no one can forget that they once made the coffee," explains Natalie.

In one sense, the job move was a step down because it involved similar responsibilities but in a much smaller market. But there were financial incentives and the possibility of using the situation to her future advantage. "As a struggling little fish in a big pond, I pushed myself to the limits to make it. I figured as a big fish in a smaller pond, I could take the time to polish skills I'd already developed," says Natalie.

Always knowing that she would someday leave Rochester, Natalie stayed in town for two years until she was offered a morning news anchor spot at WMET, a big Chicago station. Seven years after landing her first broadcasting job, Natalie feels that she has come into her own, doing what she enjoys for a good station in a major market.

It's not easy to put aside considerations about whether a city in which a good opportunity beckons is one of your top choices. If you've never spent time there, it's difficult to make the decision to take a job offer based on a short visit. When we're in our early twenties, we often think that decisions we make are irrevocable. But as Natalie discovered in her late twenties, nothing is so permanent that it can't be changed. If you've chosen to go to a city for a particular job, as she did, and after a time, you're ready to move on, you can. Still, once you've uprooted and settled in several times in quest of better job opportunities, the prospect of developing a more permanent residence becomes an extremely appealing idea.

When Jan Lewin Walter moved to New York City in 1978, it was her third relocation in seven years. She was a construction manager with the phone company in Columbus, Ohio, and her boss let her know that unless she was willing to move to Cleveland or New York, the chances of her continuing to move up were very slim. "Just a year before, I told the friend I visited in New York that no amount of money could lure me to such a dirty, noisy, rude place," says Jan.

The daughter of an Air Force officer, Jan had moved frequently as a child, although she spent her teenage and college years in the Los Angeles area. After getting a master's degree in education from California State University in Sacramento, she got married. Teaching jobs were hard to come by, but Jan's math background helped her land a job as an engineer with Pacific Telephone. She worked there for three years when an interesting opportunity came up in San Francisco, where the phone company's training center was located.

She worked in San Francisco for almost two years. Then her husband, who had been in veterinary school, got a job offer at

Ohio State University. Ohio Bell assured Jan that they could find a place for her once she arrived. What Jan had loved about San Francisco—its theater and dance, its marvelous topography, its varied ethnic groups—were missing in Columbus, where the main concerns in people's lives were their families, homes, cars and bridge clubs. In the absence of regular evening and weekend entertainment, Jan decided to enroll in a special MBA program offered by the university.

Even after she and her husband got a divorce, Jan decided to stay in Columbus. After having been there several years, she'd developed a network of friends and wasn't eager to start over again. It was only when her boss urged her to consider the promotion in New York with Ohio Bell's parent company, AT&T, that Jan toyed with the idea. Her interview trip in late March gave her a much different impression of New York than she'd gotten on her earlier visit. "My feeling was, if I could handle two cities as drastically different as San Francisco and Columbus, I could certainly deal with New York. I was willing to put in a two-year time commitment, and if it didn't work out, come back to Columbus," says Jan.

In the four years since she moved there, she has become a fan of the Big Apple. Six months after she relocated, she bought a house in a nearby suburb. Within a year, she decided to fulfill a longtime fantasy: learning to horseback ride. She soon began devoting most of her free time to the sport, and became an instructor and a judge. She met the man she subsequently married through a fellow equestrian. Now the owner of two horses, which she keeps stabled in a nearby town, Jan's dream is to own a horse farm.

Both Natalie's and Jan's relocation patterns eventually landed them in big cities where the prospects for their personal and professional lives were full of possibilities. But it's not easy to control the places where you may end up along the way, particularly if, like Jan, you're part of a dual-career couple. Being in a city in which you feel comfortable at the time when your career is beginning to jell unquestionably sets the stage for that place becoming one in which you put down roots.

Proving Your Commitment

In order to achieve a genuine career breakthrough, it's necessary not only to be good at what you do but also to convince others that you enjoy what you do and intend to stick with it. Despite the numbers of women who are flocking into the professions, there are still men and sometimes even female competitors who think women are in for the short rather than the long haul and treat them accordingly.

Chris Schindler* was 26 when she joined the staff of a renowned hospital and research center in New York City. Her husband of two years had been transferred there by his employer, a large oil company. Having answered an ad in *Science* magazine for a position with the medical center, she was disappointed when the job wasn't funded. But the woman who interviewed her thought she was talented and recommended her to a colleague who was forming a new department.

Chris asked for and got a faculty appointment, which put her in a permanent, although not necessary tenured, job track. All went well for two years. Chris, who had grown up on a farm in Pennsylvania, loved the hectic pace of New York City.

When her husband was told he was expected to move back to Los Angeles and then do a stint in Singapore, Chris protested. "I was pregnant with my first child and was just getting established at the medical center. I knew that my career would be washed up if we agreed to the move, which would have been one of many. And my husband's career would suffer if he refused to go where the company wanted him," explains Chris. She urged him to go ahead with his plan to start his own consulting business. Although he hadn't intended to do so for several years, he agreed to change his plans so that she could continue with her career.

Soon thereafter, Chris found herself in the first major show-

*A pseudonym

down in her career. A colleague, whom she had earlier recommended to the chairman of the department as a good addition to the staff, had gone through her research notes (which she did not keep locked up), repeated her experiments and then asked her if they could collaborate on the project. "I told him, 'No,' that I didn't see the advantage of having him join in after I had done all the preliminary work on my own," says Chris. "But he and the other men in the department thought that once my baby was born, I'd be gone. They didn't take me very seriously." Her colleague then went to the chairman, their mutual boss, and told him that he was trying to push Doris along on the project, that although she had great ideas, she was moving too slowly. With his help, he claimed the results could be published much faster. The chairman sided with the young male professor.

Both of them underestimated Chris. Her manner is unassuming and friendly, and she has an endearing Annie Hall speech pattern which is frequently punctuated with giggles. It was not her nature to question people's basic trustworthiness. When it dawned on her that she had become a target of this colleague's overriding ambition to make a name for himself, she reacted by working even harder to prove him wrong—and succeeded. "I had to stick it out, having just convinced my husband to pass up the promotion on the West Coast. It was an added incentive to show them that I was dead serious about my work," recalls Chris. In the months following her daughter's birth, she secretly accelerated her work on the project and submitted it for presentation at a prestigious upcoming scientific meeting. Its acceptance vindicated her of the charge that she was less than totally dedicated to her work.

The most intense part of the crisis lasted for eight or nine months, but her problems didn't end after the presentation. Several of the men, including the one who tried to move in on her project, still shunned her. When she applied to work with a visiting scientist on a project in which they had a mutual interest, he was told by several of her male colleagues that she was impossible to work with. The visiting professor decided to take her on as a collaborator anyway and discovering that that was not the truth, told her that she'd been maligned.

Most women who are subjected to job conditions that limit their opportunities for self-direction or that inject pressures or uncertainties into their work begin to think less favorably of themselves, become suspicious of others and don't operate at their intellectual peak, concludes a study, "Women and Work: The Psychological Effects of Occupational Conditions." When the going got tough, however, Chris refused to let people and events in her work environment stand in the way of her conviction in her work and herself. Like others who were destined for success, she had a gut belief that things would work out in the end.

That is the bottom line in achieving success. There will be those people who may try to shake your faith in yourself or your goals. Whatever it takes to prove your commitment—long hours, extra projects, additional training—is worth the effort so long as it's contributing to your knowledge and experience.

Since the most crucial period in consolidating your career is five to seven years after you enter the field, it's important to pay attention to the timing of events in your personal life. Asking her husband to consider moving up his own career timetable to accommodate hers was a risk that eventually benefited them both. In the eight years since then, her husband's business has become extremely successful, and Chris was named an associate professor in 1981.

12

Making Personal Commitments

〜〜〜〜〜〜〜〜〜〜〜〜〜〜〜〜〜〜〜〜〜〜〜〜〜〜〜〜〜〜〜

MAKING IT BIG in the city has less to do with how successful you are in your career than it does with how satisfied you feel with your life—who your friends are, where you live, whether you're loved.

Many women delay getting involved with people—both men and women—because they are too busy pursuing success to cultivate friends other than ones who can be helpful professionally. One woman interviewed for this book lamented not having accepted more social invitations during the early years of her career. It was only after she achieved many of her goals that it dawned on her that people might perceive her as being self-centered or unsociable. She began spending much more time with friends and interesting people she met—a personal commitment she wishes she had made earlier.

Comfortable living space is another essential ingredient in feeling that you're at home in a city. But because liking where you live involves who you're living with, your finances and familiarity with different neighbors, it's an aspect of city living that doesn't fall into place as quickly as others do. It's not until three to five years after moving to a city that the majority of women are quite or very satisfied with their living situation, according to the results of the Urban Experience Survey. There are two aspects of the housing issue that will very much affect how rooted you feel to a city: One is how frequently you move (the more gypsy-like you are the more transient you'll feel); the second is whether or not you own your own place.

Almost half of the women interviewed for this book have purchased their own place, and the majority of them did so while they were single.

For women who have longstanding love affairs with their adopted city, getting married usually increases their commitment, if only because they're likely to have found someone who shares their interests, many of which are hinged on living in an urban area. And consolidating emotional and financial resources often makes living in the city even more enjoyable than it was before.

The women who felt most comfortable with themselves and their city life-styles were those who had taken the time to build multi-dimensional lives in the city. It wasn't always a planned or conscious process; they simply knew their own minds well enough to go after the things that would make them happy, and took the risks that were necessary to achieve them.

Survey Finding

During which period did you feel you had begun to put down roots in the city?

Less than six months	12%
About a year	25%
Between one and two years	21%
Three to five years	27%
Six to ten years	4%
After ten years	1%
I haven't yet put down roots	10%

What were the main reasons? (check all that apply)

Developed network of friends	66%
Felt established in career	57%
Bought a home	22%
Got married	12%
Had a child	4%

Developing an Extended Family of Friends

I celebrated my twentieth birthday at an outdoor concert in Central Park. Hundreds of thousands of picnickers arranged their suppers on blankets, which were spread over the Sheep Meadow in a crazy quilt pattern. I was on one of them with the one person I had come to know well in my two-and-a-half-month stay in New York. Tom said he couldn't think of a more appropriate place for a young woman from Ohio to spend her birthday than watching a fireworks display as the New York Philharmonic played "The 1812 Overture." He had even thought to bring along a birthday cake of sorts; two Hostess Twinkies, with a candle in each one. I remember how pleased I was that someone had thought to make my birthday a special evening.

Ten years later, I celebrated my thirtieth birthday at a similar outdoor concert in Central Park. Tom was there, as were 30 of my closest friends. My soon-to-be husband, Joe, had organized a gourmet picnic extravaganza. The birthday cake (the three-tiered, blue-iced variety) announced its arrival by calling out in a loud voice: "Ladies and gentlemen. We're gathered here tonight to celebrate Peggy's 'Big three-0.'" The human cake then read a birthday verse and got the several hundred people in the immediate area to join in a chorus of "Happy Birthday." It was one of my most memorable birthday parties.

Having friends to share anniversaries and important moments with is not only critical to our feelings of happiness and well-being; for those who move to cities, it's the most often-mentioned factor in feeling as if they've put down roots in a new city, according to the results of the Urban Experience Survey. A 31-year-old stewardess who lives in Washington, D.C., wrote, "There are times when I yearn for the nuclear family life that is the mainstay of suburbia, but I have acclimated myself to a different environment. Six women and I have formed our own family and even refer to each other as 'Mom,' and collectively call ourselves 'the family.' We're all single career women who are geographically separated from our real families. We spend holidays and birthdays together and are emotionally supportive of one another in affairs of the head, heart and bank account. So there can be a slice of small-town cohesiveness in the urban jungle."

Building a network of friends who become your second family evolves over a period of years. Judging from the results of the Urban Experience Survey, it's not until you've lived in the city for six to ten years that you'll begin feeling very satisfied with the number of people you know and the quality of your relationships with them. That finding confirms what sociologist Claude Fischer, who studied personal networks in cities and towns, discovered—that those who had lived in one place for 11 years or more were mostly likely to have a wide and interactive circle of friends. Contrary to what many people (including some sociologists) believe, those who live in cities have many friends and tend to do many different activities together.

Behavioral scientists have established that people who are happiest and most productive, who like themselves and get along with others aren't always married, but do have a supportive group of friends. Having people to depend on is especially critical if you move to a city that is hours away from your family, whom you depended upon for emotional support in the past.

When Sue Connors decided to leave her hometown of Marinette, Wisconsin, at age 24 to attend art school in Chicago, she wasn't ready to say good-bye to her friends. They were an important part of her life, and she wasn't leaving them so much as she was a place where the possibilities of finding interesting work and eligible men were slim, or so she believed.

During her first year in Chicago, Sue had virtually no social life. Instead of living near school, Sue lived with her aunt and uncle, who were twice her age. She felt conspicuously older than her fellow students, many of whom were recent high school graduates. And she worked part-time in a department store to help cover her tuition and art supplies, which she was paying for herself. "My being shy didn't help, either. I was so lonely that I went home once a month the first year I was there," says Sue. Back home, she could be herself again, laugh with her friends, catch up on recent gossip. "I'll never forget how hard it was for me to get back on the Greyhound bus for the five-hour ride back to Chicago. Sometimes, it was so overwhelming that I felt sick to my stomach," she remembers.

It was after she had been in Chicago for three years that she finally began to feel as if she were going home when she left Marinette. After completing her two-year program, she worked for a sewing machine and fabric store for a year and moved into the apartment of a co-worker. But it wasn't until she got her first art-related job with the American Medical Association, which employs 1,000 people, that she began making friends. "I tried to hang on to my old life and old friends too long. They provided security, and until I opened myself up to finding people to replace them, I felt like a transient," explains Sue.

She was in a close-to-perfect work setting as far as making friends was concerned. She and her fellow designers shared a very large room, just far enough down the hall from their gruff, no-nonsense boss. All of her co-workers were her age, and they often talked about work triumphs and woes over lunch. Sue's trips back home became less frequent, and when she did go, she looked up old friends less often. "Once they realized that I wasn't coming back, they began letting go. I could see, too, that I was living a very different kind of life than were they, which made it impossible to be as close as we once were," says Sue.

Now that she has been in Chicago for 11 years, Sue feels that in addition to her career, her friends are one of the most important influences in her staying there. They're also one of the reasons why it would be hard for her to leave, even if a tempting job opportunity or Mr. Right were to surface in another city. "Sometimes when I'm walking down Michigan Avenue looking up at the skyscrapers, I say to myself, 'Do you believe you live here?' In high school, I could never have imagined living in Chicago, let alone feeling comfortable in a big city like this. The people I've come to know and care for have made that possible."

Having a network of friends and acquaintances is especially important if you're unattached and living alone. I discovered how very true that was when, after having lived with room-mates during my first five years in New York City, I moved into my own place. I needed people whom I felt free to call up and talk to about what had happened at work that day; people whom I wouldn't hesitate to call on the spur of the moment to have drinks or dinner; people who shared my interest in film and other free-time activities. Maintaining this network re-quired much more attention and thought than when I had a built-in set of friends in my roommates.

What also became apparent to me during that time was that some friends (both male and female) let their relationships with their own networks slip when they became romantically involved. That's understandable to some extent, but not when the new person in their life became a deterrent to their con-tinuing to keep up the most important friendships and to seek-ing out new ones. In their book *Brief Encounters,* social scientists Emily Coleman and Betty Edwards describe why we need more than just one important person in our lives: "It is by connecting with different people in different ways and places that new facets of our personality come into play and cause us to grow. You may take the lead when you are with one person, follow when with another; you may be creative with this one, analytical with that. Even when you do the same things with different people, you do them in different ways."

The supportive network that we all need, they say, consists of three concentric circles. The innermost ring consists of a core group of four to seven people with whom you are closest. Other social scientists, including Fischer, have found that hav-ing one or two key allies (outside of a spouse or boyfriend) are what's crucial to feelings of satisfaction and well-being. And during your first year or two in a new city, that may well be the extent of your innermost circle. One of the most difficult as-pects of considering someone you haven't known all that long as part of your closest circle is that unless they're also without long-standing friends in the area, they may not share your perception of the friendship. In order for a person to be consid-ered among one's best friends, it's essential, say Coleman and Edwards, that they understand you and like you for what you are, see you often and be available to you when you need them.

The second circle of friends are those whom you depend on less for support than for enrichment. A friend in this group is more likely to be someone who adds something to your life that your colleagues or friends from your intimate circle do not. You're not likely to see these friends as often as those in your intimate circle, but you are enough a part of one another's lives to meet on a regular basis.

Those who are part of the outer circle are those with whom you're least involved with as far as your time and energy are concerned, but nonetheless people whom you care about. They may be colleagues with whom you once worked, college or high school friends, ex-roommates. They are the kind of people you can depend on for stimulation, advice or favors from time to time.

All the kinds and levels of friendships that are part of one's support network take time to build, particularly if you don't know a soul when you move into town. Keeping that fact in mind is especially important during the first year or two you're in a new city when you may wonder what prompted you to leave behind established friendships. It's not until three to five years after moving into a city that you're likely to be quite or very satisfied with your friends (as were three-fourths of the respondents to the Urban Experience Survey).

Keep in mind, too, that the friends you make early on in your stay may drop out of your network because what you once had in common has disappeared, circumstances have changed, or one or both of you decide to cool off the friendship. Friends can resurface, of course, at different periods in your life. My ex-boyfriend, Tom, who took me to Central Park on my 20th birthday, has never left my life completely, although there were times when other people and changes in our lives came between us. As a writer who has been practicing his craft several years longer than I have, he has always been a trusted critic and inspiration. And during lows in our lives, we have been able to turn to one another for comfort and advice.

Many of the women interviewed for this book mentioned that few of the friends that were a part of their innermost circle five years earlier were still there today. The reason: Their friends had moved out of the city or experienced other major changes in their lives that made them less available. Coleman and Edwards suggest that it's important to ". . . savor short-term relationships because they are the very fabric of our existence." My own experience has been that while short-term relationships are exciting and an important aspect of a growing network, those that span longer periods of time are worth nurturing because they ultimately contribute the most to feeling secure in one's universe.

Buying Your Own Place

- When the building in which Nicole Cunningham had lived for six and a half years was converted to a condominium, she decided to buy her apartment. Because the mortgage and maintenance were more than double the rent she had been paying, it forced her to rethink how she was spending her money. And since the apartment is in the fashionable Back Bay section of Boston, she knew it would be a good long-term investment.
- Marsha Appel decided to buy a condominium in downtown Minneapolis after her roommate moved out of the large one they'd been co-renting. When the bank where she was negotiating a mortgage questioned her salary (which was unquestionably high enough to qualify), Marsha spoke up for herself. If they refused her, she would take the matter further with the loan committee. "Realizing that I wasn't going to let the matter drop if they turned me down worked in my favor," says Marsha.
- After living for five years in the apartment she'd moved to after her divorce, Jessica Woods wanted a change. Knowing that she was going to make Miami her home, she decided to buy a town house with a view of Biscayne Bay. "I had always enjoyed decorating the places I lived in, but once I got something that I knew was mine, I wouldn't have to limit myself to curtains and wallpaper," says Jessica, who was 31 when she bought the town house.

In making their decision to sink their savings into a down payment and make loan commitments, all three women were becoming more attached to the cities in which they lived—not only financially but emotionally. In the Urban Experience Survey, buying a home was the third most often cited explanation of why city women felt they'd begun to put down roots in their communities.

Until recently, very few young single women bought homes of their own. Only a handful of women made enough money to afford one, and if they did, they often had (and sometimes still have) trouble getting a mortgage on their own. It wasn't until the Equal Credit Opportunity Act of 1974 that the practice of requiring a male co-signer for the mortgage was outlawed. Even with financial and legal barriers disappearing, many women put off buying their own place because a first home is thought of as being part of the package that comes with getting married or starting a family.

The idea that buying alone is not a commitment to a single life-style but a smart way to use rent money, invest your earnings and get tax deductions is one that is finding increasing acceptance. In 1981, 10 percent of all residential real estate transactions were made by single women, up four percent from 1976. Roni Haggart was one of those women, and even though she was only 31, it was her second real estate transaction.

"I first thought about buying a place in 1976. I had graduated from law school, was clerking for a judge and had reasonable expectations that my earning curve would go up steadily in the next few years," explains Roni. "My roommate of five years had recently moved out of our apartment to get married, so I was thinking about changing neighborhoods. The man I was dating at the time was the real impetus behind my getting out to see what was available. We looked at several postwar brick town house developments in Virginia, about 10 minutes from downtown Washington, that were being converted to condominiums. We ultimately decided not to buy a place together, and I didn't quite have the money together for a down payment on my own. But I figured if I moved into a rental unit in a nearby development, it would only be a matter of time before it was converted."

Can You Afford to Buy Your Own Home?

Before you start looking at potential places to buy, it's smart to figure out whether your finances will allow it and, if so, what price range you ought to be considering. If the numbers you come up with from the four-step formula below look good, you can begin your search.

1. *Your income and savings.* Generally speaking, most potential home owners cannot afford to buy a home that is more than one and a half times their gross income. If you're making $25,000 a year, for example, you'll want to look in the $37,250 and under range. In addition, you should have the amount of the down payment (10–25% of the price) in savings or be able to borrow it from your family.

2. *Price and desirability.* Knowing what you can afford, investigate whether real estate in your price range is available and desirable. Scan the real estate classifieds (but keep in mind the asking price is usually higher than what the seller will accept), talk to friends who've recently purchased property or to real estate brokers.

3. *Qualifying for a mortgage.* Unless you have a good credit rating, earn a substantial income and have a solid employment history, you probably won't qualify for a loan. Every lending institution has its own formula for determining mortgage eligibility and size. But you can make an estimate of how large a loan you can get by contacting the mortgage department of several banks and asking for their guidelines.

Generally speaking, your mortgage payments plus other housing costs (taxes, maintenance on a condominium or co-op, insurance and utilities) plus payments on already incurred debts and loans cannot exceed more than one-third of your gross salary. If they do, you will have to reduce the amount of your mortgage request.

4. *Tax advantage.* Calculate your deductions (your accountant or banker can assist you). Interest on the mortgage and real estate taxes can be deducted from state and federal forms. Let's say your monthly housing expenses

total $1100, your deductions come to $1,000 (during the first few years, most of your monthly mortgage payments will go toward interest rather than principal), and your income tax bracket is 35%. That means your out-of-pocket expenses will be $750.

Total monthly expenses	$1,100
Deductions times tax bracket	− 350
($1,000 × 35%)	———
Monthly out-of-pocket expenses	$ 750

Compare your monthly out-of-pocket expenses (plus the living space it buys) to your monthly rent and current living space. If it makes financial sense, it's time to begin your house hunt.

Roni's gamble paid off; within a year, the renters were offered discounted prices on their apartments, and she bought hers. Nineteen seventy-seven was the year conversions became the rage in real estate; 50,000 apartments "went condo" that year; the number increased to over one million by 1980, when single women bought one-third of all condominiums, according to a National Association of Realtors survey.

Roni lived in her Virginia town house for almost three years, during which time the value of her place doubled. She was also making a significantly higher salary, having recently become one of five founding partners in a law firm. "I finally decided I wanted to move back inside the District. My main reason for moving out was because I knew I couldn't afford to buy there before. Life outside the city, I discovered, wasn't really for me. Even though Washington's suburbs have many high-rise apartment buildings filled with singles, they're very different from city people, who are more involved with their work, bigger risk-takers and more aggressive in pursuing goals," says Roni.

With the profit she made on her first place, Roni could afford a condominium in the city, where housing prices (coupled with high interest rates) have put home ownership beyond the reach of most singles, and even many couples. A *New York Magazine* article, "Downward Mobility," noted that even two-career professional couples, the crème de la crème of the baby boom generation, were having a tough time scraping together enough cash to make a down payment on a home.

But the dream of owning your own home isn't beyond reach if you're single and earning a good salary, *if* you're willing to consider some unconventional buying arrangements. One trend that is gaining in popularity is co-purchasing a home with one or more other singles. Some condominium developers are designing living space with this growing group of people in mind; there are two equal-size master bedrooms with baths and sometimes even separate living rooms, with only the kitchen being shared space. In a *Wall Street Journal* article, a Southern California developer predicted that 35 percent of the urban new-home market will be made of co-purchasers by 1985.

In older cities where brownstone and town house living is popular, groups of singles sometimes buy an entire building, then divide up the space among them, so that each has a completely separate apartment. A *New York Times* article described how a group of five young professionals, two women and three men, bought a brownstone and renovated it. Originally, the buyers were two groups who both wanted the same brownstone and were brought together by the real estate agent. Splitting the cost five ways gave everyone a financial break, and since two members of one group were architects, redesigning the brownstone (which had been subdivided into 17 units in its boardinghouse days) was a less costly proposition. Each person ended up with a totally renovated floor at a reasonable price.

If you're in a position to buy (that is, you have access to enough money for a 20 percent down payment and a salary that can support monthly payments), there are two caveats to keep in mind when purchasing city real estate. One is to take the time to thoroughly investigate neighborhoods and housing options. That's not so difficult if you've lived in your city for a year or more, but if you're relocating, it's smart to rent first and get to know your way around.

The second rule of thumb is to think twice about moving

into a "changing" neighborhood, where real estate is more affordable for good reason: it's not as safe as an established neighborhood. I was considering buying a co-op in an up-and-coming neighborhood and had just come from visiting one when I was attacked in a subway station. That incident clinched my decision to scratch that neighborhood—and others like it—off my list of possibilities. Unfortunately, I couldn't afford a co-op apartment in a better neighborhood, and I wasn't willing to move to another borough or to the suburbs to find affordable housing. My solution was to buy a single-family home outside of New York as an investment; I'm able to deduct both the interest on my mortgage and depreciation on the house from my taxable income.

Getting Married

Cities have traditionally been and still are places where men and women from different parts of the country meet and marry one another. But one thing has changed dramatically. In the past, getting married didn't strengthen a woman's ties with her life in a city so much as it did her ties to her husband, and where he went, she would follow. Now that women migrate to cities for much the same reasons as men do, getting married has quite a different effect: It strengthens a couple's commitment to that metropolitan area because they *both* have careers at stake.

Getting married came up fourth among the reasons why women felt they were putting down roots in their adopted city, according to the results of the Urban Experience Survey. Why? Because unless you get married within a year or two after your arrival in a city, chances are that other previously mentioned factors—a network of friends, career progress or buying a house or an apartment—will be bigger influences in your feeling comfortable and "at home." But because marriage changes the quality of your life in emotional and material ways, its impact in the "putting down roots" stage can be substantial.

Making Time to Be Together: Tips for Couples

With two demanding careers, separate and mutual friends and personal interests to pursue (the stuff of which many city marriages are made), couples often feel cheated of time together. Putting one or more of the following suggestions into practice is a good investment for any relationship.

1. Establish rituals that give you regular opportunities to talk to one another—weekday breakfasts, after-work runs, going to or from work together.

2. Set aside time that's reserved for the two of you, no matter what potential intrusion may surface. Friday nights and Sunday mornings are popular picks for at-home relaxation.

3. Agree that you'll take weekly turns making a date with one another. Whoever does the inviting selects the plans for the evening, which is an insurance against falling into the rut of just getting a bite to eat or working late simply because you have no specific plans.

4. Make it a point to keep each other up to date on what's happening at work. Sharing successes and disappointments, however small, will help you better understand your partner's moods and vice versa. Listening to your husband's problems and pressures may be fine at times, but don't hesitate to offer advice or suggest strategies when it's appropriate.

5. Develop mutual interests. If you don't already spend time together exercising or playing a sport, pursuing leisure-time activities or increasing your expertise in a particular subject, it's a good idea to explore what new interests you might develop together. It needn't be something that always requires simultaneous participation—the point is to share information, appreciate each other's "finds," and occasionally share the activity or some aspect of it together.

Shortly before her marriage on Valentine's Day in 1978, Ellie Kain and I had a celebratory dinner in a Chinese restaurant in SoHo. Although we had been friends for many years, our paths had not crossed frequently during the last two years since her life revolved around school and the Soho art community, while mine revolved around my magazine job and friends.

I had never met her boyfriend, Bruce Latimer, who had stopped in New York on an extended trip around the world and never went back to his home in Australia. He was an artist, quite well known in Sydney but unknown and untested in the art capital of America. Ellie met him at a gallery opening while she was a graduate student at Pratt Institute, a widely respected art school. Having taught the subject for four years in the greater Boston area, she was eager to find out if she could hold her own in a city where there were a dozen talented designers and artists for every good job.

What sticks in my mind most clearly about that evening was the message Ellie discovered in her fortune cookie, which read: "You will marry your present lover and be happy." It turned out to be a most accurate prediction.

In a city where creating a niche—professionally and socially—is elusive, Ellie and Bruce developed theirs together. Timing had a lot to do with why their marriage plugged them in even further to life in New York. "We had both been in the city about the same length of time and had gotten to know it on our own terms before we met," says Ellie, who was 26 when she relocated to New York. "That gave the relationship the advantage of starting out on equal footing, and we were each able to bring something to it. I had my friends and contacts from school, who were a much more conventional and less professionally established crowd than the people Bruce knew, who were avant-garde artists who congregated in hole-in-the-wall downtown bars. It was a totally new world for someone who had grown up in a comfortable suburb outside of Cleveland; I loved mingling with a much more bohemian set of people than I'd ever known."

The couple lived together in Ellie's small three-room apartment for a year and a half. Then, a combination of circumstances forced them to consider making their relationship more permanent. Bruce's visa expired, and it was uncertain how long he could reasonably expect to stay without running into legal problems. The two were also considering buying into a loft building with a group of other artists so that they could have adequate work space. And they knew that banks would be much more receptive to them if they were an "established" couple. Besides, they were in their late twenties, and getting married seemed like a reasonable proposition for two people who were crazy about one another and had similar life goals.

Their wedding reflected their life-style: After a brief ceremony at City Hall, the two went out to dinner with their immediate families and, later that evening, threw a party in the loft of one of their friends. It looked more like a costume party than a traditional wedding reception with guests, many of whom were musicians and artists, dressed in leather and sequins and tights and red hearts.

"Getting married very definitely was a catalyst in our putting down roots in the city," explains Ellie. "We had talked about spending time in Australia, perhaps even six months in New York and six months in Sydney, but all that changed when we bought a loft." The deal for the cooperative loft building Ellie and Bruce had hoped to buy into with fellow artists fell through, and it was another six months before they found comparable space. With money from their parents and savings of their own, they were able to afford the raw factory space, which in 1978 was still reasonably priced. Unlike many of their friends who slept on mattresses on the floor and used hot plates, they installed a fully-equipped kitchen, built a separate bedroom, sanded their floors and put up new walls. "After putting so much time and money into making it livable, we were reluctant to sublet it during the time we'd be gone. And we no longer had the thousands of dollars that a trip to Australia costs," explains Ellie.

Owning real estate gave them a tangible stake in the city, but other psychological developments, some of which began when they were living with one another, also contributed to Ellie's feeling that she could make a home for herself in the city. One of the most important was the peace of mind that comes with knowing that someone close by cares about your welfare. "When I was living by myself, I often thought about the fact that if something happened to me, that it might be days before it was discovered. The school I was commuting to was in a bad neighborhood, which increased my fears. And unlike an employer who would make inquiries if you didn't show up for work, none of the instructors would do that because it's up to you whether or not you show up for class. There's no question that I was more psychologically comfortable when Bruce moved in because he expected me back at certain hours. And because we usually went out together, my fear of crime diminished, not so much because I could depend on him to defend me, but because a couple is a less attractive target than a woman alone," says Ellie.

Being in a committed relationship also meant there was more time and energy that could be devoted to work instead of the social scene. "When you're single and living in a city there's pressure to date around. But I function much more smoothly when I'm with one man; complicated emotional entanglements might have distracted me from the reason I was in New York in the first place, which was to start a new career," explains Ellie.

During the first few years of their marriage, Ellie began building her reputation as a producer of multi-image slide shows. The combination of her career progress and solidifying her relationship with Bruce was the reason for her feeling strongly that all was well in her world.

Numerous studies have shown that married women are much happier than are single women. Interestingly, however, the results of the Urban Experience Survey indicated that while that was true of women living outside cities, it was not totally true of women living in cities. City women who were single but romantically involved or dating three or four times a week both said they were somewhat happier than were married women. The best explanation for this discrepancy is that for city women, satisfaction with their work is a much bigger component of their happiness than it is for other women. That was evident in another survey finding which showed that city women whose careers had not yet taken off were significantly less happy (whether they were married or single) than were successful women. In other words, a married woman living in the city (unlike her suburban counterpart) isn't likely to say she's very happy unless, as in Ellie's case, the two most important things in her life are going well: her marriage and her work.

Another factor which contributes to the feeling of well-being—whether you can comfortably support yourself—is also enhanced when one gets married. Two people pooling their resources stand a better chance of creating a comfortable lifestyle, particularly in cities, where living expenses are higher. And, as is the case for many couples like Ellie and Bruce, it made buying real estate a feasible option. Two years after renovating their first loft, the couple sold it and reinvested the money in a large loft, which they also renovated.

From the front windows of their new place, they have a view of two of New York City's most famous skyline landmarks— the Empire State Building and the Metropolitan Life Insurance Company. Their present home, which has none of the unfinished corners or undecorated areas that their first loft did, says much about how far they've come since they met six years ago, when all they had were their dreams. "Having each other reinforced our commitment to making it in the city. We've had the luxury to pursue our individual career goals and live comfortably largely because we've had one another," says Ellie.

Stage Five

Moving Out Crossroads

※※※

THERE ARE TWO KINDS of people in this world (for purposes of making a generalization about life-style): city people and everyone else. City people are "choice" addicts; they feel comfortable being surrounded by options in every aspect of their life: entertainment, jobs, friends, fashion, housing, hobbies. Cities are candy stores for choice addicts. A sure test of whether you're a city person is how distressed you feel when faced with the prospect of having to do without things you've grown accustomed to when outside a city environment. (High distress items include a good daily newspaper, fresh croissants or bagels, and foreign films.)

Many city people, particularly women, find themselves at a crossroads when major life changes occur, particularly when they marry and subsequently when they decide to have children. The traditional pattern has been for women to head to the suburbs, which has always been a ghetto of women and children. It's what their husbands want, it's what society has deemed best for the children, it's what city policymakers force upon middle-class families (because of the lack of suitable housing, schools and play areas).

But women who have moved to the cities in the seventies and eighties, most of whom are part of the "me" generation, are less willing to trade in their walking shoes for station wagons, their charming brownstone apartments for a split-level house, their mobility for isolation. They want to stay close to the action, to try to balance motherhood with an exciting career (a much more difficult feat for suburban women). Even those who take time off to raise children feel more connected if they remain in the city where good friends and museums and shopping are a short distance away.

For those women who come to cities only to discover that they can't respond to its idiosyncracies with humor, that its unique visual character is more depressing than inspiring, that its "slice of life" variety of people annoys rather than delights, leaving is inevitable. Disillusionment with a city develops for two reasons. You may have moved to a city whose character was wrong for you from the start, either because you didn't thoroughly investigate it beforehand or because you came to accommodate someone else's dream. Or, even if there was a good match between you and your adopted home, circumstances may have conspired against you and made the transition too difficult a proposition. In either case, trying a different city is probably a better bet than returning to your hometown. Until you've given city living a chance in more desirable circumstances, you probably won't get the urge to make a go of city living out of your system.

Coming to the realization that you're not a city person is another matter altogether. It's a gut feeling that your values, outlook on life and behavior are somehow out of sync with those of city people and that no person or event is likely to change those qualities. Even if you eventually become a city expatriate, you're much better off for having had the experience. Knowing what doesn't make you happy is as important as determining what does. You'll certainly appreciate the place you decide to settle in more since you have the basis to make a comparison. And, just as importantly, you'll have a richer view of life because you've been exposed to ideas, people and ways of living you might otherwise never have experienced firsthand.

The last chapter looks at the options that exist within cities today for women who are at a moving out crossroads and analyzes the personality traits of women who become committed city dwellers.

13

Staying in or Leaving the City

~~~~~~

MOST CITY DWELLERS love to complain about their living conditions. The cost of living is too high. Crime is prevalent, and getting worse. Their apartment is too small for anyone but a dwarf. So why stay in the city? Because the pluses outweigh the minuses. A San Antonio woman who is a free-lance designer of needlework and embroidery and a participant in the Urban Experience Survey sums up the feelings of many city women: "In spite of all the drawbacks of life in a large city, living in one is well worth it. There is a vitality, a stimulation that can't be matched in smaller places. Living here gives me a sense of being in the midst of the creative consciousness of the United States."

Many of the women interviewed for this book described their attachment to their adopted city in love/hate terms. Like any romantic relationship, your feelings about where you're living are bound to vacillate between periods of elation and depression. Perhaps the one big difference between city life and all other kinds is that the highs are higher and the lows lower. Not everyone thrives on this kind of dynamism. Some women function better in a less volatile environment—the kind that suburban and small-town living can provide.

Finding the Right City for You

Just because you're not satisfied with how things are working out (or not working out) in the city in which you've chosen
to live doesn't necessarily mean you should head to the suburbs or beyond. The problem may well be that you're not in the
right city.

Many women don't make a systematic comparison between
a city's advantages and disadvantages and their personal and
professional needs and interests before moving there. It's often
the case that city-bound people go to the nearest big city, one
where they have family or friends or one where they've been
offered a job. Although those reasons may seem legitimate,
they shouldn't be the only considerations in your deciding on
that city. You may find that you don't like the pace and style of
the place, two of the most important ingredients in deciding to
make it your home.

That's exactly what happened to Margaret Wong, who
moved to New York City after graduating from the State University of New York Law School in Buffalo. "I knew job opportunities for lawyers were plentiful there, and besides, I had
relatives with whom I could live in Brooklyn," says Margaret,
who grew up in Hong Kong (living such a sheltered life that
she scarcely understood what big city life was all about). She
did her undergraduate work at two universities, one in Iowa
and one in Illinois, and became accustomed to the pace of life
in college towns.

She had no problems finding a job with a small firm specializing in insurance law. But Margaret was unprepared for
the highly competitive, even cutthroat way that lawyers who
were adversaries treated one another. "During my first few
months on the job, I was taking a deposition from a client,
during which my opposing counsel was present. My adversaries kept interrupting me because they couldn't hear me. I do
speak softly, but they did it to unnerve me so that I couldn't
focus on my line of questioning," explains Margaret. Because
of her lack of experience, she didn't know what to say to put

them in their place. A regular diet of this type of confrontation began wearing on her nerves.

And there were other reasons why she couldn't picture her future in New York. Margaret had dreams of opening up a Chinese restaurant or starting an import business. "I finally decided that I couldn't be one of the best, which is what my standards are, if I were to stay in a large city. As a young Chinese woman, I didn't feel I could effectively compete with much more experienced and financially established business people," explains Margaret, who made her decision to leave six months after arriving.

Because she wanted to learn about finance, Margaret decided to look for a banking position in a smaller city, Cleveland, which is home to many Fortune 500 corporations. "I felt that Cleveland would be more manageable than New York, and once again, I felt comfortable going there because I knew several people who were living there," says Margaret, who got hired as a credit analyst.

Six months after she arrived, Margaret, who was then 26, began scouting out possible locations for her restaurant. She found a vacant storefront in what was then a rundown shopping center in Shaker Heights, which is a posh neighborhood. She struck a deal with the agent who showed it to her; she would sign the $3,000-a-month lease if the company that owned the shopping center would give her money to begin renovating the space. "That was a smart move, but I forgot to do something even more important, which was to get financing to start up the restaurant before I signed the lease," says Margaret.

At the recommendation of several people, she called a wealthy man who owned a lot of property in Shaker Heights to see if he could help her out with the financing; he turned out to be the owner of the shopping center. "He was such a powerful man that the day after I sent him a proposal, his bank called to offer me a loan," says Margaret, who had the nerve to call and ask for his help only because she didn't know how important a man he was and didn't know who else to turn to. "I think he responded because he saw me as young and energetic, and thought I could help turn around business in the shopping center. What he didn't know was that I'd never started a business before and really didn't know what I was doing," says Margaret.

Eight months later, the "Pearl of the Orient" opened for business. Margaret's family—two sisters and a brother—joined her in Cleveland to get the restaurant off the ground, and one of them, Rose, has stayed on to manage it. In the spring of 1982, three years after it opened, the restaurant was featured in a front-page article in the *Cleveland Press*. In the meantime, Margaret, who is now 32, has gone on to establish her own law practice and an import business. "So much of my good fortune has to do with being in the right city. I'm very happy here because my efforts paid off," explains Margaret.

Because Margaret's career interests all revolved around small businesses, moving to a city where there was less competition was an instinctively good decision that paid off. That's not to say she wouldn't have succeeded in an even bigger city, but it may have taken her longer and she may not have been able to divide her efforts among three separate interests.

There is no surefire way to determine which city you're likely to find the most success and satisfaction in. But if you discover after a year of living in a city that it's not what makes you happy, it's smart to consider which other cities may offer what you're looking for. One of the best ways to comparison shop for cities is by using the information in the book *Places Rated Almanac* as a starting point for narrowing down your choices. The book provides detailed facts about nine important aspects of a place: climate and terrain, housing, health care and environment, crime, transportation, education, recreation, the arts and jobs. Once you narrow your selection down to one or more cities, be sure to visit them, not as a tourist, but as someone who is sizing up the living conditions there. Check out neighborhoods you might live in, ride transportation you might be using regularly, talk to people who have moved there from elsewhere to get their impressions of its good and bad points. A decision made after a thorough investigation is much more likely to turn out favorably than is one made quickly and for capricious reasons.

When the "Burbs" Beckon

Even though nearby suburbs are usually safer and offer nicer and more spacious living quarters for lower rents, most single women don't contemplate moving to one unless it is a big singles community. Marriage is the catalyst behind 70 percent of all city-to-suburb moves. There are several reasons why. Finding suitable living space is one. It's often the case that neither person in the couple has an apartment big enough for two people. And even if one of the two of you do, there's the psychological "yours/mine" problem; finding a new space that you've selected jointly is a much more desirable situation.

The older you are when you marry, the better the chances of your wanting—and being able to afford—to buy your own place. Many city couples dismiss the feasibility of doing so in the city simply because they hear that co-op and condo prices are sky-high. Few take the time to compare the financial advantages and disadvantages of urban versus suburban housing options. Slightly more than half of the respondents to the Urban Experience Survey said that the prospect of owning a home and having a backyard would be reason enough for them to consider a move out of the city. Besides real estate reasons, it's socially acceptable (and sometimes even expected) for young couples to disengage themselves from an active social scene and emulate the living style of other married couples.

So off to the suburbs they have gone, that is, until recently. "More and more baby boom couples are deciding to stay in the city," says demographer Larry Long. "They're usually both working professionals who don't want to add commuting time on to already long days, and they can afford to rent, if not buy, nice apartments." Rather than simply acting as "staging areas" where young people could meet and marry, cities are becoming the places where couples can continue enjoying the amenities of urban living.

During the three years that my husband, Joe, and I dated one another, we maintained separate apartments. Mine (a one-bedroom rental in a brownstone) was much less spacious than his one-bedroom co-op in a modern apartment building. We could have lived in his place once we married, but decided that even that wouldn't be enough, considering that I was now working out of home rather than an office. So Joe sold his place, and we reinvested the money in an even larger place. Our "sell/buy" strategy worked out well financially, but we ended up living in my place for two years because it took time to find a "deal" and do major renovation in the apartment (it was advertised in the real estate pages under the title "Buy a Wreck"). But, in the final analysis, the wait was worthwhile; we now have the kind of apartment that makes being at home as desirable an option as going out at night.

Another option, if one of the two of you has a reasonably priced and large enough apartment, is to buy a vacation home for weekend use. The advantage of that in a tight city rental market is that you'll get more total living space for your money by buying outside a metropolitan area and get the tax benefits of being a home owner. You can even amortize your expenses by periodically renting out the house.

Survey Finding

What do you consider to be the biggest drawback of city living?

Cost of living	36%
Crime	19%
Cramped living space	13%
Obstacles to doing outdoor activities	10%
Other	9%
Pollution	6%
Difficulty of keeping a pet	2%
Lack of good public transportation	2%
Difficulty of bringing up children	1%

Children in the City—A Feasible Option?

It's understandable why and how a two-career couple could stay in the city, but what happens when the stork starts winging his way toward your apartment? There's no question that for many couples, that's the turning point in their decision to move out. Just about half of the respondents to the Urban Experience Survey said they would consider moving out of the city in order to raise children. One respondent who lives in Los Angeles commented, "I feel living in a large city takes one away from basic, perhaps old-fashioned priorities such as family. One would rather get away for the weekend than spend it at home, wrapped up in family-oriented activities. I feel children grow up much more status-oriented and a wee bit selfish in the city."

There are other reasons why cities do not enjoy a reputation as being the right kind of environment for children to grow up in, according to a 1979 Louis Harris Poll. Crime, lack of adequate space, inaccessibility of outdoor play areas, and the lack of good public schools (and the expense of private ones) are the most frequently cited reasons why.

Interestingly, married men are usually much more eager than their wives to move to the suburbs, according to several studies. Women are much more reluctant to give up the social, cultural and employment opportunities in the city. Still, many go along with their husband's wishes because they think (or their husbands convince them) that it's the right thing for the children.

"After I got pregnant, my husband suggested we move to the suburbs, but I didn't really want to bring up my child in the comfortable but vacuous environment I had been raised in," says Ilene Gordon Blustein. She and her husband had been living in downtown Chicago for two years in a condominium near the lake. Even when she decided to leave her management consulting job at the same downtown firm where her husband worked for one with a suburban company, she didn't consider moving there simply to be closer to work.

"The suburbs always seemed like a lonely place to me when I was growing up outside of Boston. I remember feeling bored, although as an adolescent, I had no choice but to try to fit in. It wasn't until I went to college at the Massachusetts Institute of Technology in Cambridge that I was exposed to people who had much different upbringings than I did. I loved the diversity of being around foreigners and people who saw things from a much different perspective than I did. It got me hooked on city living," explains Ilene.

Although her husband grew up in a similar comfortable suburban environment, he didn't share her antipathy for the sameness of life there. In fact, he rather liked the idea of being able to sit in his own backyard, rake leaves and shovel snow. "Those activities reminded him of pleasant memories from his childhood, which he thought he could recreate for our child and himself by going back," says Ilene.

And although the major change in his life would have been additional commuting time, Ilene knew the changes in hers would have been much more drastic. She would see much less of her friends, all of whom lived in the city, since her job and her child would keep her in the suburbs. "I enjoy the anonymity of the city, too. No one keeps track of your comings and goings, the way they do in many suburbs," she says.

What makes a big difference in couples like the Blusteins being able to stay in the city is having two good incomes. They could affort a spacious apartment and pay a live-in housekeeper/babysitter. The real financial crunch comes, of course, when a child is ready to go to school, if the parents decide (as many well-educated baby boom parents do) that a private school is the only option.

Ilene's hunches that her husband would be less negatively affected by the move were right. In the studies that examined the differences between families who stayed in the city versus those who headed to the suburbs, the one big change in the lives of fathers who moved was that their commuting time increased, which meant spending significantly less time with their families. Most men felt that the more relaxing atmosphere of the suburbs and the status of owning a home compensated for the decreased time with their families since they were much more satisfied with their new living situations than were their wives.

The reaction of the transplanted city women was much different. Only 14 percent of them felt more positively about the move than did their husbands. The majority felt their options for growth, stimulation and challenge were dramatically reduced. Half felt they suffered from boredom. Compared to city women who also had one or two children, they spent two hours more alone per day. Part of the reason for that statistic might be explained by the fact that city mothers were more likely to continue working after their children were born. But even when suburban mothers wanted to work, there were fewer attractive jobs available to them near their homes. The rate at which suburban jobs have increased outstrips the growth rate of jobs in the city; the catch is that the most desirable jobs, which required a high level of education, were not being created in the suburbs but in the central cities. And most mothers felt that the disadvantages of commuting to the city outweighed the benefits.

Life in the city, on the other hand, isn't idyllic for mothers either, but, according to the study, they feel the benefits outweigh the disadvantages. Two of the biggest complaints were the small size of apartments and the necessity of supervising children closely as a safety measure. The result was that city mothers suffered from a lack of privacy and spent an average of three hours more a day with their children. Still, the women were able to continue their lives in a less disrupted fashion than their suburban sisters.

Even more important, perhaps, is that city mothers (and fathers) felt that their children would grow up richer having spent their childhoods in a culturally, racially and ethnically diverse place. A quarter of both suburban and city parents in the study asserted that city children were more aware, more sophisticated, and more socially assertive and outgoing than were suburban children. One mother who returned to the city after trying suburban living commented, "The only thing suburban children know how to do is ride their bikes. They have never been to a museum. Their vocabulary is nothing like our children's, who are no geniuses." Over and over again, city parents mentioned how important they felt it was for their children to come into frequent contact with different kinds of people.

All of Chris Schindler's four daughters, for example, have gone to Jewish nursery school, even though she was raised Protestant and her husband is Chinese. "It was an early and good exposure for them and, on the practical side, it was located just across the street," says Chris. She and her husband also decided to enroll one of their school-age daughters in a good public city school (an option if you're willing to contribute time and money for extra programs) and send another to a church-affiliated private school.

When Chris was pregnant with her first child, her husband and she dutifully got on a train and went to the suburbs outside New York City to look at single-family homes. When the train taking them back to the city was late in arriving, they vowed they'd never become commuters. After the arrival of their second child, they left their modest two-bedroom apartment and bought a town house in one of Manhattan's then less desirable neighborhoods. But it was affordable, and most important, near to the hospital where Chris worked. "I'm literally five minutes away if I'm really needed, but the housekeeper we had for nine years kept order until I got home from work," explains Chris.

City mothers have developed some very effective coping strategies that make raising children in an urban setting more manageable. One of the most important ones, according to the study, was cooperative child-care arrangements. The most highly organized type was a play group in which four to ten mothers took turns watching children for a few hours each weekday. Sixty percent of the mothers who had participated in such an arrangement felt that it was beneficial to them and their children. They felt it compensated for the absence of a backyard and alleviated some of the constant supervision problems implicit in high-rise living. For play groups to function effectively, it was important for the mothers to have similar values in child-rearing, according to participants.

A second issue was dividing up the space for children and adults within the apartment. There is no ideal solution when the apartment has only two bedrooms, living room and kitchen; each family has its own preferences about whether there ought to be public or private space. But, generally speaking, life was calmer when everyone understood what their territory was and the rules were enforced.

The third coping strategy released some of the tension that inevitably built up from having to share a small amount of space, namely, taking breaks from the city. Seventy-three percent of the urban couples surveyed owned or rented a home in the country, at least during summers, or regularly visited parents or friends who did. Over half of them said this kind of outlet was important in relieving the stress of living in the city.

Determining Whether You're a City Person

Whether you're currently at a crossroads in terms of a decision to stay or leave or will be at a future point in time, the bottom line is whether you and city life are simpatico.

If, when you first moved to your city, you didn't sense its magic, you'll probably never fall under its spell. There's no question that city living is full of hassles, and unless you become hooked on its more positive aspects, you'll want to head to less stressful surroundings. Whether or not you fall in love with city living also depends on your personality. Your tolerance level may be lower and your sensibilities greater than the thresholds required for feeling comfortable in an urban setting.

If you're infatuated with the idea of big city living, however, the only way to find out for sure whether it's for you is to give it a try. One respondent to the Urban Experience Survey who grew up in Calexico on the Baja, California-Mexican border, described why she was glad she did just that: "After graduating from the University of San Diego, I moved to Los Angeles to seek the big city life—action and adventure. Well, it can swallow you up. It's easy to feel like you're just another bug among the skyscrapers. I went back to my little-big hometown and found that that's where I felt most happy. I ride my bike to work and wave to neighbors. But the only way to really know for sure that you're not cut out for big city life is to reach out and experience it."

Like three-fourths of the women who moved to cities, however, this respondent reported that living there made her feel more independent. And that's not the only positive effect that city living can have on you. More than half of the women surveyed said they felt more sophisticated, more than a third felt more tolerant and 11 percent felt more humane.

Are You a City Person?

Beneath the exterior of many a transplanted country bumpkin or suburban expatriate lurks the soul of a city-ophile. Until you've experienced city living for at least a year, however, you won't know whether your attraction to the city was infatuation or true love. How you feel about the following aspects of city living is one way to determine whether your stay will be temporary or long term. For each numbered item, select the answer that best reflects your feelings.

1. Leisure-time activities
   a. I tend to do the same activities all the time.
   b. I enjoy having so many options.
   c. I have little or no interest in activities unique to a city.
2. The fast pace
   a. It gets me down every so often.
   b. I find it stimulating most of the time.
   c. It's too hectic for my taste.
3. The variety of people
   a. Doesn't faze me one way or the other.
   b. It's what makes the city interesting.
   c. Their behavior often frightens me or puts me off.
4. The threat of crime
   a. I try to ignore it, but it sometimes affects my behavior.

    b. I wish it didn't exist, but since it does, I've learned to live with it.

    c. It keeps me from living the way I'd like to.

5. Men

    a. They're no better or worse than other men I've dated.

    b. On the whole, they're more exciting and interesting than other men I've dated.

    c. Most city men I've dated don't share my values and goals.

6. Opportunities for career satisfaction and success

    a. It would be hard to find opportunities as good as those here.

    b. I couldn't get paid or paid as much to do the kind of work I do in the city.

    c. I'd have equally good or even better chances in a less competitive environment.

7. Crowds and traffic congestion

    a. I don't like either and try to avoid them whenever possible.

    b. I maneuver through them as well as I can.

    c. I get annoyed and agitated.

8. Friendships

    a. I've met interesting people and have a few good friends in the city.

    b. Most of my good friends are people I've met since moving here.

    c. My best friends are people who live elsewhere.

9. Living in a small (or dark or rundown) space

    a. I spend more time out because it doesn't feel like home.

    b. I can live with it for the time being.

    c. I often think I can't stand it a day longer.

Now, the scoring: "a" answers count 1 point; "b" answers count 2 points; "c" answers count 0. Tally your points. If you scored:

    14–18 points   You're a confirmed city lover, who will undoubtedly enjoy a long stay in your adopted home.

| 6–13 points | The verdict is not yet in in your case, but chances are good you'll eventually leave because your commitment is not strong. |
| 0–5 points | Pack your bags and catch the next plane to Sheboygan. |

What kind of person is cut out for city living? Someone who has always considered herself a little different from her peers and the people where she grew up. Most of the women interviewed for this book felt that they were the "oddballs" in their family, the nonconformists among their peers. It was usually in college that they discovered how well they could compete among others their age. Most were not interested in getting married right after college, let alone starting a family. For them, moving to a city where there were new frontiers to be explored and conquered was the only interesting option available.

If there was one personality trait they all shared, it was that they were not quitters. Determination is a quality acquired early in life, and it is a necessity when you're making a transition from a comfortable, dependent life into a city where it's up to you to make it. This group of city women had their share of good and bad breaks; but their success lies not so much in luck as it does with recognizing and taking advantage of opportunities that came their way. They also have the common view that no matter what happens in between, everything will turn out all right in the end.

Five years after the most depressing time I spent in the city (no job, lousy apartment, stormy love life), my hometown newspaper ran a story in its life-style section entitled, "From Small Town to Big Town Via the Glamour Route: Peggy Schmidt Tackles New York Living." It made me feel like a local celebrity, mentioning that I had found time to relax at my parents' home in between television and radio appearances I was doing in nearby Cleveland in connection with my job as an editor at *Glamour* magazine. More importantly, it made me realize how much richer my life was as a result of having stuck it out through the bad times. I knew that no matter what happened in the future, I would never be content living in a place that didn't offer me the challenges that a big city such as New York does.

Even though I've known Manhattan for eleven years, I still often feel as if I'm in my own movie. The sights and sounds and smells that surround me, even in the course of everyday routines, excite me—the sight of the northern skyline of midtown shimmering silver in the morning sun as I jog around the reservoir in Central Park; the mimes, chamber music quartets and tap dancers I watch as I saunter down Columbus Avenue in the twilight of a summer's evening; the sense of purpose and importance that artists with their portfolios and business people with their briefcases project as I pass them hurrying down Madison Avenue on my way to lunch with an editor. If I didn't make my living as a writer, I would be tempted to become a tour guide—the attractions of the city are that appealing and seemingly limitless, even to the dedicated explorer.

I'm not the only one who is having a love affair with her city. Everywhere I traveled, I discovered that the women I interviewed shared similar sentiments about their adopted homes, whether they lived in a condominium overlooking Miami's Biscayne Bay, in a Victorian house on a hilly San Francisco street or a town house in a historic district in the nation's capital. I think it's no coincidence that one of the most-often heard tunes in recent times is a love song to a city—"New York, New York," which was made popular by Liza Minnelli. The lyrics never fail to make me want to tell every woman who is struggling to make it big in the city, "It's true. I'm making it happen in my own life in New York, and you can do it, too, in any city. Even if you don't get everything you want, you'll have the satisfaction of knowing that you've tried, and eventually, the recognition that what seemed like hard times were the best times of your life."

Sources

~~~~~~

Introduction

"America Falls in Love with Its Cities—Again," by Horace Sutton, *Saturday Review*, September 8, 1978.

"Demographic, Social and Economic Profiles of States: Spring 1976," *Population Characteristics*, Series P–20, No. 334, U.S. Department of Commerce, Bureau of the Census, January 1979.

"Gentrification: The Manhattan Story," by Emanuel Tobier, *New York Affairs*, Volume III, 1979.

"Geographical Mobility: March 1975 to March 1980," *Population Characteristics*, Series P–20, No. 36B, U.S. Department of Commerce, Bureau of the Census.

"Inner City Lures Young, Affluent," by Charles A. Krause and Joseph D. Whitaker, *The Washington Post*, May 29, 1977.

"New Estimates of Migration Expectancy in the United States," by Larry H. Long, *Journal of the American Statistical Association*, Volume 68, Number 341, pp. 37–43, March 1973.

"New York Still Beckons the Nation's Young," *The New York Times*, May 11, 1982.

"Population Redistribution in the United States in the 1970's," by Brian J. L. Berry and Donald C. Dahmann, National Academy of Sciences, Washington, D.C. 1977.

"The Limits of Gentrification," by Peter D. Salins, *New York Affairs*, Volume III, 1979.

"The New Elite and an Urban Renaissance," by Blake Fleetwood, *The New York Times Magazine*, January 14, 1979.

"Women in the Urban Environment," by Gerda R. Wekerle, *Signs*, Volume 5, Number 3 Supplement, Spring, 1980.

Stage One—Moving In

Chapter 1—Making the Decision to Move

"TESTING THE WATERS"

"Who Can Save the City?" (1) by Eli Ginzberg and (2) by Karen Gerard and Mary McCormick, *Across the Board*, April, 1978

Statistics obtained from: American Assembly of Collegiate Schools of Business, The American Medical Association, Society for Women Engineers and The American Bar Association.

"The Service Sector of the U.S. Economy," by Eli Ginzberg and George J. Vojta, *Scientific American*, Volume 244, Number 3, March, 1981.

"The Chosen Apple: Young Suburban Migrants to New York City," by Sylvia F. Fava and Judith DeSena, *The Big Apple Sliced: Sociological Studies of New York*, J. F. Bergin Publishers, Inc., 1983.

"ESCAPING TO A CITY"

Pathfinders, by Gail Sheehy, William Morrow & Co., 1981.

Chapter 2—Landing a Job

"TOP TEN CITIES FOR ARTISTS"

"Where Artists Live: 1970," National Endowment for the Arts, Research Division Report #5, October, 1977.

"TEMP WORK TO TIDE YOU OVER"

"'Temp' Work Becomes Full-time Way of Life," by Andree Brooks, *The New York Times*, Careers '83, October 17, 1982.

Chapter 3—Finding a Place to Call Home

"WHEN SHOULD YOU LIVE ALONE?"

"Costs Force Life of Compromise for Apartment Dwellers in City," by Robin Herman, *The New York Times*, January 22, 1980.

"THE ART OF APARTMENT HUNTING"

"Wise Rental Practices," U.S. Department of Housing and Urban Development, February, 1980.

The Newcomer's Handbook for New York City, by Jennifer Cecil, TLC & Co., Publishers, 313 West 4th Street, New York City 10014, 1982.

"Graduates' Guide to Apartment Hunting," by Deirdre Carmody, *The New York Times*, April 25, 1982.

Stage Two—Shedding Your Stranger Status

Chapter 4—Adjusting to Life in the City

"GETTING AROUND"

"Perceived Safety and Security in Transportation Systems as Determined by the Gender of the Traveler," by Larry Richards, et al., and "The Transportation Implications of Women's Fear of Assault," by Frieda Klein (an oral presentation), *Women's Travel Issues; Research Needs and Priorities*, Conference Proceedings and Papers, U.S. Department of Transportation, 1978.

"Bumper Rapists," by Lloyd Shearer, in *Parade Magazine*'s "Intelligence Report," March 14, 1982.

"ENVIRONMENTAL TRADE-OFFS"

So Human an Animal, by Rene Dubos, Charles Scribner's Sons, 1968.

"Noise: The Stress You Can Hear," by David Martindale, *Glamour*, May 1978.

"Headphone Ban," *The New York Times*, October 3, 1982.

"THE BEHAVIOR OF CITY FOLKS"

"The Experience of Living in Cities: A Psychological Analysis," by Stanley Milgram, and "Bystander 'Apathy,'" by Bibb Latane and John M. Darley, *Urbanman, The Psychology of Urban Survival*, Macmillan Publishing Co., Inc., 1973.

"DEVELOPING SOPHISTICATION"

"Taking a Sounding," by Deborah Blumenthal, *The New York Times Magazine*, August 15, 1982.

Chapter 5—Connecting with People

Loneliness: The Experience of Emotional and Social Isolation by Robert S. Weiss, The MIT Press, 1975.

"Loneliness in Two Northeastern Cities," by Carin M. Rubenstein and Phillip Shaver, *The Anatomy of Loneliness*, International Universities Press, 1980.

"HOW TO BEGIN BUILDING A NEW NETWORK"

To Dwell Among Friends: Personal Networks in Town and City, by Claude S. Fischer, The University of Chicago Press, 1982.

"Alumni Lead Renaissance of Old Clubs," *The New York Times*, November 3, 1981.

"Owning a Pet Can Have Therapeutic Value," by Jane E. Brody, *The New York Times*, August 11, 1982.

"Our Pets, Ourselves," by Patricia Curtis, *Psychology Today*, August 1982.

"MEETING INTERESTING MEN"

Singles: The New Americans by Jacqueline Simenauer and David Carroll, Simon and Schuster, 1982.

"FINDING PEOPLE LIKE OURSELVES"

The Nine Nations of North America by Joel Garreau, Avon Books, 1981.

Stage Three—Making a Go of It

Chapter 7—Pursuing Your Career Dream

"THE ATTRACTION—AND PITFALLS—OF BEING DEDICATED TO YOUR JOB"

Stress Without Distress by Hans Selye, Lippincott Co., 1979.

"Stress in the Workplace," by Alice Diamond & Sandra Kirinyer, *Human Ecology Forum*, Winter, 1982.

"LEARNING TO COMPETE"

"The Job Outlook for College Graduates During the 1980's," by Jon Sargent, *Occupational Outlook Quarterly*, Volume 26, #2, Summer, 1982.

Actors Equity figures from: "Broadway's Tough Side: Closing on Opening Night," by John Corry, *The New York Times*, November 10, 1981.

"TOP CITIES FOR AMBITIOUS WOMEN"

"Minorities & Women in Private Industry, 1979 Report," *U.S. Equal Employment Opportunity Commission*, Volume 2, September, 1981.

Chapter 8—Looking for Love

Great Expectations by Landon Y. Jones, Coward, McCann & Geoghegan, Inc., 1980.

"THE LONELINESS OF EMOTIONAL ISOLATION"

In Search of Intimacy by Carin Rubinstein, Ph.D., and Phillip Shaver, Ph.D., Delacorte, 1982.

Loneliness by Robert S. Weiss (see full reference under Chapter 5).

Figures obtained from: "Where Are the Men for the Women at the Top?" by Christine Doudna with Fern McBride, *Savvy*, February 1980.

"Where Have All the 'Good' Men Gone?"

"Hard Hearts," by Kathy Koch, *The Washington Post Magazine*, February 14, 1982.

Ratio of men to women obtained from: Census of Population and Housing, Bureau of the Census, 1980.

Percentage of homosexual men in San Francisco obtained from: *To Dwell Among Friends* (see full reference, Chapter 5).

"Relationship Roadblocks"

"Why Should a Woman Be More Like a Man?" by Carol Gilligan, *Psychology Today*, June, 1982.

Great Expectations (see full reference above)

"Ambitious Men—Can You Afford One?" by Jane Adams, *Self*, February 1982.

"Commitmentphobia," by Maxine Schnall, *Savvy*, May 1981.

"The Good News: The last expert word on what it means to be single," by Linda Wolfe, *New York Magazine*, January 4, 1982.

Chapter 9—Living with the Fear and Threat of Crime

"The Most Common City Crimes"

"Crime in the United States," *Uniform Crime Reports*, U.S. Department of Justice, August 26, 1982.

"Crime: Safe and Dangerous Places," *Places Rated Almanac*, by Richard Boyer & David Savageau, Rand McNally & Co., 1981.

"DEVELOPING STREET SMARTS"

Survival, by Hugh C. McDonald, Ballantine Books, 1982.

"Perceived Safety and Security in Transportation Systems" (see full reference, Chapter 4).

"PROTECTING YOURSELF INSIDE YOUR HOME"

Survival (see full reference above)

"LIVING WITH THE FEAR OF CRIME"

"The Figgie Report on Fear of Crime: America Afraid," sponsored by A-T-O Inc., 1980.

"Ribicoff Niece Slain in Robbery at Coast Restaurant," *The New York Times*, November 14, 1980.

"Crime, Women, and the Quality of Urban Life," by Margaret T. Gordon, et al., *Signs* (Journal of Women in Culture and Society), Volume 5, Number 3, Spring, 1980.

Stage Four—Putting Down Roots

Chapter 10—Coping with Crisis

Passages, by Gail Sheehy, E. P. Dutton, Inc., 1974.

"WHERE TO GO FOR PERSONAL COUNSELING"

"Therapy and Therapists: Making a Choice," by Patricia Paper-now, *The New York Women's Yellow Pages.*

Chapter 11—Consolidating Your Career

"The Success Capital of America," by Chris Welles, *Esquire,* July 1982.

"PROVING YOUR COMMITMENT"

"Women and Work: The Psychological Effects of Occupational Conditions," by Joanne Miller, et al., *American Journal of Sociology,* Volume 85, No. 1.

Chapter 12—Making Personal Commitments

"DEVELOPING AN EXTENDED FAMILY OF FRIENDS"

To Dwell Among Friends (see full reference, Chapter 5)

Brief Encounters by Emily Coleman and Betty Edwards, Doubleday, 1979.

"Community Attachment in Mass Society," by John D. Kasarda and Morris Janowitz, *American Sociological Review,* Volume 39, June, 1974.

"BUYING YOUR OWN PLACE"

"Population Redistribution and Changes in Housing Tenure Status in The United States," *Annual Housing Survey Studies,* No. 4, U.S. Department of Housing and Urban Development, February, 1980.

"Women in the Mortgage Market," U.S. Department of Housing and Urban Development, March, 1976.

"Downward Mobility," *New York Magazine,* August 16, 1982.

"Get a Piece of the Hottest American Dream—Not Sex, Real Estate," by Landon Y. Jones, *Self,* February 1982.

"80's Brownstoning: Divide and Conquer," by Carol Vogel, *The New York Times,* May 27, 1981.

"GETTING MARRIED"

The Sense of Well-Being in America, by Angus Campbell, McGraw-Hill Book Company, 1981.

Stage Five—Moving Out Crossroads

Chapter 13—Staying In or Leaving the City

"WHEN THE 'BURBS' BECKON"

"Reasons for Moves Out of and into Large Cities," by John L. Goodman, Jr., *American Planning Association Journal,* October, 1979.

"Back to the Countryside and Back to the City in the Same Decade," by Larry H. Long, *Back to the City: Issues in Neighborhood Renovation,* Pergamon Press, 1980.

"Survey of Citizen Views of Urban Life," Louis Harris & Associates, May, 1978.

"The Middle Income Family's Experience in an Urban Highrise Complex and the Suburban Single-family Home," by Elizabeth Mackintosh, et al., Research Report, Center for Human Environments, City University of New York, Graduate Center, 1977.

"A Woman's Place Is in the City," by Gerda R. Wekerle, Lincoln Institute of Land Policy, *Land Policy Roundtable Basic Concept Series,* Number 102, 1979.

Environmental Choice, Human Behavior, and Residential Satisfaction, by William Michelson, Oxford University Press, 1977.

Notes on the
Urban Experience Survey

〰〰〰〰〰〰〰〰〰〰〰〰〰〰〰〰〰〰〰〰〰〰〰〰〰〰〰〰〰〰〰〰

A 69-item questionnaire was sent to *Mademoiselle*'s Career Marketing Board in August 1982. The survey was completed by over 500 board members, 323 of whom live in a city. One hundred forty-four respondents had moved to a city when they were 18 or older. Michael Lenauer of Chilmark Research Associates helped design the survey and computer-tabulated the results.

Demographics of Board Members who participated:

AGE	
18–23	8%
24–28	34%
29–32	36%
33–35	15%
Over 36	6%

MARITAL STATUS

Single	29%
Married	33%
Separated or Divorced	12%
Remarried	3%

CHILDREN

Yes	16%
No	84%

RACE

White	88%
Black	11%
Other	1%

OCCUPATIONAL STATUS

Work full-time	86%
Work part-time	12%
Unemployed or a student	2%

SALARY

Less than $8,000	3%
$8,000–10,999	6%
$11,000–15,999	23%
$16,000–20,999	20%
$21,000–25,999	18%
$26,000–30,000	13%
Over $30,000	19%

TYPE OF JOB

Managerial	27%
Professional	47%
Technical	2%
Office/clerical	14%
Other	10%

Epilogue

※※※※※※※※※※※※※※※※※※※※※※※※※※※※※※※※※※※※

Since the format of this book did not always allow me to tell the entire story of the women featured in it, I have included this section to bring readers up to date on each interviewee, with the exception of those who used pseudonyms.

MARSHA APPEL, 32, is communications manager for business development at Control Data Corporation headquarters in Minneapolis. After working as a business reporter for the *St. Paul Dispatch*, she became the assistant managing editor of *Corporate Report*, and served as editor of *Twin Cities Woman* for three years. A native of Rock Rapids, Iowa, Marsha has lived in the Minneapolis–St. Paul area for 13 years.

GIDDY (GERTRUDE) BANCROFT, 27, works as an editor with the First Boston Corporation. After graduating from Harvard University in 1978, she joined the staff of *Glamour* magazine for two years. She then did corporate relations work for Barclay's Bank. In early 1983, she moved out of the apartment she shared with three roommates to live nearer her boyfriend.

ILENE GORDON BLUSTEIN, 29, is Director of Strategic Planning at Tenneco Packaging Corporation of America. She is an alumna of the Massachusetts Institute of Technology, where she earned her undergraduate degree in mathematics, and an M.S. from the Sloan School of Management. In 1976, she began working as a management consultant for the Boston Consulting Group, first in Boston, then for a year in London. She and her husband, Bram, were married in 1979 and moved to Chicago that same year. Before joining Tenneco, Ilene worked for the Sigrude Corporation. She grew up in Newton, a suburb of Boston.

JANIS CARR, 31, has been pursuing an acting career in Chicago for eight years. She has performed as a comedienne in an acting troupe and worked as a teacher and performer for the Chicago Council of Fine Arts. Her latest role was in the political satire, "We Won't Pay, We Won't Pay," at the Wisdom Bridge Theater.

JILL COCHRANE, 35, is a marketing representative for Video Net, a video teleconferencing firm. An alumna of the University of Massachusetts at Amherst, she also has a master's degree in organizational behavior and management. She was director of student activities at her alma mater, a conference organizer for the Young Presidents Organization and director of conferences and special events for the American Management Associations.

SUE CONNORS, 37, is a graphics coordinator with the American Medical Record Association in Chicago. In her job, she is responsible for all graphics for the Association's magazine and all promotional materials. After graduating from the American Academy of Art in 1972, Sue started her career as a keyliner. A native of Marinette, Wisconsin, she has lived in Chicago for 12 years.

JEFFRY CULBRETH, 28, is assistant to television personality Gene Shalit. Her job responsibilities include booking talent, researching the people Mr. Shalit interviews and scheduling screenings. Jeffry, who has lived in New York City for six years, married Tom (the man she fell in love with soon after arriving) in January 1983.

JENNIFER CULBRETH, 24, is an assistant in *Seventeen* magazine's fashion department. She moved into her own apartment in mid-1982, a year and a half after moving to New York City.

JUDSEN CULBRETH, 32, is an editor at *Redbook*. She began her career at *Seventeen* magazine in 1972, after graduating from the University of Alabama in Mobile. Before moving into her current job, Judsen worked as an editor at *Ladies' Home Journal* and at *Mademoiselle*. In 1979 she married her college boyfriend, Mark. They live in New York City with their two-year-old daughter, Brett.

CAROLINE DAVENPORT, 25, is a strategy analyst with Salomon Brothers. A 1978 graduate of Colgate University, Caroline has been published in major business journals.

PENNY FARTHING is senior counsel for the American Insurance Association in Washington, D.C. After graduating from Indiana Law School in 1970, Penny worked as an attorney with the Federal Communications Commission for two years. She was consumer affairs counsel with the American Retail Federation, congressional liaison for the Federal Trade Commission and director of legislation for the Food, Safety and Quality Service USDA. She grew up in Kennard, Indiana.

ANGELA FOWLER is an assistant manager in a retail store where she sells reproductions of art work and cultivates corporate clients. A native of Katonah, New York, Angela graduated from Boston University in 1978.

NIMA GRISSOM, 31, finished her surgical residency in June 1983, at a San Francisco hospital. She got her undergraduate degree from Trinity University (in San Antonio) and her M.D. from the University of San Antonio Medical School in 1978. She remarried in 1982. Nima is now in a private general surgical practice.

Elizabeth Haas, 27, is a consultant with McKinsey & Company, Inc., in Cleveland. Her job is to assist top management executives of businesses, governments and other organizations to refine goals, plan strategies and solve manufacturing management problems. A native of West Lafayette, Indiana, Elizabeth received her M.S. and Ph.D. from the Massachusetts Institute of Technology.

Roni (Veronica) Haggart, 33, was named a U.S. International Trade Commissioner by President Reagan in early 1982. Before becoming a member of the seven-member Commission, Roni was a senior and founding partner in the law firm of Heron, Haggart, Ford, Burchette & Ruckert. A graduate of the University of Nebraska, Roni received her J.D. from Georgetown University Law Center in 1976. She is the fourth generation of lawyers in her family, who come from St. Paul, Nebraska.

Susan Hattan, 32, is senior legislative assistant to Senator Nancy Kassebaum. A native of Concordia, Kansas, Susan graduated from Washburn University in 1973. She earned a master's degree in American politics at American University while working full-time as a legislative aide. She worked as a policy analyst at the U.S. Department of Agriculture before moving into her present position.

Bekah Herring, 26, is a Ford Model and student at New York University in Manhattan. Her photographs have appeared in *Glamour, Mademoiselle* and *Cosmopolitan* and in ads for Clairol, Avon and Almay. A native of Goldsboro, North Carolina, Bekah has lived in New York City for six years.

Melissa Howard, 29, is Director of Corporate Underwriting at WGBH-TV, the public broadcasting station in Boston. She grew up in a suburb of Cincinnati and graduated from the University of Miami in Oxford, Ohio, in 1977. She has been active in many political campaigns and is national committeewoman of the executive board of the Young Democrats of Massachusetts.

ELLIE KAIN, 32, is a producer and sales representative with Spindler Productions, a multi-media production company in New York City. After graduating from the University of Cincinnati in 1972, Ellie taught art in Massachusetts for five years before coming to New York. She grew up in Beachwood, Ohio.

NANCY KELLEY, 39, is marketing director of Sentinel Enterprises, Inc., in Miami. Raised in Queens, Nancy got her undergraduate degree from Queens College and a master's degree in painting from Marywood College in 1975. After a 10-year teaching career, Nancy switched fields and began selling store fixtures. She moved to Miami in 1980, and lives there with her son.

MARY ALICE KELLOGG, 35, is a self-employed writer and lecturer in New York City. After graduating from the University of Arizona in 1970, she moved to New York City, where she began her career at *Newsweek*. As a correspondent for that magazine, she lived in Chicago and San Francisco before returning to New York in 1977. She was an on-camera reporter for WCBS-TV, a senior editor at *Parade* magazine and is the author of *Fast Track,* a nonfiction book.

CONNIE LaPOINTE, 31, is director of the New England Governors' Conference, Inc. in Boston. A 1974 alumna of Emmanuel College, Connie received her master's degree in public administration from Northeastern University in 1977. She has been an aide to Boston Mayor Kevin White, Governor Joseph Brennan of Maine (whose campaign she managed) and Senator George J. Mitchell of Maine. Connie has coordinated international energy conferences and was elected treasurer of the Massachusetts Women's Lobby. Her hometown is Westbrook, Maine.

SUZANNE LASKY is host and producer of *Kaleidoscope,* a talk show on WCKT-TV in Miami. She graduated from Queens College and then did graduate work at Hunter College. After a brief teaching career in Queens, Suzanne moved with her husband to Miami in 1969. Suzanne got her start in television as a free-lance researcher on a documentary for a Miami station. Before moving into her present position, she was public service manager at the station. Suzanne grew up in Oceanside, New York.

VICKI MADARA, 29, is a designer with the Architects Collaborative. After graduating from the Moore School of Art in Philadelphia in 1975, Vicki moved to Boston with her husband. She has completed major space planning projects for Wang Laboratories and GSIS National Headquarters. Vicki is an instructor at the New England School of Art and Design.

ROSEMARY ANNE McCARNEY, 29, is an associate with Squire, Sanders & Dempsey in Cleveland, Ohio. She moved there in 1979 when she was offered the job of coordinator of the Canada-U.S. Law Institute and an assistant professorship at Case Western Reserve University. She worked in those two capacities for three years, during which time she also earned her M.B.A.

ELLEN MacDONALD, 33, is a partner with a Toronto law firm, Stapells & Sewell. After graduating from McGill University's law school in 1974, Ellen did a clerkship in Toronto, where she eventually built her own private practice, specializing in marital contracts. She got married in late 1982.

SHERYL LEE RALPH, 26, is starring in the Broadway show *Dreamgirls*. A 1975 graduate of Rutgers University, Sheryl has made numerous television guest appearances and had a role in the film *A Piece of the Action*. She also had a leading role in the Broadway musical *Reggae*. She grew up in Hempstead, New York, and now lives in Manhattan.

KATHY RASENBERGER, 27, is regional sales manager for four major cable trade publications in New York City. She grew up in the Washington, D.C., area and graduated from Harvard University in 1978.

CYNTHIA (CINDY) ROOT, 31, is head of the U.S. Department of Health and Human Services health legislation office. A 1973 graduate of the University of Arizona, Cindy grew up in El Paso. Washington, D.C., has been her home for nine-and-a-half years.

DEBORAH RUBIN, 35, recently sold the company she founded, City Nights Publishing, Inc., and is now involved in a new business with her husband. She grew up in Vancouver, Canada, and worked as an airline stewardess, yoga teacher and waitress before moving to Toronto in 1975.

ANN SHEETS, 30, is studying to be a paralegal secretary in New London, Connecticut. She decided to return to her hometown after living in the Washington, D.C., area for three and a half years.

SUSAN SHEETS, 30, is office manager and administrative assistant to the President of Aérospatiale, Inc. Before moving to Washington, D.C., in 1978, Susan was a French teacher in Connecticut, where she grew up. A 1976 graduate of the University of Connecticut, she is currently working on her M.B.A. She lives in Old Town, Virginia.

GALE L. SMITH, 34, is a stockbroker with Burgess & Leith in Boston. She taught English for five years and has also had extensive sales experience. She grew up in Spencerport, New York, graduated from Salem State College in 1971, and earned her master's degree in English literature in 1979.

CARRI COGGINS STOLTZ, 32, is a speech pathologist and language development specialist in the Alexandria city school system. She received her B.A. from the University of Kentucky in 1972 and her master's degree from Purdue University in 1974. She has been living in the Washington, D.C., area for six and a half years.

MIA TAYLOR, 32, was most recently manager of inside sales for a temporary help agency in Washington, D.C. She has also worked as a management consultant trainee and legislative assistant and public relations supervisor for a lobbying firm. A 1973 graduate of the University of North Carolina, Mia lives in Alexandria, Virginia.

TERRIE TEMKIN, 33, left her job as a management consultant and trainer with Hospital Learning Centers in Los Angeles in mid-1982 to pursue a doctorate in organizational communications. She is also a teaching assistant at the University of Oklahoma in Norman. Terrie grew up in Milwaukee.

WANDA URBANSKA, 27, is a contributing editor with *California Living*, a magazine supplement to the *Los Angeles Herald-Examiner*. A 1978 graduate of Harvard University, Wanda lived in New York City for a year and a half before moving to Los Angeles. She spent her childhood in Orono, Maine, and Lexington, Kentucky.

JANUS LEWIN WALTER, 34, is district manager, docket management, for AT&T in New York City. Since moving there five years ago, Jan has bought a suburban home and remarried. Jan earned her M.B.A. from Pace University in 1981.

NATALIE WINDSOR is a news anchor. A 1974 graduate of Kent State University, Natalie has worked for radio stations in Cleveland, Rochester and Chicago. Her hometown is Dayton, Ohio.

MARGARET WONG, 32, has her own law practice in Cleveland. A native of Hong Kong, she graduated from Western Illinois University and the law school at the State University of New York at Buffalo. She got married in early 1983.